THE LIBRARY
ST. MARY'S COLLEGE OF MARYLAND
ST. MARY'S CITY, MARYLAND 20686

# Chinese Business in Malaysia

Accumulation, Ascendance,
Accommodation

# Chinese Worlds

Chinese Worlds, a new series from Curzon Press and the University of Hawai'i Press, publishes high-quality scholarship, research monographs, and source collections on Chinese history and society from 1900 into the next century.

'Worlds' signals the ethnic, cultural, and political multiformity and regional diversity of China, the cycles of unity and division through which China's modern history has passed, and recent research trends toward regional studies and local issues. It also signals that Chineseness is not contained within territorial borders – overseas Chinese communities in all countries and regions are also 'Chinese worlds'. The editors see them as part of a political, economic, social, and cultural continuum that spans the Chinese mainland, Taiwan, Hong Kong, Macau, South-East Asia, and the world.

The focus of Chinese Worlds is on modern politics and society and history. It includes both history in its broader sweep and specialist monographs on Chinese politics, anthropology, political economy, sociology, education, and the social-science aspects of culture and religions.

**Chinese Business in Malaysia**
Accumulation, Ascendance, Accommodation

**Internal and International Migration**
Chinese Perspectives

**Village Inc.**
Chinese Rural Society in the 1990s

**Chen Duxiu's Last Articles and Letters, 1937–1942**

# Chinese Business in Malaysia

Accumulation, Ascendance, Accommodation

*Edmund Terence Gomez*

UNIVERSITY OF HAWAI'I PRESS
HONOLULU

© 1999 Edmund Terence Gomez
All Rights Reserved

Published in North America by
University of Hawai'i Press
2840 Kolowalu Street
Honolulu, Hawai'i 96822

First Published in the United Kingdom by
Curzon Press
15 The Quadrant, Richmond
Surrey, TW9 1BP
England

Printed in Great Britain

*Library of Congress Cataloguing-in-Publication Data*

Gomez, Edmund Terence.
Chinese business in Malaysia: accumulation, ascendance,
accommodation / Edmund Terence Gomez.
    p.  cm. – (Chinese worlds)
Includes bibliographical references and index.
ISBN 0-8248-2165-3 (alk. paper)
  1. Businesspeople–Malaysia–History.  2. Chinese–Malaysia–
Economic conditions.  3. Business enterprises–Malaysia–History.
4. Investments, Chinese–Malaysia–History.  I. Title.  II. Series.
HF3800.6.G66 1998                                   98-49976
338.8'89510595–dc21                                     CIP

*In the memory of
my selfless mother, Emelda Gomez,
my quietly loving sister, Evelyn,
and my little brother, Jeffrey, who had so much to live for*

# Contents

| | |
|---|---|
| List of Tables | ix |
| List of Figures | xi |
| Preface | xii |
| Acknowledgments | xiv |
| Note on Currency | xvi |
| List of Abbreviations | xvii |

**1 Chinese Business: Culture, Entrepreneurship or Patronage?**    1

    Chinese Business in Malaysia    1
    Literature Review: Culture, Ethnicity and Class    6
    Research Methodology    14
    Research Themes    17
        Ownership and Control    17
        Holding Company, Interlocking Stock Ownership and
            Pyramiding    19
        Interlocking Directorates    22

**2 Chinese Business, Colonialism and Accumulation**    27

    The Colonial Period    27
    From Independence to May 1969    33
    **Case Studies**
        Robert Kuok and Perlis Plantations Bhd    40
        Lim Goh Tong and Genting Bhd    49
        Loh Boon Siew and Oriental Holdings Bhd    58
    Conclusion    64

| | |
|---|---|
| **3 Chinese Business, the NEP and Accommodation** | 67 |
| The Chinese, the NEP and the Corporatization Movement | 67 |
| The Hokkien Chinese in the Banking Sector | 75 |
| Multi-Purpose Holdings | 83 |
| **Case Studies** | |
| William Cheng and Lion Corporation Bhd | 93 |
| Khoo Kay Peng and MUI Bhd | 101 |
| Vincent Tan Chee Yioun and Berjaya Group Bhd | 112 |
| Conclusion | 128 |
| **4 Chinese Business, Liberalization and Ascendance** | 133 |
| Liberalization, Authoritarianism and Patronage | 133 |
| Chinese Businessmen, Malay Patrons and Inter-Ethnic Co-operation | 153 |
| Quek Leng Chan | 153 |
| Lee Loy Seng | 157 |
| **Case Studies** | |
| Francis Yeoh and YTL Corporation Bhd | 163 |
| Ting Pek Khiing and Ekran Bhd | 171 |
| Conclusion | 179 |
| **5 Conclusion** | 183 |
| Chinese Business Networking: Dispelling the Myth | 183 |
| Corporate Growth: Patronage and Entrepreneurship | 186 |
| Postscript | 191 |
| Notes | 198 |
| References | 215 |
| Index | 224 |

# Tables

1.1 Malaysia: Ownership of Share Capital (at par values) of Limited Companies, 1969–95 (percentages) — 2
1.2 Breakdown by Ethnicity of Equity Ownership of Chinese Companies among the Top 100 Publicly-Listed Companies on the KLSE in Terms of Market Capitalization — 4
1.3 Capital Flows in East Asia as a Percentage of Gross Domestic Investment (GDI), 1990–93 — 21
1.4 Malaysia: Funds Raised in Private Securities Markets, 1995 and 1996 (RM million) — 22
1.5 Profiles of Prominent Bumiputera Directors of Chinese-Controlled Companies Among Top 100 Publicly-Listed KLSE Companies — 24
2.1 Perlis Plantations Bhd: Sectoral Breakdown in Terms of Turnover and Pre-Tax Profits, 1995 (RM million) — 44
2.2 Robert Kuok's Business Interests Outside Malaysia — 48
2.3 Genting Bhd: Share Capital, Turnover and Profit Margins, 1991–95 (RM million) — 51
2.4 Genting Bhd: Sectoral Breakdown in Terms of Turnover and Pre-Tax Profits, 1995 (RM million) — 53
2.5 Oriental Holdings Bhd: Share Capital, Turnover and Profit Margins, 1984–93 (RM million) — 59
3.1 Malaysia: Gross Domestic Product by Sector, 1955–94 (percentages) — 68
3.2 Malaysia: Exports by Major Groups, 1960–93 (percentages) — 69
3.3 Lion Corp Bhd: Share Capital, Turnover and Profit Margins, 1985–95 (RM million) — 95
3.4 Lion Corp Bhd: Sectoral Breakdown in Terms of Turnover and Pre-Tax Profits, 1995 (RM million) — 100
3.5 MUI Bhd: Share Capital, Turnover and Profit Margins, 1978–95 (RM million) — 104

3.6 MUI Bhd: Sectoral Breakdown in Terms of Turnover and Pre-Tax
Profits, 1995 (RM million) 110
3.7 Berjaya Group Bhd: Sectoral Breakdown in Terms of Turnover
and Pre-Tax Profits, 1995 (RM million) 126
4.1 DFI Flows to Southeast Asian Countries, 1985–1994
(US$ million) 134
4.2 Political Affiliation of Prominent Business Figures who are
Shareholders and/or Directors of Publicly-Listed Companies 142
4.3 YTL Corp Bhd: Share Capital, Turnover and Profit Margins,
1991–96 (RM million) 164
4.4 YTL Corp Bhd: Sectoral Breakdown in Terms of Turnover and
Pre-Tax Profits, 1995 (RM million) 168
4.5 Ekran Bhd: Share Capital, Turnover and Profit Margins (RM) 172
4.6 Ekran Bhd: Sectoral Breakdown in Terms of Turnover and
Pre-Tax Profits, 1995 (RM million) 174

# Figures

| | | |
|---|---|---|
| 2.1 | Perlis Plantations Bhd (Malaysian Operations): Simplified Corporate Structure, 1995–96 | 44 |
| 2.2 | Genting Bhd: Simplified Corporate Structure, 1995–96 | 57 |
| 2.3 | Oriental Holdings Bhd: Simplified Corporate Structure, 1995–96 | 61 |
| 3.1 | Public Bank Bhd: Simplified Corporate Structure, 1995–96 | 81 |
| 3.2 | Interlocking Stockownership in the Multi-Purpose Holding Group, 1995–96 | 91 |
| 3.3 | Lion Corp Bhd: Simplified Corporate Structure, 1995–96 | 100 |
| 3.4 | MUI Bhd: Simplified Corporate Structure, 1995–96 | 111 |
| 3.5 | Berjaya Group Bhd: Simplified Corporate Structure, 1995–96 | 127 |
| 4.1 | Hong Leong Co. Bhd: Simplified Corporate Structure, 1995–96 | 157 |
| 4.2 | KL-Kepong Bhd: Simplified Corporate Structure, 1995–96 | 161 |
| 4.3 | YTL Corporation Bhd: Simplified Corporate Structure, 1995–96 | 170 |
| 4.4 | Ekran Bhd: Simplified Corporate Structure, 1995–96 | 179 |
| P.1 | Simplified Model of the Practice of Political Patronage | 193 |

## Maps

| | |
|---|---|
| Map 1: Sabah and Sarawak | xx |
| Map 2: Peninsular Malaysia | xxi |

# Preface

Although Chinese enterprise has contributed significantly to economic growth in Malaysia, there has been surprisingly little research on the subject. This has led to various misconceptions about business practices among the Chinese, particularly of the extent of business 'networks' among the bigger Chinese firms. Such misapprehensions have also contributed to the widely held belief that Chinese enterprises, especially those in Southeast Asia, Hong Kong and Taiwan, are emerging as a major economic force through the creation of transnational business networks. The overwhelming attention given to a small number of business deals by the region's leading Chinese businessmen has also popularized the notion of a dynamic form of 'Chinese capitalism'. This volume is an attempt to contest popular stereotypes that are unsupported by empirical evidence, particularly the thesis that common ethnic identity and culture will inspire the creation of intra-ethnic business networks.

Malaysia provides an interesting case study as ethnic Chinese, who constitute about 28 per cent of the population, have maintained a huge presence in the corporate sector despite having to deal with a state that has not been supportive of its business interests. In these circumstances, it could logically be presumed that intra-ethnic business co-operation has contributed to the continued growth of Malaysian–Chinese capital. This volume provides a study of the largest Chinese companies, contextualized within an analysis of Malaysia's economic development. Case studies on eight publicly-listed Chinese companies focus on the factors that have determined forms of business practice and influenced corporate ventures. Particular attention is given to the impact of government policies, including ethnic redistribution endeavors, deregulation initiatives and industrialization drives, which have shaped ownership and control patterns, access to financial capital and government projects, and involvement in economic sectors.

While undertaking research on the largest publicly-listed Chinese companies, I have become increasingly aware that the business style of the owners of these large companies is probably vastly different from that of owners of small- and medium-scale Chinese enterprises (SMEs). Research into these Chinese SMEs would probably reveal a wholly different story of how owners of these enterprises function and develop in an environment where state policies have provided – until very recently – no support. For example, one major conclusion in this study is the heterogeneity in business style among the large Chinese firms. It is questionable if such business heterogeneity exists among the Chinese SMEs. While it is this heterogeneity among the large enterprises that brings into question a typology of 'Chinese' capital, the conclusions drawn here may not be applicable to the SMEs. Nevertheless, the history and development of the largest Chinese companies needs to be studied, recorded and put in perspective.

# Acknowledgements

This study was funded primarily by a grant from the Toyota Foundation. The Foundation, along with the Chiang Ching-kuo Foundation, also provided the funding to organize a conference on Chinese business in Southeast Asia, held at the University of Malaya, Kuala Lumpur in June 1997. A draft version of this volume, based largely on most of the case studies here, was presented at this conference. I benefited immensely from the comments made on that paper by some of the participants, particularly Lee Poh Ping, Tan Siok Choo, Donald Nonini, George Hicks, Kit Machado, Carl Trocki, Yao Souchou, Raj Brown, Loh Wei Leng, Peter Post, Paul Handley, Robert Chan and Sikko Visscher. I have also learnt much from my numerous discussions with Jamie Mackie who has been particularly supportive of my efforts to pursue research on the subject. I am especially indebted to Jomo K.S. and Lee Kam Hing, who read the manuscript, at short notice, and provided thoughtful comments and suggestions.

Being based in Leeds, England for the past two years, I have received much support from Gregor Benton, Professor of Chinese Studies at the Department of East Asian Studies, University of Leeds. Greg, who read an early draft of the manuscript and submitted it for consideration for publication, was instrumental in getting me to complete this study. Greg has also generously provided me with facilities to pursue my research at the University. I also wish to thank Flemming Christiansen who read the manuscript, raised several important points, and engaged me in numerous debates on many of the views raised here.

My research assistant, Ling Tek Soon, undertook most of the research at the Registrar of Companies and at the libraries at Star Publications Bhd and Bernama, the national news agency. His

## Acknowledgements

diligence and efficency in sending me all this material helped me to complete the research in time for presentation of the first draft at the Kuala Lumpur conference. I am also grateful to my sister, Eleanor, who responded quickly to my numerous pleas for help in tracing crucial information.

As always, I thank Sharm for her support and encouragement in completing this volume, and for providing an environment conducive to writing, even though she has herself been tied down with her doctoral research. Our two little children, Evie and Eric, often broke into the study to take a 'break' from play to help me key in parts of the manuscript. Although this meant much more editing later, they were a most welcome distraction.

Although I am indebted to all those mentioned here, I remain responsible for the views expressed in this book.

Terence Gomez
Leeds, 1998

# Note on Currency

Unless otherwise indicated, all currency values are in Malaysian ringgit (RM: ringgit Malaysia). The Malaysian ringgit is supposedly based on a bundle of international currencies, mainly the US dollar. Before the 1970s, it was pegged at RM3 : US$1. Since the beginning of flexible exchange rates in the early 1970s, it moved in the range of RM2.4–2.7 to the US dollar, before dropping precipitously from July 1997 to an all time low of RM4.9 in early January 1998.

# Abbreviations

| | |
|---|---|
| ABB | Asea Brown Boveri |
| ACCCIM | Associated Chinese Chambers of Commerce and Industry Malaysia |
| APMC | Associated Pan Malaysia Cement Sdn Bhd |
| ASN | Amanah Saham Nasional (National Unit Trust Scheme) |
| BHC | Bakun Hydroelectrical Corporation Sdn Bhd |
| Bhd | Berhad (Limited) |
| CASH | Construction and Supplies House Bhd |
| C&C Bintang | Cycle & Carriage Bintang Bhd |
| CCM | Chemical Company of Malaysia Bhd |
| CIC | Capital Issues Committee |
| Citic | China International Trust and Investment Corporation |
| CMS | Cahya Mata Sarawak Bhd |
| DAP | Democratic Action Party |
| D&C Bank | Development & Commercial Bank Bhd |
| DTC | deposit-taking co-operative |
| EOI | export-oriented industrialization |
| EON | Edaran Otomobil Nasional Bhd |
| EPF | Employees' Provident Fund |
| FCW | Federal Cables, Wires and Metal Manufacturing Bhd |
| FELDA | Federal Land Development Authority |
| FIC | Foreign Investment Committee |
| FTZ | free trade zone |
| GDP | gross domestic product |
| Gerakan | Gerakan Rakyat Malaysia (Malaysian People's Movement) |
| HICOM | Heavy Industries Corporation of Malaysia Bhd |
| ICA | Industrial Coordination Act |
| IPP | independent power producer |
| ISI | import-substituting industrialization |

| | |
|---|---|
| JMI | Jasa Megah Industries Bhd |
| KLSE | Kuala Lumpur Stock Exchange |
| KLOFFE | Kuala Lumpur Options and Financial Futures Exchange |
| KSM | Koperatif Serbaguna (M) Bhd (Multi-Purpose Co-operative Society) |
| KTM | Keretapi Tanah Melayu Bhd (Malayan Railways) |
| KUB | Koperasi Usaha Bersatu Bhd |
| LTAT | Lembaga Tabung Angkatan Tentera (Armed Forces Savings Board) |
| LUTH | Lembaga Urusan Tabung Haji (Pilgrims' Fund Management Board) |
| MARA | Majlis Amanah Rakyat (Council of Trust for Indigenous People) |
| MAS | Malaysia Airlines Bhd |
| Maybank | Malayan Banking Bhd |
| MBf | Malayan Borneo Finance Bhd |
| MCA | Malaysian Chinese Association |
| MCP | Malayan Communist Party |
| MIC | Malaysian Indian Congress |
| MIDA | Malaysian Industrial Development Authority |
| MISC | Malaysian International Shipping Corporation Bhd |
| MPHB | Multi-Purpose Holdings Bhd |
| MRCB | Malaysian Resources Corporation Bhd |
| MUI | Malayan United Industries Bhd |
| NDP | National Development Policy |
| NEP | New Economic Policy |
| NSTP | New Straits Times Press Bhd |
| OCBC | Oversea-Chinese Banking Corporation |
| Pan-El | Pan-Electric Industries Ltd |
| PAS | Parti Islam Se-Malaysia (Pan-Malaysian Islamic Party) |
| Pernas | Perbadanan Nasional Bhd (National Corporation) |
| Petronas | Petroliam Nasional (National Petroleum Corporation) |
| PIA | Promotion of Investments Act |
| PMCW | Pan Malaysia Cement Works Bhd |
| PMI | Pan Malaysia Industries Bhd (later renamed PMRI) |
| PMRI | Pan Malaysia Rubber Industries Bhd (formerly PMRI) |
| PNB | Permodalan Nasional Bhd (National Equity Corporation) |
| Proton | Perusahaan Otomobil Nasional Bhd |
| RIDA | Rural Industrial Development Authority |
| SAM | Suzuki Assemblers (M) Sdn Bhd |
| SCMP | South China Morning Post (Holdings) Ltd |

*Abbreviations*

| | |
|---|---|
| Sdn Bhd | Sendirian Berhad (Private Limited) |
| SEDC | state economic development corporation |
| Semangat 46 | Parti Melayu Semangat 46 (Spirit of 1946 Malay Party) |
| SESCO | Sarawak Electricity Supply Corporation |
| SFI | Sabah Forest Industries Sdn Bhd |
| SHMB | Shangri-La Hotels (Malaysia) Bhd |
| SKI | Sucden Kerry International |
| SME | small- and medium-scale enterprises |
| SSMC | Singer Sewing Machine Company Inc. |
| TVB | Television Broadcasts (Hong Kong) |
| UDA | Urban Development Authority |
| UEM | United Engineers (M) Bhd |
| UMBC | United Malayan Banking Corporation Bhd |
| UMG | United Merchant Group Bhd |
| UMNO | United Malays' National Organization |
| USM | Universiti Sains Malaysia |

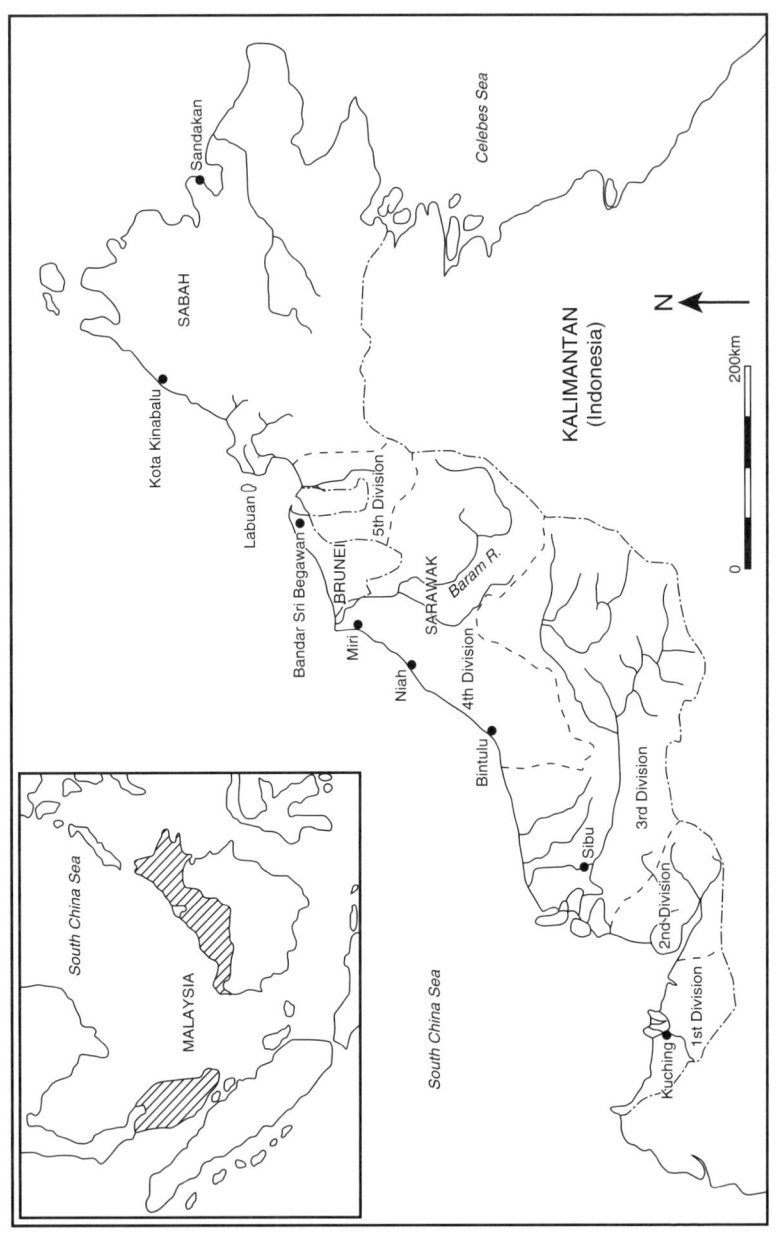

Map 1: Sabah and Sarawak

*Maps*

Map 2: Peninsular Malaysia

# Chinese Business: Culture, Entrepreneurship or Patronage?

## Chinese Business in Malaysia

In multi-ethnic Malaysia, almost all the literature on Chinese business would acknowledge the ubiquitous profile of this community in the economy, even though they now constitute less than a third of the population (see Yoshihara 1988; Jesudason 1989; Hara 1991; Heng 1992). In part, Chinese business ubiquity has been the justification for the government's concerted attempt to redistribute wealth to achieve economic parity among the major ethnic communities. In effect, this has meant positive discrimination in favor of the indigenous Bumiputera (or 'sons of the soil'), implemented through the New Economic Policy (NEP) between 1971 and 1990. In 1997, more than 60 per cent of Malaysians were Bumiputeras, a majority of whom were Malay, while the Indians made up most of the remaining tenth of the population.

The introduction and implementation of the NEP was made possible by the domination of the Malaysian state by the United Malays' National Organization (UMNO), although the government is led by a multi-party coalition, the Barisan Nasional (National Front). UMNO's leading partners in the Barisan Nasional are also ethnically-based parties, the Malaysian Chinese Association (MCA) and the Malaysian Indian Congress (MIC). During the 1980s, however, some UMNO leaders began to use party hegemony to secure control over much of Malaysia's corporate equity. By the end of the 1980s, a 'new rich,' i.e. politically well-connected Bumiputeras who had managed to gain ownership of corporate stock, had emerged (see Gomez and Jomo 1997: 117–65). UMNO hegemony and the rise of this 'new rich' were widely believed by analysts of the Malaysian economy to have hindered the accumulation and ascendance of Chinese capital in Malaysia.

Yet, at the end of the 20-year NEP period in 1990, corporate ownership figures revealed that the proportion of Chinese equity ownership had almost doubled, from 22.8 per cent in 1969 to 45.5 per cent in 1990 (see Table 1.1). During the NEP phase, a number of new Chinese businessmen had emerged as prominent business figures in control of some of the country's largest companies in terms of market capitalization. Among the most prominent of these businessmen were Khoo Kay Peng, William Cheng Heng Jem, Vincent Tan Chee Yioun, T.K. Lim, Ting Pek Khiing, Joseph Chong Chek Ah, Teh Soon Seng and Tong Kooi Ong. The well-diversified publicly-listed investment holding company, Multi-Purpose Holdings Bhd, which emerged in the mid-1970s during the MCA-led corporatization movement – an attempt to mobilize Chinese financial resources to acquire corporate assets on their behalf – remains one of the largest Chinese-controlled companies in terms of market capitalization. At the end of 1990, the Chinese were estimated to hold 50 per cent ownership of the construction sector, 82 per cent of wholesale trade, 58 per cent of retail trade, approximately 40 per cent of the manufacturing sector and almost 70 per cent of small scale enterprises (see *Malaysian Business* 16 January 1991).

The validity of these Chinese ownership estimates can, however, be questioned. The government's ethnic equity ownership figures in Table 1.1 have also been the subject of some dispute. Even the MCA president, Ling Liong Sik, was quoted in parliament in 1989 as stating, '[t]he figures don't agree with ours' (*Malaysian Business* 1 July

*Table 1.1* Malaysia: Ownership of Share Capital (at par value) of Limited Companies, 1969–95 (percentages)

|  | 1969 | 1970 | 1975 | 1980 | 1985 | 1990 | 1995 |
|---|---|---|---|---|---|---|---|
| Bumiputera Individuals and Trust Agencies | 1.5 | 2.4 | 9.2 | 12.5 | 19.1 | 19.2 | 20.6 |
| Chinese | 22.8 | 27.2 | n.a | n.a | 33.4 | 45.5 | 40.9 |
| Indians | 0.9 | 1.1 | n.a | n.a | 1.2 | 1.0 | 1.5 |
| Nominee Companies | 2.1 | 6.0 | n.a | n.a | 1.3 | 8.5 | 8.3 |
| Locally-Controlled Companies | 10.1 | – | – | – | 7.2 | 0.3 | 1.0 |
| Foreigners | 62.1 | 63.4 | 53.3 | 42.9 | 26.0 | 25.4 | 27.7 |

n.a. – not available
Sources: Third Malaysia Plan, 1976–1980 (Malaysia 1976); Seventh Malaysia Plan, 1996–2000 (Malaysia 1996)

1991). Ling was, in all probability, suggesting that the amount of equity holdings attributed to the Chinese was too high, while the Bumiputera share of corporate ownership was too low. Leaders of the Gerakan Rakyat Malaysia (Gerakan), another major party in the Barisan Nasional with mainly Chinese support, have also challenged the government's ethnic ownership figures. As far back as 1984, a Gerakan report claimed, '[o]ur own rough estimate shows that the Bumiputeras have already achieved 30 per cent of national corporate wealth at the end of 1984' (quoted in *Malaysian Business* 16 October 1986). Studies have managed to provide evidence that some equity held by nominee companies[1] is attributable to Bumiputeras, particularly politicians or politically-connected individuals (see Gomez 1990). In this respect, it is noteworthy that between 1990 and 1995, Chinese share of equity stock fell by almost five percentage points, from 45.5 per cent to 40.9 per cent (see Table 1.1). Other studies have suggested that despite significant Chinese ownership of corporate equity, dominance over the economy is now in the hands of a Malay political elite following the successful implementation of the NEP (see, for example, Gomez 1990, 1994; Jomo 1990, 1994; Gomez and Jomo 1997). A more credible indication of Chinese influence in the economy is provided by listing the number of Chinese-controlled companies among the top hundred companies on the Kuala Lumpur Stock Exchange (KLSE) (see Table 1.2).[2]

The most striking point that emerges from Table 1.2 is that almost 40 per cent of the top hundred companies are under Chinese majority ownership. Of these 40 companies, almost half are involved in manufacturing activities, i.e. they are listed as industrial and consumer products counters of the KLSE. Yoshihara (1988) suggests that one reason why Southeast Asian capital is 'ersatz' is the lack of development of a productive manufacturing base by most of the region's leading companies. From another perspective, since the implementation of the NEP, the Chinese have generally been cautious about investing in manufacturing as the government has strongly advocated greater Bumiputera participation in this sector and has shown a preference for foreign investors to forge ties with state or Bumiputera-owned enterprises to secure government economic benefits and concessions (see Jesudason 1989; Yasuda 1991). In its endeavor to develop Malaysia's manufacturing sector, the government has provided concessions in various forms, including tariff protection, depreciation allowances, tax breaks and licences, many of which, it is widely presumed, have not been captured by the Chinese. In 1970,

## Chinese Business in Malaysia

Table 1.2 Breakdown by Ethnicity of Equity Ownership of Chinese Companies Among the Top 100 Publicly-Listed Companies in Terms of Market Capitalization

| Company | KLSE Ranking | Activity | Controlling Shareholder | Size of Holdings* | Total Bumiputera Holdings* |
|---|---|---|---|---|---|
| Genting Bhd | 5 | Gaming | Lim Goh Tong | 29.13% | 5.29% |
| AC: Resorts World | 6 | Gaming | | 30.30% | 17.95% |
| AC: Asiatic Development | 81 | Plantation | | 54.65% | 28.37% |
| YTL Corp. | 13 | Construction & Manufacturing | Yeoh Tiong Lay | 47.90% | 16.29% |
| YTL-T | 65 | | | | |
| Public Bank | 16 | Banking | Teh Hong Piow | 33.72% | 29.49% |
| Berjaya Sports Toto | 23 | Gaming | Vincent Tan | 39.12% | 5.14% |
| Jaya Tiasa Holdings (formerly Berjaya Textiles) | 24 | Manufacturing | Tiong Hiew King | 29.42% | 28.71% |
| Magnum Corp | 26 | Gaming | TK Lim | 28.52% | 39.48% |
| AC: Multi-Purpose Hold. | 36 | Investment holding | | 24.04% | # |
| HC: Kamunting Corp | 94 | Construction | | 36.82% | 0.35% |
| Hong Leong Credit | 30 | Finance | Quek Leng Chan | | |
| AC: Hong Leong Bank | 32 | Banking | | 34.48% | 6.36% |
| AC: Hume Industries | 34 | Manufacturing | | 43.22% | 18.44% |
| AC: OYL Industries | 45 | Manufacturing | | 61.56% | 4.37% |
| AC: Hong Leong Prop. | 69 | Property development | | 50.54% | 3.34% |
| AC: Malaysian Pacific Industries | 73 | Manufacturing | | 55.71% | 8.50% |
| AC: Hong Leong Industries | 84 | Manufacturing | | 53.22% | 14.96% |
| Leader Universal | 35 | Manufacturing | H'ng family | 11.71% | 4.75% |
| Lingui Developments | 40 | Plantations | Samling Strategic Corp | 29.67% | 21.30% |
| KL Kepong | 41 | Plantations | Lee Loy Seng family | 42.42% | 24.81% |
| Malayan United Ind. | 42 | Manufacturing | Khoo Kay Peng | 44.82% | 1.04% |
| AC: Pan Malaysia Cement | 58 | Manufacturing | | 50.64% | 16.13% |
| Perlis Plantations | 44 | Manufacturing | Robert Kuok | 30.21% | 23.90% |
| Pacific Chemicals | 47 | Manufacturing | Ting Pek Khiing | 22.14% | 36.94% |
| HC: Ekran | 64 | Construction | | 21.11% | 17.21% |
| MBf Capital | 50 | Finance | Loy Hean Heong | 31.60% | 17.49% |
| CO: Sri Hartamas | 70 | Property Development | | 10.60% | # |
| Tan Chong Motors | 51 | Manufacturing | Tan family | 34.27% | # |
| IOI Properties | 54 | Property | Lee family | 53.73% | 15.88% |
| TA Enterprise | 55 | Finance | Tiah Thee Kian | 40.60% | 12.10% |

## Chinese Business: Culture, Entrepreneurship or Patronage?

| Company | KLSE Ranking | Activity | Controlling Shareholder | Size of Holdings* | Total Bumiputera Holdings* |
|---|---|---|---|---|---|
| Amsteel Corp | 57 | Manufacturing | William Cheng | 47.75% | 31.40% |
| Oriental Holdings | 71 | Manufacturing | Loh Boon Siew | 43.00% | 11.91% |
| Mulpha International | 79 | Manufacturing | | # | 29.18% |
| Sungei Way Holdings | 80 | Construction | Cheah Fook Ling | 34.29% | 2.99% |
| Acidchem | 85 | Manufacturing | Lim Keng Kay | 46.26% | 8.70% |
| Metroplex | 88 | Property | Dick Chan | 42.42% | 34.77% |
| Kian Joo Can Factory | 92 | Manufacturing | See family | 35.39% | 7.49% |
| Hap Seng Consolidated | 93 | Manufacturing | Lau Gek Poh | # | 23.16% |
| C&C Bintang | 96 | Manufacturing | C&C Ltd | 48.75% | 17.63% |
| CCM | 97 | Manufacturing | Lim Say Chong | 29.88% | 30.79% |

\* Estimated figures
\# Since most of the largest shareholders are nominee companies, it is difficult to estimate the volume of Bumiputera or Chinese equity ownership.
*Note*: HC – Holding Company; AC – Affiliated Company; CO – Common Ownership; T – Transferable subscription rights or warrants
(a) Acidchem has been renamed Intria Bhd, and was taken over by a Bumiputera company, Mekar Idaman Sdn Bhd, which owns the toll concession for the Penang Bridge.
(b) Chemical Company of Malaysia Bhd (CCM) was long owned by ICI (M) Holdings Sdn Bhd. In 1994, following a management-buy-out (MBO), Lim Say Chong and two other senior executives of the company, Oh Kim Sum and Chen Yeng Khan, acquired 50.1 per cent of CCM's equity (Cheong, 1995: 34–35).
*Source*: KLSE Annual Companies Handbook 21 (1–4), 1996.

Chinese ownership of manufacturing companies amounted to 22.5 per cent, Malay ownership was a mere 2.5 per cent, while the bulk was under foreign ownership (Low 1985: 26). Yet, by 1990, Chinese ownership of the manufacturing sector was estimated at 40 per cent (see *Malaysian Business* 16 January 1991). Between 1970 and 1980, the average annual growth rate of manufacturing output exceeded 10 per cent; by the end of the 1980s, manufacturing had become a major net foreign exchange earner. By 1996, manufacturing's share of Malaysia's GDP had increased to over 30 per cent.[3]

This raises two questions: How has Chinese capital managed to develop its corporate holdings, despite having to operate in the NEP environment that seemed inimical to its interests? Does this suggest that intra-ethnic business linkages have enabled Chinese capital to develop its corporate holdings in Malaysia? This volume is an attempt to address these questions, by tracing the growth of the largest Chinese enterprises in Malaysia.

## Literature Review: Culture, Ethnicity and Class

Since the early 1990s, a spate of new studies has emerged, arguing that ethnic Chinese 'networks' are spearheading Asia's economic growth and becoming a major global force (Kotkin 1993; Nasbitt 1995; Rowher 1995; East Asia Analytical Unit 1995; Weidenbaum and Hughes 1996; Hiscock 1997). To support this contention, a variety of figures has been cited. Weidenbaum and Hughes (1996: 24–5), for example, refer to the World Bank's estimate that the combined economic output of the businesses of the approximately 50 million ethnic Chinese in Asia outside of China – about 23 million in Southeast Asia, 20 million in Taiwan and the rest in Hong Kong – approached US$400 billion in 1991.[4] In 1994, the *Far Eastern Economic Review*'s (17 July 1994) conservative estimate of Southeast Asian investment in China was US$8 billion, while total investment from Taiwan was US$5.4 billion, with Hong Kong investing US$40 billion. In 1996, *Asiaweek* (19 July 1996) estimated that between 1978 and 1996, of the US$120 billion invested in China, almost 80 per cent of the total investment had originated from 'overseas Chinese'. Disclosure of such investment patterns in China has fed speculation that the Chinese of the diaspora are channeling funds to the mainland. By 1997, four World Chinese Entrepreneurs' Conventions and 21 World Chinese Traders' Conferences had been convened and attended by Chinese from all continents, suggesting that many ethnic Chinese were beginning to consider whether their common ethnic identity could be a means to facilitate business ties.

Another body of literature has fed speculation that contemporary Chinese capitalism has distinctive characteristics which have facilitated its growth. In particular, the institutions, norms and practices of ethnic Chinese have been identified as reasons for the growth of their enterprises and the emergence of Chinese business networks. Ethnic networks, based on trust and kinship ties, have reduced transaction costs, increased co-ordination and diminished risks (Redding 1990; Whitley 1992; Kotkin 1993). Fukuyama (1995) also subscribes to such a cultural perspective, but argues that there is very little trust among Chinese outside of immediate family members. For Fukuyama, equal division of family wealth among sons tends to undermine the development of Chinese business groups. Such a practice also leads to dissipation of corporate holdings and competition among family companies, hindering the development of large Chinese corporations. There is little empirical evidence to support either of these two hypotheses in the Malaysian context, particularly among larger Chinese enterprises.

This strengthens the growing body of literature that contests the presumptions that the values and socio-economic institutions characteristic of some Chinese are universal within the community and that ethnic Chinese overseas are identical with those in China (see, for example, Hodder 1996). Such homogenizing assumptions fail to take into account the specific and particular experiences of Chinese business communities in different countries. In Malaysia, as Jesudason (1997) has noted, cultural changes had begun to weaken ethnic solidarity in business even before implementation of the NEP; clan and guild associations, for example, have diminished in importance among the Chinese. Moreover, such static general cultural assumptions can be contested by reference to cross-border comparisons. Why, for example, have ethnic Chinese entrepreneurs in Thailand managed to accumulate a far greater proportion of corporate equity than, say, the far more numerous Chinese in Singapore? Yet, Sino-Thais constitute just 10 per cent of the Thai population while more than 75 per cent of Singaporeans are ethnic Chinese. This suggests that the use of culture as the primary conceptual tool to explain the growth of ethnic enterprises is problematic.

Another major problem in much of the current literature is that all Chinese are treated as a homogenous and monolithic group. It is possible, however, to disaggregate the Chinese into sub-ethnic groups that have played different roles within the larger Chinese ethnic community. In Malaysia, which probably has among the largest number of ethnic Chinese in Southeast Asia, the community has not managed to transcend internal divisions to act as a unified ethnic force, even in the face of blatant ethnic discrimination by the state. Among the major dialect groups in Malaysia – including Hokkiens, Cantonese, Teochews, Hainanese and Hakkas – the Hokkiens comprise the largest sub-ethnic community, and have played the most prominent role in business. Some Hokkiens have also had a long tradition of being involved in trade. Particularly in the Malayan peninsula, Yong (1987: 10) noted that Hokkiens 'had been the merchant princes during the 19th century, and in the 20th century dominated the more modern sectors of the economy, such as banking, insurance, shipping, rubber-milling and manufacturing, and the export and import trade.'[5] Recently, it seems that the most effective and long-term business co-operation among Chinese in

Malaysia and elsewhere in East Asia has been among the Foochows (*Asian Wall Street Journal* 21 December 1994).[6]

Another significant cleavage among the Chinese which is ignored in much of the existing literature is class difference. In Southeast Asia, Chinese in Thailand comprise about 10 per cent of the population, but own approximately 85 per cent of the economy. In the late 1980s, Sino-Thai business groups owned 37 of the 100 largest companies in Thailand; most of this wealth was concentrated in the hands of just five key Teochew families (Suehiro 1989; Lim 1996). Ethnic Chinese constitute only three per cent of Indonesia's 182 million population but own an estimated 70 per cent of the country's corporate assets. One Indonesian, Liem Sioe Liong, the second wealthiest man in Southeast Asia after the Sultan of Brunei, controls the Salim Group which recorded sales estimated at US$9 billion in 1992, then approximately five per cent of Indonesia's GDP (*Business Week* 11 November 1991). About two per cent of the Filipino population is believed to be ethnic Chinese, but they own about 40 per cent of corporate equity (Lim 1996).[7] In Malaysia, by the mid-1990s, although the country's 28 per cent ethnic Chinese owned 41 per cent of total corporate equity, there is evidence that much of this wealth is highly concentrated (see Hara 1991; Heng 1992; Gomez and Jomo 1997). Recent studies of the political economy of the region in general, and of some of the largest Chinese companies in Malaysia, Indonesia, the Philippines and Thailand in particular, also provide evidence that Chinese business growth has been determined not by 'Chinese' traits, but by their ability to forge close ties with the indigenous elite (Robison 1986; Yoshihara 1988; Suehiro 1989; Hutchcroft 1994; Gomez and Jomo 1997).

Popular notions like 'global tribe' and 'bamboo network' refer mainly to the business activities of the Chinese elite who owns much of this wealth – Malaysia's Robert Kuok and Quek Leng Chan, Indonesia's Liem Sioe Liong, Eka Tjipta Widjaja and the Lippo Group, Singapore's Ong Beng Seng, the Philippines' Henry Sy and John Gokongwei, Thailand's Sophonpanich family and Charoen Pokphand group, and Hong Kong's Li Ka Shing and Lee Shau Kee (see Kotkin 1993; East Asia Analytical Unit 1995; Weidenbaum and Hughes 1996). The business deals among these businessmen have been the primary basis for arguing that there exists growing business cooperation in East Asia among Chinese enterprises which will ensure their emergence as a dynamic global business force.

Kotkin has been principally responsible for the argument that a common ethnic identity and culture has inspired the creation of intra-ethnic business networks. Kotkin asserts that 'global tribes combine a strong sense of common origin and shared values' and that 'success in the new global economy is determined by the connections which immigrant entrepreneurs carry with them around the world' (Kotkin 1993: 4). Kotkin seems to be influenced by a number of ideas in the literature on ethnic enterprises. One major influence is the Weberian view that belief systems drive entrepreneurial behavior in capitalist economies. Weber argued that the 'Protestant ethic' encouraged hard work and economic rationality, thus explaining the industrial transformation of Western Europe. Weber also argued that the development of capitalism in China had been hindered by Confucian traits, i.e. a kinship system based on the extended family, bureaucratic centralization of power in a patrimonial state that obstructed development of a capitalist class, and a religious tradition that did not encourage an activist asceticism required in entrepreneurial pursuits.

This culturalist perspective has been revised by Redding (1990) and Kotkin, among others.[8] As Dirlik (1997) has noted, the revised argument now being propounded

> represents a 'Weberizing' of Confucianism; the critique of Max Weber's views on the relationship between Confucianism and capitalism has taken the form not of a critical evaluation of Weber's views on capitalism, but rather of an assertion that Confucianism shares in the values that Weber ascribed to the Protestant ethic in Europe.

Kotkin's thesis also appears to be influenced by the business experience of immigrant communities in the United States. Much of the literature on ethnic enterprise and entrepreneurship in the United States and Europe argues that immigrant businessmen, especially Asians, share common behavioral characteristics in the way they do business (see, for example, Bonacich and Modell 1980; Light 1980; Ward and Jenkins 1984). In the United States, Light (1980) contends that there is a specific 'ethnic business style' among Chinese, Japanese and Korean immigrants, which has ensured the growth of their enterprises; some of the common business characteristics of these immigrant ethnic communities include the use of family firms, trade guilds, rotating credit associations and considerable intra-ethnic business transactions, locally and with their 'homeland'.

An attempt to use this line of argument in the Southeast Asian context is problematic. Large scale migratory movements in the United States and Europe have continued in the modern era, for political and economic reasons. For example, the Cubans in Miami and the Koreans in Los Angeles and New York, among most recent migrants in the United States, have – as Kotkin has noted – emerged as a dynamic business communities (Portes and Manning 1986; Park 1997). However, in Malaysia (and most other countries in Southeast Asia), large scale immigration ceased before the Second World War. Following the economic depression of the early 1930s, demand for labor in Malaya's tin mines and plantations dropped. After the Pacific war, and especially following independence, strict immigration curbs were introduced. Most of the literature on the Chinese in Malaysia (and Southeast Asia) argues that the Chinese have come to identify themselves with the country of their birth and no longer look to China as their 'homeland,' while investment in China is seen by entrepreneurs as a business proposition, rather than as a commitment to rebuild an ancestral homeland (see Ho 1995; Jesudason 1997; Suryadinata 1997).

The belief that there is much ethnic Chinese business networking is attributable to the role of certain Southeast Asian leaders. Lee Kuan Yew, Singapore's influential Senior Minister, has been a particularly strong advocate of business networking among members of the Chinese diaspora.[9] While Prime Minister of Singapore, Lee had experienced the capacity for Chinese capitalists to mobilize funds quickly. In 1988, when Lee's government wanted to build Suntec City in Singapore, a US$460 million office and convention center, the investors included some of Hong Kong's leading businessmen, including Li Ka Shing, Lee Shau Kee, Run Run Shaw and Cheng Yu Tung; the investment banker who put together the financing later claimed: 'We got it all arranged in one week' (quoted in *Business Week* 11 November 1991). Chinese businessmen of the diaspora have been encouraged by Lee Kuan Yew to view ethnic networking as an effective way to move into potentially lucrative markets in China, to compete more effectively with multinational corporations, and to transform the handicap they may feel as ethnic minorities into an advantage, not just in the region, but in the global economy.

Another proponent of the potential economic impact in Asia of the Chinese outside China is Robert Kuok, a contemporary of Lee Kuan Yew at Singapore's Raffles College (*Far Eastern Economic Review* 7 February 1991). According to Kuok, because of the sheer size of their capital flows, and increasing all the time, they make an enormous impact on the economies of the region, particularly as they possess considerable entrepreneurial and organizational abilities. By and large, they are a very thrifty lot, and very careful with money. Therefore, in a region where capital is in perennial short supply and at the same time development schemes are both plentiful as well as crying out for action, the Overseas Chinese capitalists are really the best medicine that can be prescribed because they tend to start a project or an industry with a small money investment but with large investments of time, skill and energy (*New Straits Times* 5–6 October 1991).[10]

The encouragement and privileges accorded by the government of China to 'Overseas Chinese' – as they have been viewed by the Chinese authorities – has resulted in increased investments by Chinese businessmen in East and Southeast Asia. Government leaders in Singapore and Malaysia have also encouraged investments in China. Malaysian Prime Minister Mahathir Mohamad, for example, also appears to see much benefit from getting indigenous businessmen to work with Chinese capitalists to enable Malaysian companies to tap into the economic potential that the market in China offers. In 1993, he led an almost 300-strong delegation to China, with half his delegation comprising businessmen (see Ho 1995: 230–48; Yong 1995: 249–54; Chan 1996). This raises another question: Have increased investments in China been due to trust, 'tribalism' and shared cultural values, or to the fact that governments have framed policies to support such investments?

Some studies have suggested that the big enterprises owned by the key Chinese capitalists in Southeast Asia are not large-scale firms run along the lines of the Western model of a corporation. Rather, most of these companies are a conglomeration of small- and medium-scale enterprises (SMEs) in a varied number of businesses, often not even remotely related (see Gomez and Jomo 1997; Robison 1986; Sato 1993; Suehiro 1989). Rather than build horizontal and vertical roots in a particular business, these companies prefer to diversify into any field that promises huge profit margins. This situation can be compared with Taiwan, where the economy has relied heavily on the SMEs to drive manufacturing, in spite of the presence of a few large business groups (Hamilton 1997: 246–58).[11]

Although it is economic rationalism, rather than ethnic identity, which determines business behaviour, it is possible at various stages of economic development and in situations where state policies are implemented which can have a bearing on the operation of Chinese enterprises, co-ethnic cooperation can emerge as an economic and political strategy. It is quite probable that co-ethnic business co-operation tends to occur more among the SMEs, as Chinese businessmen who lead large enterprises have been able to accommodate the state more in order to continue to ascend. Such accommodation by owners of large Chinese companies can be in the form of divesting a portion of their corporate equity to state enterprises, thus relinquishing some ownership of stock yet retaining control of their enterprise. Joint-ventures normally are formed between larger Chinese companies and state-owned enterprises. These measures can enable the large enterprises to secure concessions from the state. Large Chinese enterprises are also able to bypass the state by venturing abroad. Since such avenues of accommodation are limited among the SMEs, greater intra-ethnic business cooperation may emerge as a means to deal with the state policies. SMEs may also form or belong to ethnic-based associations in order to act collectively. However, while membership in such associations can promote greater intra-ethnic business networks and facilitate business deals based on 'trust' which helps reduce transaction costs, this does not negate the possibility that inter-ethnic business transactions are simultaneously undertaken. Moreover, while institutions tend to see other ethnic or state enterprises as competitors, thus reinforcing ethnic identity, individual businessmen tend to be more multi-racial and independent in business ventures.

Some of the existing studies on large Chinese enterprises in Malaysia provide useful insights, but their research covers too wide a range of companies, thus furnishing inadequate evidence to conclusively substantiate their primary arguments (see, for example, Yoshihara 1988; Jesudason 1989, 1997; Hara 1991; Heng 1992). Yoshihara (1988) argues that most large enterprises are led by 'comprador capitalists,' who are merely rent-seekers who have emerged by forging ties with influential state leaders. Such capitalists are 'ersatz' since they tend to concentrate on activities that are rentier and speculative rather than entrepreneurial. For Yoshihara (1988), Chinese SMEs in Southeast Asia are more entrepreneurial and could have contributed much more to the region's rapid industrial progress if the states had given them more support instead of depending primarily on state enterprises and foreign capital. This is a contention which Jesudason (1989) and Bowie (1991) have developed for the

Malaysian case, where ethnic Chinese comprise a large portion of SMEs, which have been, until fairly recently, largely left alone or ignored by the state.[12] Hara (1991) and Heng (1992), however, dispute Yoshihara's contentions regarding the leading Chinese capitalists, asserting that although these businessmen have had to establish ties with the Malay political elite, there has been much more competitive use of the opportunities secured through such collusion.

The corporatization movement, led by the MCA in response to active state involvement in the economy, involved the establishment of investment holding companies and cooperatives, both small and large. The primary focus of research was the leading large-scale investment holding enterprise promoted by the MCA, i.e. Multi-Purpose Holdings Bhd, and the implications of the mix between politics and business (see, for example, Gale 1985; Yeoh 1989; Heng 1988, 1992; Gomez 1991, 1994).

Heng (1992) has researched both Chinese enterprises owned by leading Chinese businessmen and companies that emerged during the corporatization movement. Heng came to the conclusion that the failure of the latter group of companies to emerge as a significant economic force, despite MCA backing, was the absence of support from the Malay political elite. While providing a rather broad historical overview of the implications of state involvement in the economy for Chinese businesses and the reasons why the latter failed to establish an alliance with state capital, Jesudason (1989) drew attention to some conflicts that emerged between Chinese businessmen and MCA leaders when companies led by the latter began acquiring other Chinese companies. The corporatization movement thus not only posed a threat to established Chinese businessmen, but also appeared to cause distrust among them and the new breed of MCA leaders leading the movement. Even though the corporatization movement failed to take root and most MCA-led companies and cooperatives came close to bankruptcy in the mid-1980s, the party's links with big Chinese business appear to have diminished considerably.

Even though most existing studies on Chinese business have been on large-scale enterprises, there is no in-depth study that traces the creation, organization and growth of these big companies. Nor has there been any thorough analysis of how these enterprises have conducted their business and increased their corporate assets despite the declining influence of their primary patron in government, the MCA, and the promulgation of state policies that positively discriminated in favor of Bumiputera capital. This study is an attempt to redress the gaps in this field by undertaking a detailed case study of some of Malaysia's largest Chinese companies.

## Research Methodology

This study employs a multi-disciplinary approach to trace the historical development of Chinese companies in Malaysia. Since this is, in effect, an attempt to study and understand entrepreneurial behavior of individual ethnic Chinese businessmen, it calls for an approach that will explore a wide range of variables. By using an historical approach showing changes in Malaysian society, the implications of these for Chinese capital can be better understood. This will focus on the interplay between Chinese businessmen and the state, particularly influential politicians in government, and the impact of ethnic politics on the business sector. Attempts will be made to identify the events and factors that have determined business behavior, corporate strategies and organizational structure of companies under Chinese ownership.

To capture the peculiarities in the style of business operations of Chinese businessmen, some insights will be provided on the development of most of the major Chinese companies listed in Table 1.2. Eight companies from among the nearly 40 Chinese-controlled concerns listed in Table 1.2 have been selected for detailed study. The first criterion for selection was the time period in which the groups came to prominence. An attempt was made to select companies of three types, namely those led by Chinese businessmen who emerged during the 1950s and 1960s, i.e. the pre- and immediate post-Independence period, those who emerged following implementation of the NEP (during the 1970s and early 1980s), and those who attained prominence since the late 1980s. Between these periods, significant policy changes were introduced, which have had profound implications for the operations of Chinese capital. For the companies selected for each of these three categories, an attempt has been made to distinguish – based on existing studies and secondary sources, particularly newspaper reports – between businessmen considered relatively independent of links to the Malay (or Chinese) political elite and those who have forged close ties with influential politicians. For each category, an attempt was also made to select companies that have grown in different ways, i.e. those that appear to have grown in a vertical or horizontal manner, as opposed to those that appear to have had a conglomerate style of growth.[13] Based on these guidelines, the following companies were selected:

Group 1: Robert Kuok (Perlis Plantations Bhd), Lim Goh Tong (Genting Bhd) and Loh Boon Siew (Oriental Holdings Bhd)

While Lim Goh Tong and Loh Boon Siew were born in China and migrated to Malaya virtually penniless, Robert Kuok was born in Malaya, the son of a successful trader. Yet, all three men had emerged by 1970 as among the richest businessmen in the country. Kuok developed a reputation as a sugar trader, ventured into shipping and hotels and, from the mid-1970s, diversified his operations abroad, establishing his headquarters in Hong Kong. Kuok has diversified his business abroad, particularly to Hong Kong and China, also moving into media and manufacturing. Lim started out as a contractor, established his reputation in gaming, and has moved into plantations, manufacturing, power generation and leisure services. Lim has ventured abroad, concentrating primarily on developing his leisure and gaming activities, but many of these ventures have not been very profitable. Genting is the leading Chinese publicly-listed company in Malaysia in terms of market capitalization; its associate company, Resorts World Bhd, is the second largest (see Table 1.2). Loh had a diversified business base, but is now primarily associated with the motor industry. While Kuok and Lim have been closely associated with UMNO leaders, Kuok has operated more independently than Lim; Kuok also had close ties with some MCA leaders. Loh was an MCA member before his death in 1995.

Group 2: William Cheng (Amsteel Corp. Bhd), Khoo Kay Peng (MUI Bhd) and Vincent Tan Chee Yioun (Berjaya Group Bhd)

While William Cheng and Khoo Kay Peng attained prominence in the 1970s, Vincent Tan emerged as a major corporate figure in the mid-1980s when he secured control of the McDonald's franchise and the privatized gaming operation Sports Toto. Cheng and Tan come from families with business backgrounds, and both went into business at an early age. Khoo's family had no business background, and he was long employed in banks before moving into business on his own. All the three business groups they lead are diversified, but while Cheng is widely known as Malaysia's 'steel king' and Khoo developed MUI Bank and MUI Finance quickly into major financial companies, the Berjaya Group has not acquired a strong reputation in any particular sector. While Cheng appears relatively unreliant on intimate ties with the political elite, Khoo has been closely associated with politicians in both UMNO and the MCA. Tan is reputedly linked with some leading UMNO leaders and has benefited from a number of other concessions from the state, including the award of the privatized multi-billion ringgit sewerage contract and licences to move into the media and telecommunications sectors. Tan does not have close links with Chinese politicians and some of his business deals with other Chinese have become publicly acrimonious battles for control of major companies. Unlike Cheng's limited links with ethnic Chinese businessmen, Khoo has had some publicized business ties with some leading local and foreign ethnic Chinese corporate figures.

### Group 3: Francis Yeoh (YTL Corp. Bhd) and Ting Pek Khiing (Ekran Bhd)

Both Francis Yeoh and Ting Pek Khiing lead companies which have developed strong reputations in the construction industry, while remaining rather small concerns with limited impact on the corporate sector before the early 1990s. While Yeoh's family has a long history of active involvement in construction, dating back to the beginning of this century, Ting's father was a small businessman with no presence outside Kuching in Sarawak. Both men achieved prominence after securing lucrative concessions from the government, which contributed to the rapid growth of their groups. Ting, however, appears to have much more extensive business deals with businessmen associated with the political elite than Yeoh. Both companies are also currently involved in manufacturing and power supply, although construction remains their primary business.[14]

These case studies of Chinese businessmen[15] should provide some understanding of how large Chinese companies have coped with government policies to ensure at least 30 per cent ownership of all publicly-listed companies. Other key questions will be addressed: how, and to what extent, has there been a coalition of Chinese and Malay capital, and of Chinese capital with other Chinese capital, both local and foreign? How has government policy, especially the NEP, affected the family company style of ownership, and what have been the changes in terms of management? To what extent have leading Chinese businessmen been privy to government-allocated benefits, under what conditions have they been obtained, and how effectively have they been used to enhance profits as opposed to productivity and competitiveness and to develop export capability?

## Research Themes

Ownership and Control

Since public listing is an effective means for raising funds, it is not uncommon for owners of profitable concerns to bring down their shareholdings while retaining control of the company. This method is only effective if there is significant diffusion of shares among the other major shareholders. If other shareholders manage to concentrate sufficient equity, control over the company can be finely balanced, influencing corporate decisions. Thus, an important distinction has to be drawn between ownership and control.

Chandler (1977: 13) defines control as the ability to determine the 'basic long-term goals and objectives of the enterprise, and the adoption of courses of action and the allocation of resources necessary for carrying out these goals.' Berle and Means (1967) stress the importance of control over ownership of stocks, and argue that in companies with a large capital base, 10 per cent equity ownership is sufficient to maintain control, particularly if there is a considerable diffusion of share ownership.[16]

There are a number of reasons why Chinese businessmen were able to relinquish majority ownership of their enterprises from the 1970s without too much concern that this would lead to loss of control over their companies. In the early 1970s, the main new owners of their equity were state agencies which were primarily passive investors. The majority of Bumiputeras who secured such stock were not active in management. Thus, the Chinese, who had managerial or technical expertise, could effectively retain control over the companies, even if one Bumiputera agency or individual secured, say, 30 per cent or even half the stock. Another phenomenon that emerged during the 1970s was that many Bumiputera individuals who secured stock in quoted companies divested their equity in return for quick profits, to 'get rich quick'. This meant that even though at least 30 per cent of such stock was in Bumiputera hands, there was some diffusion of ownership which enabled the Chinese to retain control of the companies.

However, although many individual Bumiputeras quickly divested the equity they had obtained in Chinese companies, Chinese businessmen found that they had to ensure at least 30 per cent ownership remained in Bumiputera hands to enable them to secure access to some state contracts. For example, large, publicly-listed construction companies could find their bids for government contracts rejected, ostensibly because their Bumiputera shareholdings had fallen below the stipulated share. This would inevitably mean another round of special Bumiputera share issues. IJM Corporation Bhd, controlled by Tan Chin Nam, had such an experience (see *Malaysian Business* 1 July 1991).

The distinction between ownership and control has become more pronounced with the rise of a Bumiputera middle class and a powerful well-connected Malay 'class' of 'new rich' which has emerged following the dizzying takeovers and mergers since the 1980s. Many of this new breed of Malay businessmen are professionally qualified, have managerial experience and are capable of acquiring the technical expertise they require to be productive, competitive and innovative. These businessmen are no longer merely interested in equity participation, but desire to take over and manage the companies themselves, and to develop their own corporate bases. The development of this trend is partly attributable to Prime Minister Mahathir's exhortations to Bumiputeras to discard 'get-rich-quick' practices and to instead utilize the privileges they have obtained from the state more effectively and productively. Rather than remain as mere stock owners, Mahathir has encouraged Bumiputeras to actively participate in the management of companies and to develop entrepreneurial skills which would enable them to develop independently of state patronage.[17]

The complexity of the concept of control and the fact that large stock ownership need not necessarily ensure control are reflected in the following example. The Ban Hin Lee Bank has been under the control of the Penang-based Yeap family since its incorporation. The Hong Leong group tried to secure control of the bank by acquiring almost 40 per cent of its equity. Despite this, Hong Leong was prevented from obtaining control of the bank when the Yeap family obtained the support of minority shareholders to ensure that Hong Leong could not even secure board representation. In 1994, Hong Leong eventually relinquished most of its equity in the bank to Advance Synergy Bhd, controlled by Ahmad Sebi Bakar.[18] Advance Synergy raised its stake in Ban Hin Lee Bank to almost 45 per cent, but has still not managed to gain control of the bank.

The case of Ban Hin Lee Bank reveals that control can be achieved or retained with minority stock ownership, and if control over appointments to the board of directors and key management posts, in particular that of the chief executive, remains in the hands of the family. Thus, even holding a large percentage of stock ownership may not be sufficient to secure control of a company.

Holding Company, Interlocking Stock Ownership and Pyramiding

Bonbright and Means (1969: 10–11) define a holding company as 'any company, incorporated or unincorporated, which is in a position to control, or materially to influence, the management of one or more other companies by virtue, in part at least, of its ownership of securities in the other company or companies.' Scott (1985: 135) notes that a holding company 'is designed explicitly to control or influence other companies without taking full ownership of them.' Scott (1985: 136) adds that holding companies can 'dominate the flow of capital to other business enterprises.'

In Malaysia, family-owned holding enterprises normally control one main publicly-listed company which functions as the holding company for most of the family's corporate activities. Most holding companies use pyramid systems to secure ownership over a number of companies. Pyramiding involves creating a multi-layered structure of companies, with the directors of the family holding company controlling the enterprises acquired. This allows for the emergence of interlocking stock ownership. Pyramiding is also a means to conceal the extent of corporate control.

In Malaysia, it has been quite common for a businessman to take control of a publicly-listed company and to use it to develop crossholdings with other quoted companies in which he has an interest. By getting one publicly-listed company to buy another publicly-listed company held by him, the businessman is relieved of the burden of holding the stock in his own name. The money received from divesting his equity to another company, now under his indirect control, can be used to repay loans taken to make the original acquisition. Such ownership patterns are considered legitimate market transactions by the authorities as these publicly-listed companies, which now own each other, benefit in the form of the dividends being paid. Minority shareholders also benefit as their company has, presumably, invested in shares that are profitable. The crossholding system, however, is open to abuse if it is not properly monitored by the authorities. One stockbroker highlighted the possibility of such abuse succinctly: 'Crossholdings are generally done to protect the majority shareholder who manages to secure control of the companies with largely minority money' (quoted in *Malaysian Business* 16 August 1992).

Probably one of the first businessmen to use pyramiding effectively to build up his interest in the rubber industry was the late Lee Loy Seng, whose family had made a fortune in tin-mining in Perak. In the 1950s, when the Malayan rubber industry was dominated by British companies, Lee discovered that Parit Perak Bhd, a quoted European-controlled rubber company with a small paid-up capital, had 'hard cash reserves.' Lee acquired a controlling stake in the company and, according to him, then 'used Parit Perak money to buy a controlling share in Glenealy. Then Glenealy and Parit Perak together bought Batu Lintang. Then with the help of a few friends, Batu Lintang, Glenealy and Parit Perak bought control of Batu Kawan. We just rolled on like this' (quoted in *Malaysian Business* May 1973; see Chapter 4). Lee eventually emerged as the largest local owner of plantations.

During the 1970s and 1980s, i.e. the NEP decades, most of the major Chinese groups used a holding company using a pyramiding system to develop extensive interlocking stock ownership. Among the most notable examples were William Cheng's Lion Corporation group, Khoo Kay Peng's MUI group and Vincent Tan Chee Yioun's Berjaya Group Bhd. Multi-Purpose Holdings, which is controlled by two other listed companies, Kamunting Bhd and Malaysian Plantations Bhd, and ultimately controlled by T.K. Lim's family through private holding companies, probably has the most intricate corporate structure (see Chapter 3). This pattern of growth using publicly-listed companies as holding companies also points to the increasing use of the stock market to raise funds.

The growth of Malaysia's only bourse, the Kuala Lumpur Stock Exchange (KLSE) and its impact on the local capital market, has increased phenomenally during the last two decades. In 1973, when the KLSE was established, 262 companies were listed on the bourse. The nominal value of the total shares listed then was RM3.8 billion, while its market valuation was RM13.3 billion (Faridah 1997: 21). By 1995, the number of companies on the KLSE had increased by more than 100 per cent, even though companies incorporated in Singapore had been delisted from the KLSE in 1990. Of the 529 companies listed on the KLSE in 1995, 369 companies were on the main board with 160 on the second board. The second board was introduced in 1989 to enable profitable small- and medium-sized companies to secure additional funding through the stock market. The nominal value of the shares of these 529 companies in 1995 was RM92.4 billion, while their market valuation was RM565.6 billion (*KLSE Annual Companies Handbook* 21 (1) 1996: 634). In 1980, market capitalization of the KLSE was about 80 per cent of GDP; by 1995, it had increased by more than threefold, to 265 per cent of GDP (Callen and Reynolds 1997: 185).[19] By 1992, the KLSE had become the largest stock market in Southeast Asia and the fourth largest in Asia (*Malaysian Business* 16 August 1992).

Other factors contributed to the increase in the KLSE's market capitalization. The government's active promotion of privatization from the mid-1980s led to the listing of 24 public enterprises on the KLSE. The market capitalization of these privatized agencies accounted for 22 per cent of the KLSE's total market capitalization in 1995 (Callen and Reynolds 1997: 185).[20] The new middle class that had emerged had also begun investing significantly in the stock market from the early 1990s.[21] From 1988, the amount of investment capital moving about freely in international finance markets had grown phenomenally, augmenting increasing domestic investment. In East Asia, between the period 1990 to 1993, Malaysia registered the highest rate of net capital inflows as a percentage of gross domestic investment (see Table 1.3). Such investments contributed to the potential that the securities markets in Malaysia could provide as a source for funds (see Table 1.4). Between 1995 and 1996, for example, there was an almost 40 per cent increase in funds raised through the private capital market. From the early 1980s, a new jargon began to permeate the stock-market vocabulary. Among the

*Table 1.3* Capital Flows in East Asia as a Percentage of Gross Domestic Investment (GDI), 1990–93

| Country | 1990–92 | 1991–93 |
| --- | --- | --- |
| China | 10.2 | 15.1 |
| Indonesia | 16.9 | 18.8 |
| Rep. of Korea | 4.1 | 6.1 |
| Philippines | 14.1 | 16.8 |
| Thailand | 11.9 | 11.2 |
| Malaysia | 22.4 | 29.3 |

*Note*: Percentages reflect a three-year average.
*Source*: World Bank 1996: 21

Table 1.4 Malaysia: Funds Raised in Private Securities Markets, 1995 and 1996 (RM million)

|  | 1995 Jan–Aug | 1996[a] Jan–Aug |
|---|---|---|
| **Equity Market** | | |
| Shares[b] | 8,165 | 11,198 |
| Public issues | 3,598 | 1,692 |
| Rights issues | 3,316 | 4,435 |
| Special Issues[c] | 483 | 1,878 |
| Private placements[d] | 645 | 3,193 |
| Warrants | 123 | 0 |
| *Debt securities* (gross) | | |
| Conventional bonds | 4,825 | 5,797 |
| Convertible bonds | 708 | 698 |
| Islamic notes | 800 | 2,350 |
| Cagamas bonds | 1,572 | 3,365 |
| Less: Redemptions | (2,999) | (2,145) |
| Net issues of debt securities | 4,906 | 10,065 |
| NET FUNDS RAISED | 13,071 | 21,263 |

[a] Preliminary data
[b] Refers to share issues by companies listed on the KLSE.
[c] Includes special issues to Bumiputeras and selected investors.
[d] Includes restricted offer for sales.
[e] Refers to securities with maturity of more than one year.

Source: *Malaysian Business* 16 November 1996

most common new corporate terms were 'dawn raids,' 'green mail' and 'poison pill' tactics, 'hostile takeovers,' 'white knights' and 'leveraged buy-outs'. During this merger and acquisition boom period, worrying developments involving the financial system became common place; many of these takeovers were highly leveraged and collaterized against the assets of the target company itself.

Interlocking Directorates

Interlocking directorships refer to a situation in which a director of one company also sits on the boards of directors of one or more other companies. With such interlocking, as Pennings (1980: 2) notes, 'the individual who sits on two corporate boards provides a connection by which the firms can communicate, establish a common body of information, and develop a uniform structure for superior organizational intelligence.' Through pyramiding, the directors of the holding company have the power to appoint one or more directors to the boards of the companies acquired. This often results in the possibility of inter-company transactions, like the sale of one subsidiary to another subsidiary, the routing of profitable business to one subsidiary in preference to another, and the concealment of losses or creation of non-existent deficits (Berle and Means 1967: 183).

With regard to directors of companies not interlocked through share ownership, Scott (1997: 7) points out that 'at the very least, interlocking directorships constitute channels of communication between enterprises: a person who sits on two or more boards – a "multiple director" – has access to the inside information of each company and has an opportunity to "transmit" this information from one board to another.'

Thus, it is widely presumed that a study of interlocking directorships would provide insights that would help identify and trace complex corporate connections between politically-linked Malay directors and Chinese majority shareholders of the companies. However, a systematic investigation of the background of the Malay directors of Chinese corporations who figure among the top one hundred companies on the KLSE does not appear to bear this out (see Table 1.5).

It appears from Table 1.5 that the Bumiputera directors of large Chinese companies are not as prominent or as politically influential as presumed. A number of Bumiputera directors are former bureaucrats or members of the nine royal houses. A few are former cabinet members or relatives of former or serving ministers and other prominent politicians. There are some interlocking ties, but the common personalities do not involve significant business linkages.

Although Table 1.5 indicates that are there are no major political figures or their close business associates on the lists of directors, several important qualifying points have to be made. First, Table 1.5 cannot be said to be representative of all directorships involving politically-linked businessmen. The pattern of interlocking directorships among publicly-listed companies indicates that some politically well-connected individuals are directors and shareholders of a large number of companies, including a number of Chinese companies with smaller market capitalization (see Gomez 1997a). The fact that interlocking directorship ties do not appear significant among large Chinese companies raises important questions. Second, one should

## Chinese Business in Malaysia

*Table 1.5* Profiles of Prominent Bumiputera Directors of Chinese-Controlled Companies Among Top 100 Publicly-Listed KLSE Companies

| Company | Name of Director | Background |
|---|---|---|
| Genting Bhd | Mohd Haniff Omar | Ex-Inspector General of Police |
|  | Nik Hashim Nik Yusoff | Lawyer and banker |
|  | Mohd Amin Osman | Ex-Deputy Inspector General of Police |
| Resorts World | Mohd Haniff Omar | Ex-Inspector General of Police |
|  | Alwi Jantan | Ex-ministry Secretary General |
| Asiatic Development | Mohd Amin Osman | Ex-Deputy Inspector General of Police |
| YTL Corp. | Yahya Ismail | UMNO business proxy |
|  | Raja Mohar Raja Badiozaman | Ex-ministry Secretary General |
| Public Bank | Mohd Nizam Tun Razak | Son of former PM Razak |
| Berjaya Toto | — |  |
| Jaya Tiasa Holdings | Abu Talib Othman | Ex-Attorney General |
| Magnum Corp | Mohd Khir Johari | Ex-UMNO Minister |
|  | Mohd Ghazali Mohd Seth | Ex-Armed Forces Chief of Staff |
| Multi-Purpose Holdings | — |  |
| Kamunting Corp | — |  |
| Hong Leong Credit | Hashim Mohd Ali | Ex-General; PM Mahathir's brother-in-law |
| Hong Leong Bank | Nik Hashim Nik Yusoff | Lawyer and banker |
| Hume Industries | — |  |
| OYL Industries | Zailah Tun Dr Ismail | Daughter of former Deputy PM |
|  | Mohd Nazim Tun Razak | Son of ex-PM Razak |
| Hong Leong Prop. | — |  |
| Malaysian Pacific Ind. | Syed Zaid Syed Jaffar Albar | Brother of UMNO minister |
| Hong Leong Industries | Tunku Dara Naqiah | Negeri Sembilan royalty |
|  | Ahmad Johari Tun Razak | Son of former PM Razak |
|  | Nasruddin Mohamed | Ex-ministry Secretary General |
| Lingui Developments | — |  |
| Kuala Lumpur Kepong | Robert Hamzah | Brother of ex-Finance Minister Razaleigh |
| Leader Universal | — |  |
| Ekran | — |  |
| Pacific Chemicals | — |  |
| Malayan United Ind. | Mohd Khir Johari | Former UMNO Minister |
|  | Nik Hashim Nik Yusoff | Lawyer and banker |
| Pan Malaysia Cement | Mohd Yassin Jaffar | Brother of Deputy PM Anwar confidante Kamaruddin Jaffar; ex-Prisons Chief |
| Perlis Plantations | — |  |
| MBf Capital | Tunku Abdullah Tuanku Abd Rahman | King's brother; son of first king |
| Sri Hartamas | — |  |
| Tan Chong Motors | — |  |
| IOI Properties | Nasruddin Mohamed | Ex-ministry Secretary General |

*Chinese Business: Culture, Entrepreneurship or Patronage?*

| Company | Name of Director | Background |
|---|---|---|
| Amsteel Corp | Zain Hashim | Ex-army chief |
|  | Nasruddin Mohamed | Ex-ministry Secretary General |
| Oriental Holdings | Hamzah Sendut | Ex-USM Vice Chancellor |
| Sungei Way Holdings | Nasruddin Mohamed | Ex-ministry Secretary General |
| Acidchem | Hamzah Sendut | Ex-USM Vice Chancellor |
| Metroplex | Yahya Ismail | UMNO business proxy |
| Kian Joo Can Factory | Tunku Nadzaruddin Tuanku Jaafar | Negeri Sembilan royalty |
|  | Raja Ashman Shah Azlan Shah | Son of Perak Sultan |
| Hap Seng Consol. | Hamzah Sendut | Ex-USM Vice Chancellor |
| C&C Bintang | Sallehuddin Mohamed | Ex-Government Chief Secetary |
|  | Hassan Abas | UMNO-linked businessman |
|  | Jaffar Mohd Ali | Brother-in-law of PM Mahathir |
|  | Abd Rashid Mohd Hussain | Robert Kuok's son-in-law |
|  | Yahya Ahmad | President of National Chamber of Commerce |
| CCM | Mohd Sheriff Mohd Kassim | Ex-ministry Secretary General |
|  | Mohd Ghazali Seth | Ex-Armed Forces Chief of Staff |

Sources: *KLSE Annual Companies Handbook* 21 (1–4), 1996

not underestimate the significance of bureaucrats as businessmen. Following implementation of the NEP, many public enterprises became directly involved in business. This propelled bureaucrats into business, where they developed management skills and made important business contacts. They also became very familiar with the local business environment and problems of doing business. Moreover, their knowledge of government machinery has often been crucial, especially to Chinese businesses, in facilitating decision-making and circumventing red tape (Sieh 1992; Jesudason 1989).[22]

Yet, the actual roles these Bumiputera directors play in the management of Chinese companies are debatable. For example, Nasruddin Mohamed, who served as the secretary-general of the important Ministry of Trade & Industry, is a director of Hong Leong Industries, IOI Properties, Amsteel Corporation and Sungei Way Holdings, but there are no major business links between these companies controlled by different Chinese businessmen. Hamzah Sendut, the late former vice-chancellor of Universiti Sains Malaysia (USM), sat on the board of Oriental Holdings and Hap Seng Consolidated, but there are no corporate links between these two companies. Ghazali Seth, a former armed forces chief of staff, is on the board of Magnum and CCM, but again there are no significant ties between these companies. Nik Hashim Nik Yusof, a lawyer and a banker, serves on the board of some major companies like MUI, Genting and Hong Leong Bank, yet this tie does not appear to have contributed to any business cooperation among these companies. This suggests that the Bumiputera directors of large Chinese-controlled companies are not links for interlocking directorates, but simply reflect their utility to the companies which have invited them to serve on their boards.

# Chinese Business, Colonialism and Accumulation

## 2

### The Colonial Period

Western colonization of Malaya commenced in 1511 with the capture of Malacca, a major seaport on the west coast of the peninsula, first by the Portuguese and then by the Dutch (in 1641); both these European colonizers made little attempt to penetrate further into the peninsula. Similarly, when the British first colonized Malaya in 1786 with their occupation of Penang (an island off the north-west coast of the peninsula), and then of Malacca in 1795 and of Singapore (an island off the southern tip of the peninsula), the emphasis of the colonizers was to use these ports to spearhead their commercial penetration into various parts of Southeast Asia (Parmer 1969: 281–84). It was only after industrialization in Europe gained momentum in the late 19th century that the British became aware that the other states in the peninsula had tremendous economic potential, with their rich deposits of tin ore and vast areas of land suitable for rubber.

Chinese trade links and settlements in the Malay archipelago, particularly in Malacca, predated those by the European by at least two centuries. After the British secured control over the major trade routes, Chinese spread deep into the interior where tin had been discovered. The growing involvement of Chinese in the tin industry required their mass immigration from during the mid-19th century (Gullick and Gale 1986: 52–6).

British involvement in the rest of the peninsula began in 1874, when they secured control of the state of Perak, where some of the largest deposits of tin had been discovered and many Chinese had moved in the ensuing tin rush. This soon led to problems among the Chinese who were allied with rival Malay chiefs. When the position of the Sultan of Perak became tenuous, he asked the British to mediate in these disputes. This provided an avenue for the British to intervene in and take over the affairs of the state; eventually, the sultan was replaced and his role reduced to that of a mere figurehead.[1] Despite this, the Chinese managed to retain control of tin mining as they had the capacity to secure immigrant labor from China for the labor-intensive industry.

Most of these Chinese immigrants came from Southern China and comprised members of various dialect groups. These dialect differences were further complicated by the division of the Chinese into clans and guild associations. By 1947, of the 2.6 million Chinese in Malaya, around 32 per cent were Hokkiens, 25 per cent were Cantonese, 17 per cent were Hakkas, 14 per cent Teochews, and six per cent were Hainanese. Of the other smaller dialect groups, 2.76 per cent were Kwongsai, 1.84 per cent were Hokchiu, 0.66 per cent were Henghwa, 0.49 per cent were Hokchia, with other groups making up the remaining figure (Ratnam 1965: 5). Another division among the Chinese was between more recent migrants and the Straits-born Chinese – also known as Babas – who were more likely to be westernized, English-educated and English-speaking; a majority of the Straits-born Chinese spoke little or no Chinese.[2]

Many Chinese in Malaya soon developed and adapted frontier community institutions and arrangements to meet the need for new social and economic organization in the face of generally unsympathetic colonial authorities. Since financial institutions were not then available to them, the founders of business enterprises had to rely primarily on their own resources and Straits Chinese credit to develop their businesses. By the mid-1930s, although the Chinese had emerged as an economic force, their commercial interests in the country were not as extensive as those of the British. Most of these Chinese enterprises were family-owned and based primarily on small-scale trade and petty business ventures (see Puthucheary 1960). Given the size of their operations, Chinese businesses rarely posed a serious threat to the bigger, better financed, and politically favored British enterprises. Despite these impediments to the development of Chinese capital, by the beginning of the 20th century, a number of Chinese had come to own a number of large rubber plantations. In the tin mining industry, some Chinese had managed to secure a huge presence before the advent of the capital-intensive dredge tilted the balance in favor of the bigger British mining companies.[3]

Malay involvement in the emerging capitalist economy was not encouraged by the British, who preferred the Malays to remain in the more rural sectors of the economy, primarily in fish and rice production. When Malay peasants turned to rubber production, the British tried to block their efforts by imposing restrictive cultivation conditions on land. After 1910, for example, the colonial government insisted that the Malays could not grow rubber on newly-acquired land. Those who did so had to pay higher land taxes than those who cultivated food crops (Lim 1977). Although the Malay Reservation Act (1913) and the Land Enactment Act (1917) were enforced, ostensibly to protect Malay peasant land from being taken over by non-Malays, implementation of these laws led to the ghettoization of Malay peasants on their 'reserves' (Hing 1984). These early discriminatory policies in favor of British plantation interests severely limited the potential development of indigenous capital and shackled Malays to traditional economic activities. The ways in which the British hindered the development of Malays were later used to justify the post-1969 policies that positively discriminated in favor of the Malays.

Among the most prominent Chinese businessmen of the colonial era were Eu Tong Sen, Lau Pak Kuan, Loke Yew, Tan Kah Kee and Lee Kong Chian, all of whom secured significant stakes in tin mining or rubber plantations (see Chan and Chiang 1994; Lee and Chow 1997).[4] With the exception of Eu Tong Sen, the others were born in China. However, a number of Straits-born Chinese emerged as major business figures in Malacca and Singapore, with interests in plantations, trading and shipping. Among the more prominent of these Straits-born Chinese businessmen were Chan Kang Swi (a rubber planter and banker from Malacca), Singaporean Tan Jiak Kim and Malaccan Tan Jiak Hoe (associated with the Straits Steamship Company),[5] Lee Keng Hee (a shipping, property and plantation magnate born in Singapore, but whose family roots could be traced back seven generations to Malacca) and the Malaccan E Kong Guan (a leading owner of rubber plantations whose father was a merchant in Singapore) (Khoo 1988; Lee and Chow 1997).

Eu Tong Sen, a Cantonese, was born in 1877 in Penang, but educated in China. The son of Eu Kong, a wealthy tin miner in Perak, Eu took over his father's business at the age of 21, diversified into rubber plantations, founded the Lee Wah Bank in Singapore and expanded his operations into Hong Kong and Canton. Loke Yew, a Cantonese, was born in Guangdong province in 1846, and migrated to Singapore at the age of 13. He started out as a sundry shop assistant and, after saving some funds, moved to Perak to open his own tin mines. Loke Yew expanded his mining operations to a number of other states – particularly Selangor and Pahang – and diversified into revenue farming, rubber plantations, tobacco cultivation and trading and banking. In 1903, he helped found the Kwong Yik Banking Corporation Ltd, the first Chinese bank to be incorporated in Malaya. By the early 1900s, Loke Yew was reputed to have become the richest man in Malaya. Lau Pak Khuan, a Hakka, was also born in Guangdong in 1895. At the age of 12, Lau came to Malaya to work for a relative in Perak. He later took over a tin mine and expanded his business in the state. Lau later diversified his operations and helped establish two banks, the Chung Khiaw Bank and the Overseas Union Bank, an insurance company, Public Insurance Company, and the Oriental Smelting Company (Lee and Chow 1997: 42, 82, 123–5; Khoo 1988).

One of the leading Chinese businessmen at the turn of this century was Tan Kah Kee, a Hokkien, born in Fujian province in 1874. After receiving his early education in China, Tan came to Singapore at the age of 17 to help run a thriving business his father, Tan Kee Peck, had established in the 1870s. Through his company, Soon Ann, Tan Kee Peck started out as a rice trader, then ventured into real estate and rice and sago milling, before establishing a reputation in the pineapple industry. Although Tan Kee Peck became the largest pineapple producer in the peninsula and controlled about 70 per cent of canned pineapple exports by the early 1900s, Soon Ann ran up huge debts and was liquidated in 1904. Kah Kee managed to pay off much of Soon Ann's debts, establishing his own reputation in the process. Kah Kee initially remained in the pineapple and rice business, then diversified into the rubber industry, expanding his various operations into Malaya, and then Thailand, Indonesia, Hong Kong and China. Kah Kee moved into shipping in 1905, and bought a stake in the Chinese Commercial Bank in 1912. In 1919, he incorporated Tan Kah Kee and Company and established vertically integrated operations in the rubber industry. He acquired a number rubber factories and began manufacturing rubber products, including tyres, shoes and toys. In 1923, Kah Kee established a Chinese newspaper, the *Nanyang Siang Pau*. His total capital investments during the 1920s was estimated at around eight million Straits dollars (then approximately US$4.54 million). However, during the depression years in the early 1930s, Kah Kee's business ventures suffered significantly. He was bailed out with the help of his son-in-law Lee Kong Chian, who bought over a number of assets owned by Tan Kah

Kee & Co. By the early 1930s, Kah Kee had begun to be actively involved in events in China: first, with the war involving Japan, then with the activities of Mao's Communist party. Kah Kee later returned to China, where he died in 1961 (Yong 1987: 20–2; Lee 1997: 155–8; Pan 1990: 181–5; Huff 1994: 219–30).

Lee Kong Chian founded the Lee Rubber group, and his family retains a prominent presence in Singapore's corporate sector, particularly through the Oversea-Chinese Banking Corporation Ltd (OCBC) group.[6] Lee, who was born in 1894 in Fujian province, joined his father in Singapore in 1903. In 1916, Lee was employed by Tan Kah Kee as the latter began to expand his rubber trade to Europe. Lee worked with Tan until 1927, when he established the Lee Smoke House – the predecessor of Lee Rubber – in Johore. By 1937, Lee was described by one newspaper, the *Pinang Gazette*, as the 'rubber and pineapple king of Malaya' (quoted in Khoo 1988). Like Tan, Lee soon developed an integrated operation in both industries – planting, processing, packaging and exporting – and expanded his operations to Thailand and Indonesia. Lee soon diversified extensively, with interests in biscuits, printing, and the Chinese Commercial Bank (formed in 1912), before helping to establish OCBC in 1932. In 1938, Lee became the second chairman of OCBC, a post he held until 1964. Under Lee's control, the OCBC group developed an interest in a number of British-controlled companies, including Fraser & Neave Ltd, Straits Trading Ltd, Wearne Brothers Ltd, Sime Darby Holding Ltd, United Engineers Ltd and Malayan Breweries Ltd. Lee died in 1967, but his family remained the largest shareholder of OCBC stock (Lim 1981: 93–4; Yoshihara 1988: 240–1; Huff 1994: 221–30; Lee and Chow 1997: 88–90).

These brief accounts of the rise of some leading Chinese businessmen during the colonial period reflected a more general trend among most Chinese capitalists, namely the predominantly family-owned and managed nature of their enterprises. This was one reason why Chinese capitalists were compelled to form the Malayan Chinese Association (MCA); they hoped that effective political representation in a post-colonial government would enable them to protect their economic interests. The British also encouraged Chinese businessmen and professionals to form an organization which would serve as an alternative to the Malayan Communist Party (MCP), which then had much support from within the Chinese community.[7] When the MCA was established in 1949, its leadership inevitably comprised anti-communist Guomindang (KMT) leaders and wealthy

Chinese businessmen. Among the original leaders of the MCA were the tin miner Lau Pak Khuan, H.S. Lee, a graduate of Cambridge University and another wealthy tin miner, and Tan Cheng Lock and his son Tan Siew Sin, from a prominent Baba family from Malacca with vast interests in rubber plantations (Heng 1988: 63–5).[8]

The move made by Chinese businessmen into politics was not a difficult one as many MCA leaders were then serving as presidents of the Chinese Chambers of Commerce in most states in the peninsula, as well as leaders of important Chinese associations such as the Selangor Chinese Assembly Hall, the Perak Chinese Association, the Penang Chinese Assembly Hall and the Johore Baru Chinese Association. They also led the trade guilds, cultural, social and recreational association and numerous dialect associations (Heng 1988: 64–5). Tan Cheng Lock, for example, was also the chairman of the Malacca Chinese Chamber of Commerce. In view of the MCA's history of bourgeois leadership, the party has rarely been able to muster the support of working-class Chinese.

Since the British colonial government insisted on some form of multi-racial co-operation before independence could be granted, in 1952, the MCA helped form the Alliance, a coalition with another ethnically-based and elite-led party, the United Malays' National Organization (UMNO).[9] An agreement, popularly referred to as the 'bargain,' was reached between the leaders of UMNO and the MCA. The bargain basically involved an understanding among the multi-racial elite that Malays would dominate politics, leaving the Chinese relatively unaffected by state intrusion in the economy. The Alliance was also an effective way for UMNO and the MCA to retain their ethnic identity while mobilizing broad multi-ethnic support. In 1954, the Malayan Indian Congress (MIC), another ethnically-based party led by professionals, joined the Alliance. This tripartite coalition was also an expedient arrangement for these political parties since the mass-based UMNO, whose members comprised primarily peasants, found that it could depend on the MCA for financial support. The success of this collaboration was reflected in the results of the country's first general election in 1955, when the Alliance won 51 of the 52 parliamentary seats.

When the Alliance was formed, the leaders were primarily concerned with capturing power – the aristocratic Malays were keen to secure political power, while the Chinese bourgeoisie wanted to preserve and enhance their economic base. Thus, it was doubtful if the three parties in the Alliance shared a common political ideology.

The objectives of UMNO, MCA and MIC have been described as being based on 'ethnic ideologies' (see Brown 1994: 206–57). In view of the bourgeois orientation of these party leaders, ethno-populism has camouflaged class dominance; this has also enabled these parties to represent their leaders as ethnic patrons.

The hegemony of ethno-populism among politicians was facilitated by the elimination of the parliamentary left in the mid-1960s and, with it, more ideological debates in Malaysian politics. The legitimacy of ethnic mobilization has sustained ethno-populism, resulting in the inability of leaders who advocate inter-ethnic solidarity to receive much support. With limited inter-ethnic interaction, there have been fears among all ethnic communities that their interests would be marginalized in multi-racial organizations.

## From Independence to May 1969

After independence in 1957, MCA leaders were given the important Finance and Trade & Industry portfolios in the post-colonial government which provided them with means to protect and advance favored Chinese economic interests. Since the Alliance had assured the British against nationalization of their vast investments in their former colony if independence was granted early,[10] foreign – particularly British – capital continued to dominate the major economic sectors in the country. Though the Alliance viewed foreign investments in Malaya as crucial for economic development, UMNO also believed that permitting foreigners control of a large stake in the economy would curb the post-colonial expansion of Chinese capital (Golay 1969: 346–7).

During the first decade after independence, there is much evidence that Chinese businessmen were privy to various types of concessions from the state. When Malaysia's first Finance Minister Henry H.S. Lee resigned, he asked for and received a licence from the government to establish a bank, the Development & Commercial (D&C) Bank Bhd.[11] A number of other Chinese also secured banking licences from the government, including Khoo Teck Puat (who established Malayan Banking Bhd in 1960) and Teh Hong Piow (who set up Public Bank Bhd in 1966). Lim Goh Tong obtained a licence to run a casino. In manufacturing, Robert Kuok benefited from the government's import-substituting industrialization (ISI) incentives by setting up sugar and flour mills.

The government, recognizing the economy's over-dependence on export earnings from tin and rubber, had promoted the production of other commodities, including cocoa and oil palm, while ISI was introduced to encourage industrialization on the basis of manufacture of goods previously imported. ISI was pursued by offering infrastructure and credit facilities as well as tariff protection, to the mainly foreign manufacturing companies seeking to secure or increase their local market shares.[12] British investors, particularly anxious to preserve (if not expand) their market share from the colonial period, took good advantage of incentives offered by the government.[13] Through the Pioneer Industries Ordinance introduced in 1958, the government offered, among other incentives, tax relief on profits to new import-substituting manufacturing firms, with the length of such relief dependent on the size of the company's investments. The Pioneer Industries Ordinance was legislated to be temporary, but tariff protection tended to be more long term. These investment incentives were also not structured to encourage eventual exports of initially import-substituting manufacturing.

One local businessman who secured pioneer status to venture into sugar and flour production and milling was Robert Kuok (Sia 1993: 59–63). Sia (1993: 56) claims that Kuok had also been encouraged by Abdul Razak, Prime Minister from 1971 to 1976, to go into the plywood and veneer industry; these ventures were not very successful. This was quite significant since the incentives offered by the government tended to favor large, capital-intensive companies. Moreover, there was some Malay concern that ethnic Chinese would be the primary beneficiaries of protected domestic industrialization. Since the technological base among domestic, particularly Chinese, companies was rather modest, foreign enterprises benefited most from ISI. Inevitably, the development of domestic industry remained limited. The extent of domestic capital participation in ISI initiatives in the 1960s was rather small, mainly involving ethnic Chinese in fairly simple food, plastic and wood-based industries.

During the period 1957 to 1970, the Malaysian economy grew appreciably, registering an average annual growth rate of 5.8 per cent. Malaysia's considerable export earnings ensured large savings and foreign exchange reserves, contributing to investments, growth and structural change. Despite this, by the late 1960s, the deliberate bifurcation of political and economic power between Malay aristocrats and Chinese businessmen respectively was increasingly untenable for the Malays. Even after a decade of independence, only minimal changes had been made to the power sharing arrangements. In spite of Malay political dominance, the community had made little economic progress. The government's rural development efforts, introduced primarily to help the Malays, emphasized productivity increases, but did not involve redistribution of land or capital. Furthermore, the government's commitment to limited regulation was viewed by many Malays as the primary cause of increased economic inequality and the concentration of wealth in foreign and Chinese hands.

As Malay frustration increased over insignificant changes in ethnic ownership patterns, the UMNO leadership came under severe criticism from within its own ranks for the government's non-interventionist policy. Many of these criticisms were voiced during two Bumiputera Economic Congresses held in 1965 and in 1968, and organized by Malay politicians and civil servants. The government's response to these criticisms was to increase allocations for the establishment of new public enterprises. The Majlis Amanah Rakyat (MARA, or the Council of Trust for Indigenous People) was incorporated to establish and manage new industrial enterprises for eventual transfer over to Bumiputeras. MARA was also responsible for establishing training institutions and underwriting or acquiring corporate equity (Gale 1981: 5–85).[14] In 1966, Bank Bumiputra (M) Bhd was established to encourage and develop Bumiputera businesses, principally through financial assistance. Bank Bumiputra's incorporation was viewed by some non-Malays as an attempt to break Chinese and foreign domination of the banking industry (Snodgrass 1980: 53). However, among the original directors of Bank Bumiputra was Robert Kuok, while one Chinese who played a key role in the bank's management soon after it was established was Khoo Kay Peng, who went on to develop the MUI Bank group. In 1969, a Bumiputera trust agency, Perbadanan Nasional Bhd (Pernas, or the National Corporation) was incorporated to acquire corporate equity on behalf of the community.[15]

The establishment and promotion of these new enterprises by the government led to growing concern among the Chinese that these enterprises would eventually encroach into the economic sectors they controlled. Subsequently, there was increasing Chinese dissatisfaction with the MCA over the party's reticence in checking pro-Malay state intervention in the economy.

This pattern of economic development exacerbated already existing social inequalities. Between 1957 and 1970, distribution of income worsened, while inequality among all the major ethnic groups grew, with inequality within the Malay community increasing most. This growing inequality was perceived primarily in racial terms. Malay resentment over their limited ownership of corporate wealth was expressed mainly against ubiquitous Chinese businesses, while non-Malay frustrations were directed against the UMNO-dominated state.

This led to popular discontent with the ruling coalition, resulting in the Alliance's worst electoral performance in the 1969 general election. Although the Alliance narrowly retained control of the federal government, in the state-level elections, Kelantan and Penang fell to the opposition, while the ruling coalition only barely secured majorities in the Selangor, Perak and Terengganu legislatures. Since the Alliance had retained control of the government with a severely diminished majority, communal tensions were high as the results were perceived by some quarters in UMNO as a diminution of the party's – and hence, Malay – political hegemony. This, and other factors, triggered off severe race riots in the capital on 13 May 1969.

Following the 1969 general election and the subsequent riots, UMNO embarked on a series of discussions with all major political parties to regroup the Alliance into an enlarged coalition, the Barisan Nasional. The MCA, which had fared very badly in the election, found its position in government weakened considerably when the Gerakan Rakyat Malaysia (Gerakan, or Peoples' Movement Party) and the People's Progressive Party (PPP) were incorporated into the Barisan Nasional; both these ostensibly multi-racial parties enjoyed much Chinese support. The leading Malay opposition party, Parti Islam Se-Malaysia (PAS, or the Malaysian Islamic Party) was also co-opted into the Barisan Nasional. UMNO's accommodationist initiative, through the consociationalist arrangements of the Barisan Nasional, meant that the significant Chinese support enjoyed by the Gerakan and the PPP eroded the MCA's influence. Meanwhile, the incorporation of PAS, which was very influential in the east coast and north of the peninsula, enhanced Malay electoral support. PAS, however, left the coalition in 1977.[16]

UMNO's hegemony in the Barisan Nasional gave the Malay party leverage to pursue affirmative action policies in favor of Bumiputeras. Since the race riots were mainly ascribed to the inequitable distribution of wealth between the Malays and the Chinese, the New Economic Policy (NEP) was introduced in 1970. The goals of the NEP were to achieve national unity by 'eradicating poverty,' irrespective of race, and by 'restructuring society' so as to achieve inter-ethnic economic parity between the predominantly Malay Bumiputeras and the predominantly Chinese non-Bumiputeras.

The NEP entailed partial abandonment of the previously more *laissez-faire* style of economic management in favor of greater state intervention, primarily for ethnic affirmative action, including the accelerated expansion of the Bumiputera middle class, capital accumulation on behalf of the Bumiputeras and the creation of Malay capitalists. This was to be attained by increasing Bumiputera corporate equity ownership from a mere 2.4 per cent in 1970 to 30 per cent in 1990, and by reducing the poverty level from over 50 per cent in 1970 to 16 per cent by 1990.

A number of measures were taken to achieve the NEP goals: improving access of the poor to training, capital and land; changing education and employment patterns among Bumiputeras, through scholarships and ethnic quotas favoring Bumiputera entry into tertiary institutions; requiring companies to restructure their corporate holdings to ensure at least 30 per cent Bumiputera ownership; and by allotting publicly-listed shares at par value or at only nominal premiums to Bumiputeras.

The need for Chinese businessmen to cultivate ties with influential Malays became imperative when it became obvious that UMNO hegemony in the Barisan Nasional meant that Chinese capitalists could not depend on the MCA to protect their interests. When it became clear the NEP's second objective, the restructuring of society, was the main emphasis of the policy, the need to find ways to accommodate Malays became urgent if Chinese businessmen were to continue to have access to the means to accumulate wealth.

In 1969, Chinese equity ownership stood at 22.8 per cent, compared to the Bumiputera share of a mere 1.5 per cent, while the bulk of the remaining equity was under foreign ownership (see Table 1.1). To ensure more parity in ethnic ownership patterns, the government increased public sector expenditure, particularly to fund the growing number of government-owned enterprises participating in business activities. Public enterprises, which included Bumiputera trust agencies, were used by the government to actively participate in almost all sectors of the economy and acquire assets on behalf of Bumiputeras.[17] In contrast to the 10 public enterprises in 1957, there were 1014 by 1985 (Rugayah 1995: 66).

Increased state funding for public enterprises and trust agencies, which allowed them to go on a massive acquisition drive, was facilitated by a gradual shift to deficit financing and the fortuitous availability of oil from off the east coast of the peninsula from the mid-1970s. Oil's contribution to total export earnings increased appreciably after the international oil price hikes in 1973. The acquisition drive of these public enterprises was aided by a 1975 government ruling that each publicly-listed company had to ensure that a minimum 30 per cent of its equity was allocated to Bumiputera agencies or individuals. Apart from this, wholly-owned companies were incorporated by state enterprises to venture into most areas of business. Public enterprises also established joint-ventures with Bumiputera, non-Bumiputera and foreign companies. In many cases, public enterprises merely acquired between 20 to 50 per cent of equity in companies for investment purposes.

By the late 1970s, public enterprises had acquired controlling interests in a number of major foreign-owned companies. In 1975, Pernas acquired the British-owned London Tin (now the Malaysia Mining Corporation), the country's leading tin mining group. The following year, Pernas secured control of the British-owned Southeast Asian-based multinational Sime Darby Bhd. In 1981, the British-controlled Guthrie Corporation, the largest plantation company in Malaysia, was taken over by another major trust agency Permodalan Nasional Bhd (PNB, or the National Equity Corporation), which was soon to emerge as the country's largest institutional investor. By 1993, the assets owned by PNB amounted to almost RM22.654 billion, making it the largest single holder of corporate stock (*Malaysian Business* 1 December 1993). PNB's assets then comprised 26 per cent of the finance sector, 26 per cent of the hotel industry, 57 per cent of the manufacturing sector, five per cent of the plantation sector, six per cent of the property sector and six per cent of the mining sector (*New Straits Times* 8 June 1994).

State intervention as well as public sector investments became important means for private wealth accumulation and political patronage. Public and Bumiputera enterprises were generally assured of favorable government treatment, particularly through licences, contracts and access to finance and information, especially if supported by influential politicians. This enabled many such enterprises to advance rapidly in areas of business in which government regulation and political patronage has been crucial, such as real estate, transport, plantations, mining and finance. As Chinese involvement in most of these sectors was significant, they tried, but were unable to get the state enterprises to focus attention only on businesses controlled by foreigners (see Jesudason 1989: 128–65).

The reactions of individual Chinese businessmen to the NEP were different. Some adopted a rather offensive approach. One prominent example of this type of reaction was that of the Singaporean banker Tan Chin Tuan, chairman of the major financial institution and holding company, the Oversea-Chinese Banking Corporation (OCBC). There was some speculation that Tan was trying to merge OCBC's business operations with those of two other Singaporean-based businessmen, Khoo Teck Puat (who had worked for OCBC) and Lee Kong Chian (who had helped establish OCBC), to create a huge Chinese enterprise. This proposed merger did not materialize (see *Insight* July 1983). Concerned with the possible impact of the government's new ownership restructuring requirements on the numerous quoted companies in the OCBC group, like the Straits Trading Company, Great Eastern Life Assurance Company, Malayan Breweries, Fraser & Neave and Wearne Brothers, Tan reportedly showed his displeasure by stepping down as chairman of some of these Malaysian-based companies (see *The Star* 19 May 1983).

Some Malaysian-based Chinese businessmen took non-confrontational approaches. The late Lee Loy Seng, of the KL-Kepong group, divested his interests in companies in which government-owned enterprises bought into. For example, when one such government enterprise acquired a stake in publicly-listed Highlands & Lowlands Bhd, Lee sold of his equity in the company because he 'didn't want to compete with a government company' (*Asiaweek* 19 May 1985). Lee would, however, later help lead Multi-Purpose Holdings, the investment holding company established by the MCA as a means to mobilize Chinese capital to act collectively to protect their economic interests.[18]

Teh Hong Piow, who owned Public Bank Bhd, claims that his response to the NEP was to make it a point to study and follow all government policies (see *Malaysian Business* 1/9/91). In 1982, Public Bank was granted 'Approved Status' by the Ministry of Finance for meeting all of Bank Negara's (the central bank) priority lending guidelines and for fulfilling the NEP's Bumiputera ownership and employment quotas (*Malaysian Business* January 1983). The following case studies of Robert Kuok, Lim Goh Tong and Loh Boon Siew deal with how the three, who control some of the leading companies on the KLSE, developed their corporate assets in the colonial and early post-colonial period and dealt with the implementation of the NEP.

*Chinese Business in Malaysia*

Robert Kuok and Perlis Plantations Bhd　　　　　　　**CASE STUDY**

Robert Kuok Hock Nien, the most internationally renowned – and probably the most enigmatic – of Chinese businessmen to have emerged in the post-independence period, reportedly owned assets amounting to between RM4 billion to RM5 billion in the early 1990s (*Business Week* 11 November 1991; *Malaysian Business* 16 February 1993). Kuok, a Foochow, was born in Johore Bahru in 1923. His father, Kuok Keng Kang, had migrated from Fujian province in 1909, and had established a reputation distributing rice, sugar and flour through his Johore-based firm Tong Seng & Company. The licence to trade in these commodities was obtained by Kuok Keng Kang from the Sultan of Johore. Robert Kuok had an upper-middle-class upbringing. Educated at the English College in Johore Baru and Singapore's Raffles College, Kuok is believed to have had a stint in the United Kingdom during the Japanese Occupation, where he picked up experience in international commodities trading.[19] On his return to Malaya, Kuok worked with Mitsubishi Shoji Kaisha, which traded in salt, sugar and rice. Following the death of Kuok's father in 1948, Tong Seng & Co was liquidated, although the reasons for this are still unclear since the company had emerged as a major trading establishment in Johore. On 1 April 1949, Robert Kuok formed Kuok Brothers Sdn Bhd to take over most of Tong Seng & Co's operations (Tan 1982: 292; Sia 1993: 55–69; *Malaysian Business* 16 February 1993).

Kuok, like his father, has had close links with many prominent Malay leaders. Hussein Onn, Prime Minister from 1976 to 1981, and the wife of former Deputy Prime Minister Ismail Abdul Rahman – both men were from Johore – have held equity in companies owned by Kuok, while Hussein's cousin, Taib Andak,[20] another prominent Malay, was a director of Kuok's publicly-listed concern, Federal Flour Mills Bhd. Kuok's close links with government leaders were obvious in his appointments to the boards of state-owned enterprises – as chairman of the Malayan-Singapore Airlines in the late 1960s and to lead the then newly-founded (in 1968) Malaysian International Shipping Corporation Bhd (MISC) which was to become the national shipping company. Kuok was also appointed director of two major government-owned institutions founded to promote Bumiputera capital: Bank Bumiputra, established in 1966 to ensure more funds were channeled to Malays to facilitate their participation in business, and Pernas, the trust agency established in 1969 to acquire assets on behalf of the community.[21] Kuok and Government Economic Adviser Daim Zainuddin, the Finance Minister from 1984 to 1991 and now the country's most influential business figure, forged a partnership to buy into the Malaysian French Bank Bhd (now renamed the Multi-Purpose Bank). Kuok also had a stake in UBN Holdings Sdn Bhd, co-owned by Peremba Bhd,[22] a government-owned property development company founded by Daim; UBN Holdings owned the Shangri-La complex in Kuala Lumpur (Tan 1982: 173: Sia 1993: 55–69; *Far Eastern Economic Review* 30 October 1986; *Investors' Digest* March 1987).[23]

Kuok also benefited from economic concessions provided by the government. In 1968, when Kuok incorporated Perlis Plantations to handle sugar-cane cultivation and sugar refining operations, this was after he had secured 14,490 acres of land from the Perlis state government (*Insight* August 1983). This was an interesting development considering that the federal government was then already under some pressure from UMNO members to augment state intervention in the economy to promote Malay economic interests.

Kuok also managed to establish ties with government leaders in other countries. In the early 1960s, Kuok so impressed the mainland Chinese authorities when he managed to fend off their attempts to corner the sugar market in Malaya by sourcing sugar from India at a lower price, he secured the franchise from them to distribute China-made products locally (*New Nation* 19 March 1971). Kuok subsequently built on this early link with the Chinese authorities. In 1993, he was selected as one of the advisers to the Chinese authorities on the future of Hong Kong and was appointed a director and made a shareholder of Citic Pacific, the Hong Kong-listed arm of the Beijing-based government agency, China International Trust and Investment Corporation (Citic) (*New Straits Times* 14 September 1993).[24] Citic was formed by the Chinese authorities to secure foreign investments, particularly from ethnic Chinese of the diaspora. Another prominent director on Citic's board is Hong Kong's Li Ka Shing (Chan 1996: 5–6). In 1996, Kuok was selected by the Chinese authorities to sit on the 150-member Preparatory Committee established to oversee the return of Hong Kong to China (Chan 1996: 211–12). Kuok has significant investments in China – he is believed to have been investing in the country since 1983 – through his Shangri-La hotel chain and his Hong Kong-based firm Kerry Trading, which has had joint-ventures with the Chinese central government. Kuok is reportedly also well acquainted with the president of the Philippines, Fidel Ramos (see *New Straits Times* 14 September 1993). Interestingly, in the 1990s, through Kuok Philippines Properties Inc. (KPPI), Kuok emerged as the second largest property developer in the country (*Far Eastern Economic Review* 1 February 1990).

Until the early 1970s, most of Kuok's business activities were concentrated in Malaysia. From 1971, he began venturing more into Singapore, before settling in Hong Kong in 1975 (*Far Eastern Economic Review* 30 October 1986 *Business Times* 14 September 1993). This was the period when state intervention in the Malaysian economy was growing through the NEP. Kuok has, however, never revealed his reasons for establishing the headquarters for his businesses in Hong Kong, probably the most *laissez-faire* economy in Asia.

One incident cited as a reason for Kuok's move abroad was his unsuccessful attempt to secure government approval to export sugar in the early 1970s. Between the late 1950s and early 1970s, through Perlis Plantations, Kuok had developed a vertically integrated sugar operation in Malaysia. However, when he sought a licence to export sugar produced by Perlis Plantations, the government withheld approval. In 1974, when there were violent fluctuations in the price of sugar in the international commodities market, Kuok estimated that if Perlis Plantations had been allowed to export sugar, the company could have made a 'windfall profit' of between RM15 million to RM20 million (cited in Cheong 1992: 45–6).[25] During the 1960s, Kuok was already actively involved in international sugar trading, having forged alliances with Indonesia's Salim Group, Thai sugar producers and refiners Thai Ruen Rueng, and the major British commodities trading companies E.D. & F. Man and Tate & Lyle; in 1971, with the two British firms, Kuok sold one million tonnes of sugar to China (*Far Eastern Economic Review* 7 February 1991; Sia 1993: 62).

Kuok's view that extensive regulations impaired the development of capital was obvious in a speech he delivered in Malaysia in 1989, when he said: '. . . over-regulation is not conducive for economic expansion. Sometimes we throw in a whole lot of regulations and then offer incentives in the way of exemptions from some of these regulations. Malaysia . . . is perceived as being over-regulated' (see *New Straits Times* 27 February 1989).[26] Kuok has also questioned the wisdom of the Malaysian government's extensive ownership (and control) of equity in the corporate sector and has recommended greater government–business co-operation (ibid). Another reason for Kuok's business expansion abroad was disclosed by Geh Ik Cheong, the former chairman of Perlis Plantations, who stated, 'A lot of the opportunities here (in Malaysia) have attracted many up-and-coming Bumiputera companies. We haven't always felt comfortable competing with them. So as a group we have taken the step to expand internationally' (quoted in *Malaysian Business* 16 February 1993).

Despite his close ties with Malay politicians and his business co-operation with some of them, Kuok also played a key role in helping to revive the MCA-controlled Multi-Purpose Holdings when the company came close to bankruptcy in the mid-1980s. In 1986, the normally reclusive Kuok was also open in his support for the discredited MCA president Tan Koon Swan. Kuok even personally turned up in Singapore to post a S$2 million bail for the businessman-cum-politician. Kuok was also open in his support of Khoo Kay Peng who had fallen out of favor with UMNO leaders for supporting Razaleigh Hamzah, who had narrowly lost his challenge to Prime Minister Mahathir Mohamad for the presidency of the party in 1987. Razaleigh later formed a new opposition Malay party and helped create a new multi-racial opposition coalition which emerged as a serious threat to the Barisan Nasional during the 1990 general election (see Chapter 3).

Kuok's main publicly-listed holding company in Malaysia has been Perlis Plantations, a diversified corporation involved in commodities trading, food industries, hotels, shipping, plantations, mining, property, retailing and entertainment (see Table 2.1). The other publicly-listed companies in the Perlis Plantations group are Federal Flour Mills Bhd and Shangri-La Hotels (Malaysia) Bhd (SHMB). SHMB was listed on the KLSE in 1992 after a merger between UBN Holdings and Kuok's Rasa Sayang Beach Hotels (Penang) Bhd. Rasa Sayang had been de-listed in 1987 when Perlis Plantations made a general offer for the company and eventually increased its equity to almost 98 per cent (*Malaysian Business* 16 October 1992). A similar merger exercise was undertaken in 1987, when most of Kuok's Malaysian companies, including Federal Flour Mills, were brought under the Perlis Plantations umbrella. Among the major unlisted companies in the group are Malayan Sugar Manufacturing Company Bhd (sugar refining), Malaysian Bulk Carriers Sdn Bhd (shipping), Cathay Cinemas Sdn Bhd and Golden Communications (M) Sdn Bhd (film distribution and exhibition) (see Figure 2.1).

*Table 2.1* Perlis Plantations Bhd: Sectoral Breakdown in Terms of Turnover and Pre-Tax Profits, 1995 (RM million)

| Sector | Turnover | Pre-Tax Profit |
|---|---|---|
| Food Industries | 5778.8 | 190.0 |
| Commodity trading | 3148.5 | 56.4 |
| Hotels | 85.1 | 26.4 |
| Shipping | 28.0 | 20.5 |
| Plantations & Mining | 227.2 | 77.2 |
| Property, Entertainment & Retailing | 224.8 | (5.8) |
| Others | 228.1 | 27.3 |

Source: *KLSE Annual Companies Handbook* 21 (4), 1996: 79

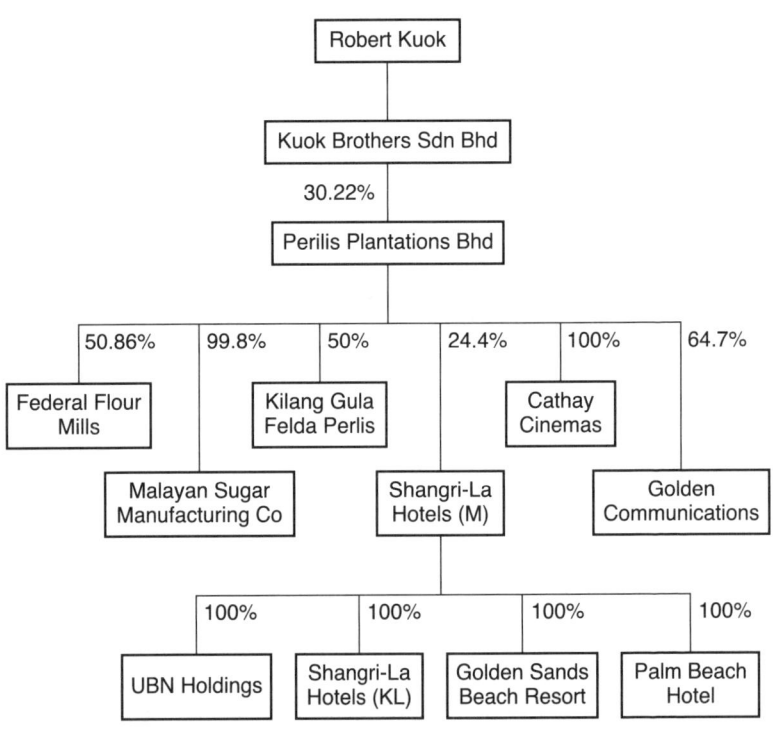

*Figure 2.1* Perlis Plantations Bhd (Malaysian Operations): Simplified Corporate Structure, 1995–96

Sources: *KLSE Annual Companies Handbook* 21 (4): 6–11; 72–9; 835–40

The current chairman of Perlis Plantations is Kuok's son, Kuok Khoon Ean, who is also deputy chairman of Federal Flour Mills and a director of SHMB. Robert Kuok has seven children,[27] but Khoon Ean is the only one who sits on the boards of directors of his three Malaysian publicly-listed companies (*Malaysian Business* 16 February 1993; *KLSE Annual Companies Handbook* 21 (4), 1996: 6–11; 72–79; 835–40). Kuok Brothers is Perlis Plantations largest shareholder with a 30.22 per cent stake. The second largest shareholder is the armed forces' provident fund, Lembaga Tabung Angkatan Tentera (LTAT), with a 9.08 per cent interest, while another government agency, Amanah Saham Nasional (ASN, or National Unit Trust Scheme), has a 4.65 per cent stake. Among the other top 10 shareholders of Perlis Plantations are four nominee companies which collectively own 18.03 per cent of the company's equity (*KLSE Annual Companies Handbook* 21 (4), 1996: 72–9). Although Kuok Brothers has majority ownership of Perlis Plantations, Federal Flour Mills and SHMB, these three companies are managed by professionals.

Perlis Plantations was incorporated on 1 November 1968 to cultivate sugar cane in Perlis, although the fore-runner for Kuok's involvement in the sugar industry was Malayan Sugar Manufacturing. In October 1959, Kuok formed a joint-venture with two Japanese companies, Mitsui Bussan Kaisha Ltd and Nissin Sugar Manufacturing Company, to establish a sugar refinery. The project, operated through Malayan Sugar Manufacturing, took off in 1964. Another partner in this joint-venture was the government's Lembaga Urusan Tabung Haji (LUTH, or Pilgrims' Management and Fund Board).

From here, the move into sugar cultivation was made. Perlis Plantations was incorporated to take over land obtained from the Perlis state government and to start a sugar plantation. In 1974, a second sugar refinery plant was established next to the plantation through a joint-venture, Kilang Gula Felda Perlis Sdn Bhd; Perlis Plantations' partner in the venture was the government's land development agency, FELDA (*Malaysian Business* 16 February 1993; Sia 1993: 61–4). The chairman of FELDA at that time was Taib Andak, with whom Kuok was already well acquainted. Kuok made it a point to involve state-owned institutions in his ventures in the sugar industry, which probably put him in good stead with government leaders, particularly when he began to diversify into shipping. In 1976, Perlis Plantations acquired Malayan Sugar Manufacturing and became engaged in all principal areas of the sugar industry, from cane growing to sugar milling, refining and distribution (*KLSE Annual Companies Handbook* 21 (4), 1996: 72–7). By the 1970s, Kuok had reputedly managed to control 10 per cent of the world's sugar trade, and London sugar brokers christened him the 'Sugar King' (see Cheong 1992: 43). Kuok is still popularly referred to by this title in Asia.

Kuok's ability to seize opportunities as they cropped up in the Malaysian economy was also obvious from his involvement in the flour milling and shipping industries. The decision to move into flour milling complemented Kuok's sugar refining. There were lucrative opportunities, particularly tax reliefs to be tapped, under the government's incentives to promote import-substituting industries (ISI). Federal Flour Mills Bhd was incorporated in February 1962, and, with its ownership of four flour mills, is the largest flour miller in the country (Sia 1993: 63; *KLSE Annual Companies Handbook* 21 (4), 1996: 6–9).

When the Malaysian government attempted to develop a national shipping line to reduce its dependence on foreign freighters to handle its two main exports, rubber and tin, Kuok was invited to do a feasibility study. Kuok, recognizing the potential this venture offered to his own trading business, helped incorporate the Malaysian International Shipping Corporation Bhd (MISC) in November 1968. Although the MISC project was an attempt by the government to develop a national shipping line, Kuok also invested some of his own funds in the company. Since Kuok had no experience then in the industry, he secured the services of, and investment from, the Hong Kong shipowner Frank Tsao Wen-king; Kuok also managed to secure investments from members of the local Chinese Chamber of Commerce, reflecting his standing in the community. Kuok was chairman of MISC from 1968 to 1979 (*New Nation* 19 March 1971; *New Straits Times* 21 November 1985). Kuok would later admit that when he went into shipping, he approached Frank Tsao, telling him, 'I know nothing about ships. I can't even distinguish between the front end and the rear end' (quoted in *The Edge* 5 June 1995). The original shareholders of MISC were Kuok Brothers, Frank Tsao & Co. Ltd and LUTH (Sia 1993: 64–5). Although Kuok eventually divested his interests in MISC,[28] he currently owns the Singapore-based Pacific Carriers Ltd, a publicly-listed company which is the largest dry-bulk shipping line in Southeast Asia (*Far Eastern Economic Review* 7 February 1991).

From his roots as a trader in Kuok Brothers, Kuok established an international reputation in trading. He is quoted as stating: 'Everything else I'm in is just a natural extension of trading' (*New Nation* 19

March 1971). There seems to be some justification to this claim as Kuok has built on the early experience he garnered as a sugar trader. His venture into sugar cultivation and refinery was an astute move when he pioneered entry into a field as yet untapped in the peninsula then. In this regard, there was some vertical integration in his business growth. Kuok's diversification into shipping was a logical extension of his involvement in trade. The two activities that contribute most to Perlis Plantations' pre-tax profit are food industries and commodities trading (see Table 2.1). Kuok owns a 30 per cent stake in the world's largest sugar trader, Sucden Kerry International (SKI); the company's remaining 70 per cent equity is owned by the Paris-based commodities giant Cie Commercial Sucres et Denrees. SKI's owns 66.7 per cent of the Hamburg-based Marimpex, a international oil trader. In 1990, SKI acquired a 30 per cent stake in Industria Azucarera Nacional de Chile (IANSA), Chile's sugar monopoly (*Far Eastern Economic Review* 7 February 1991).

Kuok's involvement in hotels through the Shangri-La chain, for which he has also gained international repute, seems to have occurred in the 1970s, after implementation of the NEP, as he began to venture abroad. When he moved to Singapore in 1971, it was to establish the Shangri-La hotel, and his entry into Hong Kong was for a similar reason. From this initial venture in Hong Kong, Kuok has diversified extensively, into electronic and publishing media, property development, manufacturing and trading. Through Hong Kong, he has effectively gained entry into China, establishing a similar pattern of growth – first setting up a chain of Shangri-La hotels, then moving into property development and eventually developing a manufacturing base; he has set up vegetable oil refining and Coca-Cola bottling plants in the country. In some major property development schemes in Beijing and Shanghai, Kuok has worked with Li Ka Shing, and in Chengdu in Sichuan province, he was involved in developing a huge shopping complex with T.T. Tsui, who controls the Hong Kong-listed company, China Paint Holdings (*Far Eastern Economic Review* 30 October 1986; *New Straits Times* 14 September 1993; *Business Times* (Singapore) 23 July 1992; see also Table 2.2).

In Asia, although Kuok's most conspicuous landmark is the Shangri-La hotel chain, his interests in the media sector have been growing. In September 1993, through his Hong Kong-based Kerry Group, Kuok acquired a 35 per cent stake in the South China Morning Post Holdings, which publishes Hong Kong's leading English-language newspaper, the *South China Morning Post*; the

Table 2.2 Robert Kuok's Business Interests Outside Malaysia

| China | Singapore | Indonesia |
|---|---|---|
| World Trade Centre Beijing[c] | Pacific Carriers[e] | Gunung Madu[c] |
| Bu Ye Cheng Centre[c] | Shangri-La Hotel[a] | TKA[c] |
| Regency Park and Top Spring[c] | Rasa Sentosa Beach Resort[a] | Jakarta Shangri-La[a] |
| Kerry Oil and Grains[d] | Allgreen Properties[c] | Bali Dynasty[a] |
| Kerry Beverages[d] | Leo Properties[c] | Broderick Trading[b] |
| | | |
| Hong Kong | Thailand | Canada |
| Shangri-La Asia[a] | Shangri-La Hotel[a] | Abbey Woods Development[c] |
| TVB Ltd[f] | Wattanathani[c] | Pacific Palisades Hotel[a] |
| Kerry Properties[c] | Thai Ruen Rueng-Kerry Development[c] | |
| Kerry Trading[b] | | |
| Kerry Financial Services | | |
| South China Morning Post[f] | | |
| Citic Pacific | The Philippines | France |
| | Kuok Philippines Properties Int.[c] | Sucden Kerry Int.[b] |
| | Makati Shangri-La[a] | SKIP[b] |
| | Mactan Shangri-La Beach Resort[a] | |
| Fiji | | |
| The Fijian[a] | ESDA Plaza-ESDA Shangri-La[a] | Germany |
| Fiji Macambo[a] | | Marimax[b] |
| | Chile | |
| | IANSA[b] | |

[a] Hotels
[b] Trading
[c] Property Development
[d] Manufacturing
[e] Shipping
[f] Media

Sources: *Business Times* 14 September 1993; *Far Eastern Economic Review* 7 February 1991

newspaper publishing company was acquired from News Corp, owned by the Australian media magnate Rupert Murdoch. The South China Morning Post owns a 15 per cent stake in Thailand's Post Publishing Company which owns the influential Thai daily, the *Bangkok Post*. Kuok also owns a 32 per cent stake in Television Broadcasts (TVB), Hong Kong's leading television station. Following Kuok's move into the media sector, in which he had no previous experience, one regional magazine reported that, 'Some analysts speculate that Peking blessed – if not bankrolled – Kuok's purchase of SCMP (South China Morning Post)' (see *Far Eastern Economic Review* 16 September 1993). This was seen as an attempt to channel ownership and control of the influential newspaper into the hands of businessmen associated with the Chinese authorities. It was also reported that Kuok had acquired TVB as a favor to the company's chairman, Run Run Shaw, and that Kuok received modest returns on his investment in the private television company (see *Far Eastern Economic Review* 7 February 1991).

Kuok, who has advocated ethnic Chinese businessmen of the diaspora working together, has himself been involved in business deals with a number of Asia's leading Chinese capitalists. There is evidence that Kuok has been involved with Indonesia's Liem Sioe Liong through his sugar business, and in property development ventures in China with Hong Kong's Li Ka Shing and T.T. Tsui. With Run Run Shaw, Kuok has a joint interest in Hong Kong's TVB. Kuok has had some business deals with Thailand's Chatri Sophonpanich, another of Southeast Asia's leading Chinese capitalists who controls Bangkok Bank which, according to *Asiaweek* (9 June 1989), was one of 'Kuok's initial bankrollers.' In Malaysia, Kuok has worked closely with Malayan United Industries (MUI) Bhd's Khoo Kay Peng – they jointly hold equity in South China Morning Post Holdings – and the major property developer Tan Chin Nam who controls IGB Corporation Bhd, IJM Corporation Bhd and Tan & Tan Development Bhd (see *Business Week* 11 November 1991; *Far Eastern Economic Review* 7 February 1991; see also Chapter 3).

---

Lim Goh Tong and Genting Bhd                    **CASE STUDY**

Lim Goh Tong, a Hokkien, with corporate assets worth RM2.8 billion in 1992, is reputedly the wealthiest man in Malaysia (*The Star* 19 May 1992). In March 1996, Lim's main publicly-listed corporations, Genting Bhd and Resorts World Bhd, were the fifth and sixth largest publicly-listed companies respectively on the KLSE in terms of market value. Genting was capitalized at RM16.1 billion while Resorts World was capitalized at RM15.7 billion (*KLSE Annual Companies Handbook* 21 (2), 1996: 740). The four companies ranked above Genting and Resorts World were Malayan Banking Bhd, Malaysia's largest (government-controlled) bank, and three major privatized companies, the telephone and electricity utilities, Telekom Malaysia Bhd and Tenaga Nasional Bhd, and Petronas Gas Bhd, controlled by the government's petroleum agency, Petronas. The combined market value of Genting and Resorts World's stock – Genting is Resorts World's major shareholder – would make them the third largest company on the KLSE, after the two utilities giants.

Lim left Fujian province in China for Malaya in 1937 at the age of 20. He started out as a carpenter, then sold food stuff, ventured into petty trading of scrap metal, before establishing a profitable interest in tin and iron mining in Johore. Lim established himself in the construction industry that in the 1950s. Through his company, Kien Huat Construction Sdn Bhd, Lim secured contracts to construct several major government projects – including dams, bridges, roads and water supply, sewerage and irrigation schemes – throughout the country. Kien Huat Construction went on to become one of Malaysia's largest construction companies in the 1960s (*Insight* June 1980; *Malaysian Business* March 1981).

In 1950, Lim established contact with Mohammad Noah Omar, then an Assistant District Officer in Batu Pahat, Johore, who went on to become a Johore state assemblyman and Speaker of the *Dewan Rakyat* (House of Representatives). Noah was the father-in-law of two future Prime Ministers, Abdul Razak (1971–76) and Hussein Onn (1976–81). In 1965, Lim and Noah established Genting Highlands Bhd, with the former as managing director and Noah as the chairman.[29] That year, Genting Highlands secured approval from the government to develop a resort on a mountain top on the border between the states of Selangor and Pahang. The contract also involved developing the infrastructure required to access the resort, which entailed cutting through virgin jungle. The government approved the sale of a 12,000 acre property to develop the hill resort, also known as Genting Highlands, located around 50 kilometers from the national capital. On completion of the road to the proposed resort, Genting Highlands Hotel Sdn Bhd was incorporated to construct hotels and promote the area. To ensure the profitability of the resort, Lim was given a licence, renewable every three months, to operate a casino. Genting Highlands Hotel was listed on the KLSE in December 1971 and renamed Genting in June 1978. The hillside resort spearheaded Lim's venture into the leisure industry, but the casino, the only one in the country, became the main revenue earner for the Genting group and made it one of the fastest growing publicly-listed companies in the 1980s. In 1995, despite the diversified nature of the Genting group's activities, almost 80 per cent of its revenue was still derived from its casino operations (*New Straits Times* 17 June 1979; *Asiaweek* 5 March

1980; *Malaysian Business* 1 December 1987; *Far Eastern Economic Review* 5 January 1995). In 1995, Genting's turnover was RM2.5 billion, while its profit-before-tax was RM1.088 billion, both almost double the figures registered in 1991 (see Table 2.3). Genting is among the country's largest corporate taxpayers (*Malaysian Business* 16 March 1995).

In January 1982, the hotel business operated through Genting Hotel was transferred to a subsidiary, Resorts World Sdn Bhd, increasing the latter's paid-up capital from RM3 to approximately RM99 million. Resorts World had then reportedly secured five-year pioneer status, on the condition that it complied with the NEP's redistribution requirements by 1987 (see *Business Times* 18 August 1989). In August 1989, in a major restructuring exercise involving another shares-for-assets swap, Resorts World's capitalization was increased to RM475 million when it took over Genting's gaming, resort and other hotel operations. Touted officially as a rationalization exercise to enhance efficiency, Genting retained control of its property and plantation activities, and re-emerged primarily as an investment holding company, while Resorts World was listed on the KLSE (see *New Straits Times* 8 August 1989). Genting's restructuring, involving the transfer of most of its primary assets to Resorts World, was already two years behind schedule. Despite the transfer of Genting's main assets, particularly its casino operations, to Resorts World, under the restructuring exercise, certain allowances favoring Genting were made. For example, Genting Hotel & Resorts Management Sdn Bhd, a wholly-owned subsidiary of Genting, was appointed the operator and manager of the gaming, hotel and resort operations that had been transferred to Resorts World, for which a lucrative management fee was charged (see *Malaysian Business* 1 March 1990).[30]

Following Resorts World's listing, Genting's interest in the company was reduced from almost 99 per cent to around 54 per

*Table 2.3* Genting Bhd: Share Capital, Turnover and Profit Margins, 1991–95 (RM million)

|  | 1991 | 1992 | 1993 | 1994 | 1995 |
|---|---|---|---|---|---|
| Paid-Up Capital | 231.84 | 232.16 | 233.31 | 351.05 | 351.10 |
| Turnover | 1214.67 | 1638.45 | 2004.19 | 2378.00 | 2496.00 |
| Pre-tax Profit | 581.49 | 694.85 | 958.54 | 1128.40 | 1088.60 |

*Source:* KLSE *Annual Companies Handbook* 21 (3), 1996: 174–83

cent, with Bumiputera parties holding 30 per cent. Through the restructuring and from the sale of almost half of its interests in Resorts World, Genting raised almost half a billion ringgit (*Business Times* 8 and 18 August 1989). The new major Bumiputera shareholders of Resorts World remained unclear. The armed forces provident fund, LTAT, and members of the Pahang royal family were believed to be among the Bumiputera investors, holding their stock through nominee companies (*Malaysian Business* 16 March 1995). In 1995, Genting was listed as Resorts World's largest shareholder with 30.3 per cent equity, but this figure is probably understated as the other nine major shareholders were all nominee companies which collectively owned almost 39 per cent of the company's stock. This was confirmed by the further disclosure that Kien Huat Realty Sdn Bhd, Lim's holding company, was listed as owning an indirect stake of 55.77 per cent in Resorts World.

Since nine of the ten largest shareholders of both Genting and Resorts World are nominee companies, it is difficult to ascertain the Bumiputera shareholders of both companies. In 1995, individual Bumiputeras held only 0.26 per cent of Genting's equity, while Bumiputera corporations and agencies owned 32.9 per cent of the company's stock. As for Resorts World, individual Bumiputeras owned only 0.14 per cent of the company's stock while Bumiputera agencies owned just over 1.0 per cent of the stock. Interestingly, Bumiputera interests in the company, held through nominees, amount to a significant 16.59 per cent.

Gambling is forbidden by Islam, so given the profitability of the industry, it is understandable why the Bumiputera owners of Genting and Resorts World have not publicly disclosed their interests. Resorts World's turnover at the end of 1995 was RM1.867 billion, compared to RM1.925 billion, RM1.704 billion and RM1.347 billion respectively for the previous three years. Resorts World's pre-tax profit in 1995 was RM736.2 million, compared to RM792.2 million, RM672.8 million and RM474.9 million respectively for the previous three years (*KLSE Annual Companies Handbook* 21 (3), 1996: 174–81, 235–9).

Genting moved into the plantation sector in 1980 when its wholly-owned subsidiary, Asiatic Development Sdn Bhd, acquired three interlocked Malaysian rubber companies for RM180 million from Hong Kong-based companies (*Far Eastern Economic Review* 5 January 1989). In June 1983, Asiatic Development was publicly-listed and quickly developed its interests in the sector, emerging as one of

Malaysia's top five companies in the plantation sector in terms of hectarage by 1990. Given the decline of the plantation industry, however, the returns to Genting of its investments in Asiatic Development have not been very lucrative, although the company has registered profits (see Table 2.4). There are plans to convert some of its plantations into industrial areas (*Malaysian Business* 16 March 1992).

Lim also owns an interest in, and is a director of, Genting International Ltd, an investment holding, manufacturing and management consultancy company which was listed on the Luxembourg Stock Exchange in 1990.[31] Lim's 15 per cent interest in Genting International is held through Kazzon Ltd. Through another company, Golden Hope, Lim is said to hold more equity in Genting International. Kazzon and Golden Hope's collective interest in Genting International in 1989 was reportedly at least 54 per cent (see *Far Eastern Economic Review* 5 January 1989). Genting International also acts as a management consultant for casino operations in Adelaide and Perth in Australia (*Malaysian Business* 16 March 1992).

In 1990, Lim announced that the Genting group would participate more actively in the manufacturing sector to reduce its dependency on the gaming and leisure industry (*Business Times* 30 June 1990; see also Table 2.4). Asiatic Development first ventured into manufacturing rubber gloves and then neo-pneumatic tyre segments. In June 1993, Asiatic Development joined a RM50 million joint-venture in China's Guangdong province to build a palm oil refinery and oleochemical operations. Genting established Malaysia's largest paper mill in October 1990. In 1994, Genting took up a 40 per

*Table 2.4* Genting Bhd: Sectoral Breakdown in Terms of Turnover and Pre-Tax Profits, 1995 (RM million)

| Sector | Turnover | Pre-Tax Profit |
|---|---|---|
| Resorts | 1830.8 | 821.5 |
| Plantations | 177.0 | 62.8 |
| Properties | 76.9 | 29.6 |
| Manufacturing | 282.0 | 37.6 |
| Power | 94.5 | 100.8 |
| Others | 129.6 | 36.3 |

Source: *KLSE Annual Companies Handbook* 21 (3), 1996: 183

cent stake in a 720-megawatt independent power plant (*Malaysian Business* 16 March 1992; *Far Eastern Economic Review* 5 January 1995).

Genting's paper manufacturing activities have been handled by its 97.7 per cent subsidiary, Genting Sanyen Newsprint Sdn Bhd, which has also constructed a RM740 million paper industrial complex which, when fully operational in mid 1997, was expected to produce at least one million tonnes of various types of paper. The profit potential from this activity was phenomenal since almost 90 per cent of Malaysia's paper requirements in 1994 were being imported; Genting Sanyen Newsprint was expected to produce at least 85 per cent of Malaysian paper requirements (Cheong 1995: 71–2; *KLSE Annual Companies Handbook* 21 (3), 1996: 179–81; *Business Times* 8 May 1996). Yet, in August 1996, Genting divested its interest in Genting Sanyen Newsprint for RM99.8 million to Malaysian Newsprint Industries Sdn Bhd, a company incorporated in 1995 to develop its own newsprint mill. The shareholders of Malaysian Newsprint Industries include the politically well-connected New Straits Times Press Bhd (30 percent), the Hong Leong group's Malaysian Pacific Industries Bhd (30 per cent) and Rimbunan Hijau Estate Sdn Bhd (20 per cent) controlled by Sarawak timber tycoon, Tiong Hiew King (*The Star* 9 August 1996). Genting is to concentrate on the production of industrial grade paper, manufacturing approximately 50 per cent of Malaysia's total requirements (*New Straits Times* 14 August 1996; *Far Eastern Economic Review* 6 January 1997). Although Genting secured an extraordinary capital gain of RM72.8 million from its divestment of Genting Sanyen Newsprint, and even though part of the latter's equity was to be owned by two Chinese-controlled companies, it does not appear that the sale of the paper manufacturing company was motivated by these two factors (*Business Times* 14 August 1996).[32]

Genting's attempts to work with other Chinese businessmen have not been very successful. For example, Genting Australia Investment Holdings formed a joint-venture with Singapore-based Hotel Properties Ltd, owned by Ong Beng Seng, to venture into a hotel and property project in Sydney; the joint-venture was eventually disbanded, amicably (*The Sun* 15 January 1997). There is not much evidence that the Genting group has worked closely with other Chinese companies in Malaysia or in other countries in the region.

Genting's participation in the power supply sector has been through its 39.1 per cent stake in Genting Sanyen Power Sdn Bhd

(GSP), which began operating a 720mw power station in Kuala Langat in the state of Selangor in January 1996 (*KLSE Annual Companies Handbook* 21 (3), 1996: 174–81). GSP, reportedly Malaysia's third largest independent power producer (IPP), has secured power supply projects in Guangdong province in China and Madhya Pradesh in India (*Business Times* 3 July 1996).

In September 1993, Lim established Singapore Star Cruise Pte Ltd to move into the cruise industry in the region. Starting out with two cruise vessels, the venture is an attempt to develop the company into Asia's largest cruise hotel resort.[33] Barely two years later, in 1995, with an expanded fleet of five vessels, Star Cruise had emerged as the region's largest cruise operator and the world's eighth in terms of total fleet tonnage and passenger volume (*The Straits Times* (Singapore) 22 October 1993; *Malaysian Industry* April 1995; *Malaysian Business* 16 March 1995). In 1994, Lim sold 100 per cent of the cruise operation and 50 per cent of the gaming operations owned by Star Cruise to Genting International, probably to increase the latter's profitability (*Malaysian Industry* April 1995).

Since it is not possible for Lim to expand his casino operations in Malaysia, he has endeavored to become a major international casino operator, through Genting International. His efforts to expand his operations abroad have not, however, been very successful. In Australia, an attempt to operate a casino in Queensland was aborted, while a proposal to build a casino in Sydney was rejected. Genting International, however, did acquire a majority stake in a casino operation in Perth, which was subsequently sold for a modest profit. Presently, Genting International has management contracts only for three casinos in Australia. Genting International's acquisition of a 50 per cent stake in the Lucayan Beach Resort and Casino, a Bahamas-based government-controlled operation, proved to be loss-making (*Far Eastern Economic Review* 5 January 1989).

Some of Lim's family members have participated in the management of his business interests. His eldest son, Tee Keong, studied at Rochester in New York, while his second son, Kok Thay, and youngest son, Chee Wah, both graduated from London University with degrees in engineering and economics respectively. Lim has a daughter, Siew Lay. Until the early 1980s, Lim and his immediate family members held directorships in his main listed companies and were actively involved in the management of these interests. For example, in 1980, six of Genting's nine directors were members of the Lim clan – his wife Kim Hua, sons Kok Thay and Chee Wah, daughter Siew Lay and her husband Tan Teong Hean (*Insight* June 1980). Chee Wah was made managing director of Asiatic Development in 1980. Kok Thay was appointed deputy managing director of Genting at the age of 28 (*New Straits Times* 17 June 1979).

By 1995, however, although Goh Tong remained chairman and joint managing director of Genting and Resorts World, the only other family member on the board of directors of both companies was his son Kok Thay, the joint managing director. Lim's eldest son, Tee Keong, is only a director of Genting. Goh Tong is the joint chief executive of Asiatic Development, while Kok Thay is a director of the company. The other joint chief executive of Asiatic Development is Baharuddin Musa, while the chairman is Mohd Amin Osman, also a director of Genting; Mohd Amin is a former Deputy Inspector General of Police. The deputy chairman of Genting is Haniff Omar, the former Inspector General of Police, who holds a similar post at Resorts World.

Lim's main family holding company is Kien Huat Realty Sdn Bhd, which is Genting's major shareholder with 29.13 per cent of the company's equity (see Figure 2.2). As mentioned, Lim's shareholding is probably higher since the rest of the nine largest shareholders, with a combined total of almost 40 per cent of equity, are all nominee companies (*KLSE Annual Companies Handbook* 21 (3), 1996: 174–81). According to company records, Kien Huat Realty was incorporated as an investment holding company on 5 November 1959. The directors of the company are Lim, his wife and his children, while the majority shareholder was another private company, Asola Sdn Bhd.

Lim's links with Malay politicians enabled him to obtain and keep a casino licence despite criticism from Islamic elements. Abdullah Ahmad, a former Member of Parliament and political secretary to Prime Minister Razak, attributed Lim's success to 'foresight,' but added that 'it helps when you've got powerful friends,' a clear reference to Noah (quoted in *Malaysian Business* 1 December 1987).[34] Lim himself has acknowledged state patronage, stating that 'without its strong support, I could not have made it' (ibid.). Indication of the tenuous nature of Genting's gaming operations in Malaysia can be garnered from a comment made by the late opposition leader Tan Chee Khoon. According to Tan, when he criticized the government in parliament for promoting gambling, he was told that 'Genting would slowly wind down its gambling operations and at the same time make greater efforts to promote

## Chinese Business, Colonialism and Accumulation

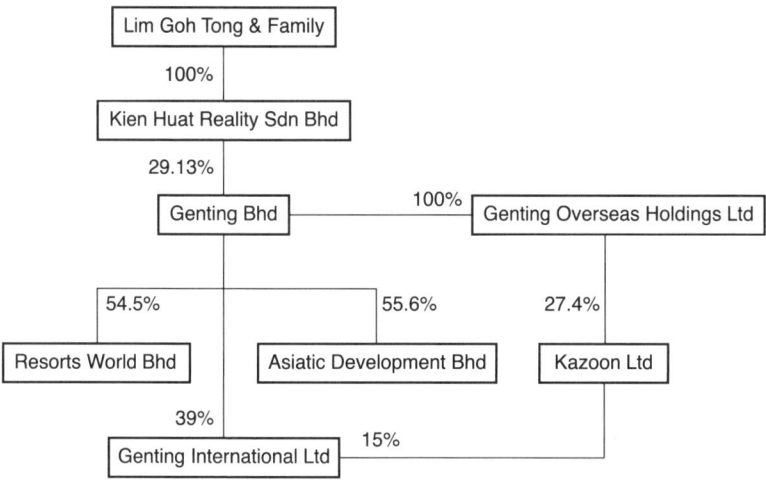

*Figure 2.2* Genting Bhd: Simplified Corporate Structure, 1995–96
Sources: *Malaysian Business*, 16 March 1995; *KLSE Annual Companies Handbook* 21 (3), 1996: 174–81

the hotel part of the business' (*The Star* 17 September 1986). Though this assurance was given by the government in the 1970s, there is no indication that the Genting group is winding down its gaming activities.

Thus, it is not surprising that there have been controversies over Lim's alleged relations to the political elite. In 1990, there were allegations that Genting had ingratiated itself with UMNO by giving politically well-connected individuals RM570 million worth of Resorts World shares, which were apparently pledged to banks as collateral for loans (see *Far Eastern Economic Review* 23 August 1990). That Lim contributes funds to political parties has not been disputed. According to another source, '[H]e's even donated to some opposition parties on the principle that they need money too. Of course, he doesn't give them as much as he gives Barisan parties' (quoted in *Malaysian Business* 1 December 1987).

Apart from the casino licence, Lim appears to have benefited from other concessions from the state, particularly through his participation in the power supply industry. However, since Genting's casino licence is renewable quarterly and given the group's overwhelming dependence on the casino for revenue (see Table 2.4), Lim is even more vulnerable to political changes, especially in UMNO's top leadership; thus, the interests in funds given by him to UMNO. In this light, Lim's decision to relinquish his interests in the potentially profitable Genting Sanyen Newsprint to, *inter alia*, the politically well-connected New Straits Times Press is noteworthy. Whether this is one reason why Lim has diversified his business overseas is, however, questionable. Genting's joint-ventures in China (in manufacturing and power), for example, are in sectors where it has relatively little experience but are none the less potentially very lucrative.

Loh Boon Siew and Oriental Holdings Bhd **CASE STUDY**

Loh Boon Siew, who died in January 1995, was reportedly the second richest Malaysian businessman in 1992, with corporate assets worth approximately RM1.8 billion (see *The Star* 19 May 1992). Although Loh, a Hokkien, is best known for his Honda motor vehicles franchise his business interests were diversified, with involvements in construction, property development, cement manufacturing, hotel and plantation sectors. Operating from the state of Penang, Loh was one of the state's earliest housing developers and was responsible for the development of many of the state capital's most prominent areas. Loh also established the Bayview chain of hotels, predominantly located in Penang (*Malaysian Business* June 1974). Loh had four daughters and his business interests were consolidated under a few family holding companies, like Boon Siew Sdn Bhd and Loh Boon Siew Holdings Sdn Bhd, and one publicly-listed company, Oriental Holdings Bhd.

Born in Fukien province in China in 1916, Loh came to Malaya with his father at the age of 12. Having very little formal education, Loh started out as a mechanic. At the age of 18, Loh set up his own workshop, and by the following year, he had saved enough to purchase a fleet of 11 buses, operating through his Penang Yellow Bus Company Sdn Bhd. Within three years, the thriving company had a fleet of 41 buses. By this time, apart from the bus company and his mechanic shop, Loh had ventured into the sale of used cars, spare parts, batteries and tyres. Loh also secured the franchise to distribute the British-made Aerial motorcycles in the northern regions of Malaya. During the Japanese Occupation of Malaya, most of his buses were confiscated; after the war, Loh restarted these businesses, rapidly expanding (*Malaysian Business* January 1974; *The Star* 20 November 1985; *The Sun* 19 December 1994).

Through his association with Honda, Loh came to national prominence. In 1958, during a visit to Japan, Loh's attention was drawn to Honda motorcycles. That year, his family company, Boon Siew, secured the franchise to be the sole distributor of Honda motorcycles. It was the first Japanese-made motorcycle in Malaya. The Japanese were then trying to break into the Malayan motor vehicle distribution industry, controlled by the British. After a rather lukewarm start, demand increased appreciably and by the mid-1970s, Honda had captured 60 per cent of the motorcycle market. Loh's distribution network also expanded to Singapore and Brunei. In 1969, as demand grew, Loh set up a plant in Penang to assemble Honda motorcycles, through his Kah Motor Co Sdn Bhd. Later, Kah Motor secured the franchise to also distribute Honda motorcars and commercial vehicles. Kah Motor was originally the sole agent for Toyota cars, but relinquished this franchise in 1966 in favor of the Honda franchise. Honda cars are assembled by Oriental Assemblers Sdn Bhd,[35] in which Oriental Holdings has a 65.94 per cent stake; the Honda car assembly plant in Johore was bought from General Motors in 1980. The assembly and distribution of Honda motorcycles and cars have yielded a significant portion of the turnover and profits of the Oriental Holdings group (see Table 2.5). In the motorcycle distribution market, however, competition has increased with the introduction of other Japanese motorcycles, particularly the Suzuki and Yamaha, distributed by the Lion group and the Hong Leong group respectively (*Malaysian Business* 16 June 1988).

Oriental Holdings owns the entire equity of Kah Motor, which has been consistently registering profitable turnovers. In 1995, for

*Table 2.5* Oriental Holdings Bhd: Share Capital, Turnover and Profit Margins, 1984–93 (RM million)

|  | 1984 | 1985 | 1986 | 1987 | 1988 | 1989 | 1990 | 1991 | 1993 | 1994 | 1995 |
|---|---|---|---|---|---|---|---|---|---|---|---|
| Paid-Up Capital | 100.2 | 100.2 | 100.2 | 100.2 | 100.2 | 100.2 | 100.2 | 120.2 | 144.3 | 144.3 | 144.3 |
| Turnover | 489.6 | 298.5 | 247.4 | 318.3 | n.a | n.a | 1155.1 | 1246.5 | 1527.9 | 2060.3 | 3413.6 |
| Pre-Tax Profit | 65.4 | 32.6 | 10.5 | 23.3 | 57.0 | 125.2 | 259.3 | 254.1 | 214.8 | 310.9 | 353.9 |

*Sources: Malaysian Business* 16 June 1988; *KLSE Annual Companies Handbook* 21 (4), 1996: 70

example, it registered a turnover of RM1509 million, compared to RM1566 million in 1994. Kah Motor has local and foreign-incorporated subsidiaries involved in a myriad activities, including motor dealing and repairs (through Happy Motoring Co Sdn Bhd, incorporated in Brunei, in which it has a 51 per cent stake), motor vehicle distribution (through Boon Siew [Borneo] Sdn Bhd, in which it owns 98.8 per cent equity), property development (through wholly-owned Ultra Green Sdn Bhd and Singapore-based B.S. Kah Pte Ltd, in which it has a 40 per cent stake), hotels (through wholly-owned Kah New Zealand Ltd and Kah Australia Pty Ltd, and its 51 per cent Australian subsidiary, Geographe Bay Motel Unit Trust). The chairman of Kah Motor is Loh's daughter, Loh Cheng Yean, while the managing director is Loh's son-in-law, Wong Lum Kong. Other directors of the company included Penang Malay bigwig S.M. Aidid and the late Hamzah Sendut.[36]

Oriental Holdings was incorporated in 1963 as an investment holding company and was publicly-listed in 1964. By 1979, its paid-up capital was only RM18 million, which was increased to RM46.8 million through a bonus issue, followed immediately by a special Bumiputera issue of 20 million shares. The bonus issue appeared to be an attempt to consolidate control over Oriental Holdings before the Bumiputera issue was made. Since then, between 1981 and 1993, Oriental Holdings has had four more bonus issues, augmenting its paid-up capital to RM144.288 million (*KLSE Annual Companies Handbook* 21 (4), 1996: 65–71; also see Table 2.5).

Oriental Holdings has concentrated much attention on manufacturing, diversifying its range of motor component parts (see Figure 2.3). Among the group's component-manufacturing subsidiaries are Oriental Assemblers Sdn Bhd (manufacturer of engines and assembler of motor vehicles), Armstrong Auto Parts Sdn Bhd (manufacturer of seats, diecast parts, shock absorbers, suspension and electrical components for motorcycles and motor vehicles) and Armstrong Cycle Parts Sdn Bhd (manufacturer of automotive control cables, clutches, brakes and speedometers). The group is also heavily involved in the manufacture of plastics, particularly through its subsidiary Teck See Plastics Sdn Bhd which, in turn, has a number of subsidiaries – Lipro Sdn Bhd (manufacturer and assembler of plastic part components), Lipro Electronics Sdn Bhd (assembler and distributor of electrical and electronics products) and Lipro Electrical Manufacturing Sdn Bhd (manufacturer and distributor of electrical parts).[37]

## Chinese Business, Colonialism and Accumulation

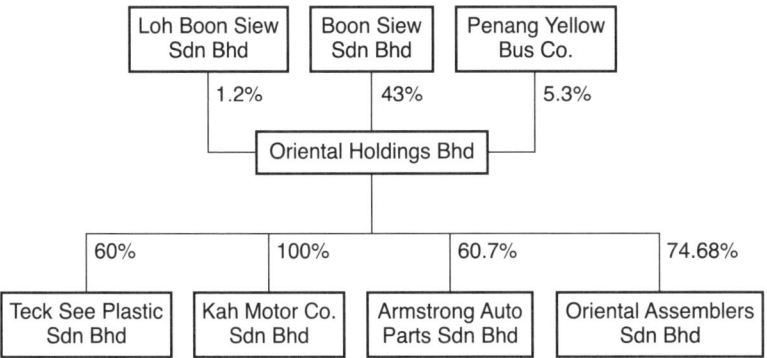

*Figure 2.3* Oriental Holdings Bhd: Simplified Corporate Structure, 1995–96
Sources: KLSE Annual Companies Handbook 21 (4), 1996: 65–9

Oriental Holdings' car assembly, component parts and plastic manufacturing activities contribute a major portion of the group's total earnings. In 1995, for example, it was estimated that the motor division contributed a 65 per cent share of the group's total earnings, while the autoparts and assembling divisions contributed another six per cent and seven per cent respectively. This sector is expected to generate further earnings for the Oriental Holdings group since the government intends to reduce the import content of material used in the automotive sector (*The Sun* 17 June 1996). The plastic division, which manufactures plastic parts for the automotive industry, as well as the electrical and electronic industries, contributed another 11 per cent. Oriental Holdings has an interest in companies which manufacture steel products in China.[38]

Following Loh's death, his daughter Cheng Yean took over as chairman of Oriental Holdings, while Loh's son-in-law, Wong Lum Kong, was appointed managing director. Another of Loh's children, daughter Say Bee, is also a director of the company. In terms of its shareholding structure, Loh's family companies collectively own almost 52 per cent of Oriental Holdings' equity – Boon Siew Sdn Bhd (43 per cent), Penang Yellow Bus Company (5.3 per cent) and Bayview Hotel (3.5 per cent) (*KLSE Annual Companies Handbook* 21 (4), 1996: 65–9).

The Penang Yellow Bus Company was incorporated on 3 January 1949 and is led by Lim Su Tong; it has a long list of shareholders, but the company is majority-owned by two of Loh's family companies,

Boon Siew Sdn Bhd and Loh Boon Siew Holdings Sdn Bhd. The latter, an investment holding company, was incorporated on 3 March 1980, and its equity is primarily held by Loh's family members. Boon Siew Sdn Bhd has a longer history; incorporated on 10 December 1957 to sell motorcycles, grow rubber, lend money and hold investments, its original directors were Loh and his wife Ong Lay Wah (she died in May 1980). Boon Siew Sdn Bhd has an issued capital of RM60 million, and its main shareholders are other family-owned companies, such as Loh Cheng Yean Holdings Sdn Bhd, Loh Ean Holdings Sdn Bhd, Loh Phoy Yen Holdings Sdn Bhd, Loh Gim Ean Holdings Sdn Bhd (each of which own 6.6 million shares), Loh Kar Bee Holdings Sdn Bhd (10.786 million shares) and Loh Kah Kheng Holdings Sdn Bhd (10.813 million shares), while Boontong Estates Sdn Bhd and Bayview Hotel Sdn Bhd each own six million shares. In 1995, the directors of Boon Siew Sdn Bhd were Loh Kar Bee, Loh Cheng Yean, Loh Gim Ean, Wong Lum Kong, Lim Su Tong and Tan Heng Teong. Wong was the managing director, and Tan, his deputy. Apart from its interests in Oriental Holdings, Boon Siew Sdn Bhd has a list of subsidiaries and associate companies, involved in a diverse range of activities, including finance (Boon Siew Finance Sdn Bhd – 45.1 per cent equity; Onward Leasing & Credit Sdn Bhd – 49 per cent), plantations (Southern Perak Plantations Sdn Bhd – 51.85 per cent; Boon Siew Development Sdn Bhd – 76.55 per cent; A1 Emas Sdn Bhd – 65.75 per cent), newspaper publisher (Kwong Wah Yit Poh Press Bhd – 32.5 per cent), hotels (Bayview Hotel Sdn Bhd – 37.5 per cent), manufacturing (NGK Spark Plugs (M) Bhd – 40 per cent; Yuasa Battery (M) Sdn Bhd – 20.9 per cent) and property development and rental of premises (Chainferry Development Sdn Bhd – 27.7 per cent; The Corner Club Bhd – 20.7 per cent).[39]

There are a number of Bumiputeras listed as shareholders of private holding companies controlled by Loh, most of whom are Penang-based businessmen, particularly S.M. Aidid. The most prominent Bumiputera in Loh's group of companies who figured as a director of Oriental Holdings and Kah Motor was the late Hamzah Sendut, the first vice-chancellor of USM. Hamzah was also a director of publicly-listed Carlsberg Brewery (M) Bhd, Hap Seng Consolidated Bhd, Paramount Corporation Bhd and The East Asiatic Co (M) Bhd.

The business operations of the Oriental Holdings group also indicate that it has not been privy to any concessions by the state; nor have any of the companies in the group worked with well-connected Bumiputera businesses even though Loh was an active member of the MCA, once Deputy Chairman of the Penang MCA.

Loh's case provides further credence to the view that MCA's participation in government has not significantly benefited major companies owned by MCA leaders since the 1970s implementation of the NEP,[40] reflecting the MCA's declining influence in government. An indication of how some Chinese businessmen who were involved in the MCA viewed their role in politics can be gauged in what one prominent Chinese businessman Lee Loy Seng said. 'I'm no good in politics. Let's leave politics to the politicians. I'll do my bit as an industrialist' (*Malaysian Business* May 1973). Yet, Lee served as the MCA Perak treasurer from 1974 to 1978, and as a senator from 1971 to 1980.

In terms of links with other Chinese companies, Loh was also a director of Southern Bank Bhd and Tasek Cement Bhd, in which he had a 10 per cent stake. Lim Goh Tong was also a director of Southern Bank, which was seen as a Hokkien bank. Despite their common interests in the bank, and although both men are Hokkien, there were no major business deals involving the two. Other shareholders of Tasek Cement have included Quek Leng Chan of the Hong Leong group, but here too, there are no major business links involving the companies in these groups.

Loh proved himself to have been quite entrepreneurial. The intermediary role that Loh had played between the British and the local economy in the distribution of motorcycles in the colonial period held him in good stead in the immediate post-colonial period when he secured the franchise to distribute Honda vehicles. From the role of trader, Loh later moved into the assembly of motor vehicles. Further vertical integration was achieved when the group began to manufacture component parts. A historical review of Loh's business style suggests concentration on vertical integration in the motor vehicle industry despite the diversified nature of his business operations. Unlike Lim, who has not worked closely with foreign companies, Loh established links with the British and then the Japanese, and managed to gain expertise from them to develop independently. Meanwhile, the Japanese have probably also benefited from the distribution network that Loh managed to create in the country and region.

## Conclusion

Unlike Lim and Loh, who were penniless emigrants from China with little formal education, Malaya-born Kuok had a more bourgeois upbringing and is much better educated. Kuok's father had a medium-sized trading firm, while Kuok also received training in reputable international commodities trading firms before venturing into business on his own. Kuok's inherited wealth facilitated the development of his corporate base through his private investment holding company, Kuok Brothers. Kuok's background enabled him to establish ties with Malay leaders at an early age (most of Malaya's Malay leaders in the immediate post-Independent period were of aristocratic origin). These ties also helped Kuok secure some important economic concessions from the government, particularly to venture further into the commodities and shipping industries. Kuok, however, also accommodated state agencies, allowing them some ownership of his companies before this was required by the NEP. Kuok also played a role in developing some key government-owned enterprises, like Bank Bumiputra, MISC and Pernas, before the dawn of the NEP era. Kuok has shown an entrepreneurial capacity, developing the concessions he has secured from the state – for sugar and shipping – and has established a reputation for himself in Asia through the Shangri-La hotel chain and as a sugar trader. The head start that Kuok had over Lim and Loh, his class background and the privileges he had in terms of education and training in trading, help explain the far greater expansion of his corporate base. The development of the corporate holdings of Kuok and Lim is also attributable to the more liberal conditions in the distribution of economic concessions by the Malay political elite in the immediate post-colonial period.

All three men built their corporate base by venturing into diverse activities. However, all three men had a core business activity that facilitated this conglomerate style of growth. Kuok created a niche in sugar and flour refinery, trading and hotels. Loh concentrated primarily on vehicle assembly as his core activity, while Lim's main business was construction, until he secured the licence to operate a casino. There is evidence of much vertical integration in Kuok and Loh's primary businesses. Kuok's involvement in the sugar industry includes ownership of plantations, refineries and trading companies. Kuok has developed a strong reputation in Asia as a trader and hotelier. Loh's involvement in the auto industry includes the manufacture of component parts, assembly of motor vehicles and distribution of these vehicles. There is, however, little evidence that Lim has managed to develop his gaming activities outside Malaysia; his ventures into the casino business in Australia and the USA have not been very successful. Lim has since moved into leisure, power production and manufacturing, all of which still contribute significantly less to the group's turnover compared to its gaming operations (see Table 2.4).

Further credence to this view can be garnered from a 1997 tabulation by *Asiaweek* (21 November 1997) of the top 1000 companies in Asia in terms of sales. The Malaysian companies to make this *Asiaweek* list include Kuok's Perlis Plantations (ranked 559) and Federal Flour Mills (at 881). Lim's Genting and Loh's Oriental Holdings did not make it onto the *Asiaweek* list in terms of sales.[41] However, while Oriental Holdings recorded a total sales volume of US$1250.4 million, Genting's sales volume was appreciably lower at US$1031.7 million. If the tabulation was based on profits, Genting would attain the highest ranking among the three groups, registering a profit of US$227.1 million, compared to Oriental Holdings' US$156.8 million, Perlis Plantations' US$71.2 million and Federal Flour Mills' US$45.6 million. In terms of profits as a percentage of sales, Genting would again secure the highest ranking, at 22 per cent, compared to Oriental Holdings' 12.5 per cent and Perlis Plantations' 3 per cent and Federal Flour Mills' 3.1 per cent (*Asiaweek* 21 November 1997). These figures are indicative of the lucrativeness of Genting's casino operations in Malaysia.

These sales figures by *Asiaweek* also provide further evidence of Loh's entrepreneurial capacity as he has managed to build up Oriental Holdings without any state patronage. Kuok and Lim have cultivated close links with politically well-connected Bumiputera businessmen or politicians who have contributed to the development of the Perlis Plantations and Genting groups. While Kuok was privy to licences to move into sugar refining, flour milling and shipping, Lim was given two licences, to run a casino – a monopoly – and to move into power production. On the other hand, Loh was rather independent of Malay politicians, and basically relied on his own business acumen to develop the Oriental Holdings group. Despite his involvement in hotels and property development, Loh developed Oriental Holdings through an obvious commitment to vertical style growth in manufacturing, particularly in the production and assembly of component parts for the automotive industry, after

## Chinese Business in Malaysia

securing franchises from the British and then the Japanese to distribute motor vehicles.

Although Loh was a member of the MCA, he has no important business links with other Chinese capitalists, apart from his ownership of equity in the Southern Bank in which Lim also has an interest. Lim also has no major business links with other Chinese in Malaysia. Lim's attempt to work with the Singaporean businessman, Ong Beng Seng, through a joint-venture in a hotel and property project in Australia, did not succeed. Kuok, in contrast, has developed ties with a number of other Chinese businessmen in Asia. Although Kuok, Lim and Loh have all acquired or established hotels abroad, and have invested in the manufacturing sector in China, only Kuok has developed very significant corporate holdings outside Malaysia.

In all three groups, a new generation has emerged. Despite this, there is no evidence of much dispersion of ownership and control through division of stock among the family members themselves, even in the case of Loh's family, which uses a large number of private holding companies to hold Oriental Holdings' shares. These three businessmen also do not appear to have lost much control of their companies despite the restructuring required to accommodate Bumiputera equity participation. Policy and management decisions still remain in the hands of an individual or family. And even though there is clear evidence that professional management has been hired for the administration of Kuok and Loh's companies, there is little evidence of managerial control in Chandler's sense, i.e. where the family business gives way to modern business enterprise run by managerial experts (see Chandler 1977). The corporate structure of all three groups also does not indicate that these men have implemented an intricate system of inter-company holdings to consolidate their corporate holdings in Malaysia.

# Chinese Business, The NEP and Accommodation

## The Chinese, the NEP and the Corporatization Movement

Although the NEP sought to reduce ethnic inequalities in wealth, income and employment, the government declared that no particular group would experience loss or feel any sense of deprivation due to implementation of the policy. According to the government, 'restructuring' was to be primarily achieved through economic growth. Asset redistribution was to be undertaken through various forms: taxation, funding public enterprises, and through the banking system which would provide Bumiputeras with preferential credit access and funding for the acquisition of corporate equity. In spite of this, affirmative action endeavors soon aroused non-Bumiputera dissatisfaction with the NEP.

These fears were exacerbated when public enterprises began to move into economic sectors in which the Chinese had been prominent, particularly banking, property, construction and manufacturing. The Urban Development Authority (UDA), established in 1971, rapidly ventured into construction and property development. By 1976, two Chinese-controlled banks, Malayan Banking Bhd and the United Malayan Banking Corporation Bhd (UMBC), had fallen under state control following runs on the banks; during the next decade, the D&C Bank, Kwong Yik Bank, Bank of Commerce, all financial institutions established by the Chinese, and the Indian-controlled United Asian Bank, would fall under state or Bumiputera control (see Gomez and Jomo 1997: 60–6).[1] As manufacturing enjoyed numerous incentives provided by the government to promote industrialization, there was growing interest in gaining access to companies dominant in the sector.

Economic diversification had remained limited between 1957 and 1970 (see Table 3.1). From the late 1960s onwards, the government actively promoted export-oriented industrialization (EOI) as the problems of its import-substituting industrialization (ISI) drive during the 1960s had become apparent. ISI had generated relatively little employment, while the government found it increasingly untenable that most foreign companies participating in ISI merely established subsidiaries for assembling, finishing and packing goods produced with imported materials for profitable sale within the protected domestic market. In 1968, the more employment and export-oriented Investment Incentives Act, which provided tax holidays to approved firms for up to eight years, was introduced. Other incentives were offered: to encourage employment, tax breaks were given if industries employed a certain number of workers. The labor laws were also amended in 1969 to help create more attractive labor regulations and industrial relations for such industries (see Jomo and Todd 1994). In 1971, the Free Trade Zone Act was promulgated which allowed for the creation of new industrial estates or export processing zones known as free trade zones (FTZs) to encourage investments by companies manufacturing for export. This Act, which provided FTZ companies with exemptions from customs regulations for equipment, materials and products imported and exported for export-oriented industries, attracted huge investments, particularly from the United States.

Within a decade, firms in the free trade zones had come to dominate Malaysian manufactured exports, overtaking the resource-based industries processing raw materials for export. With the incentives provided to promote EOI, the average annual growth rate of manufacturing output exceeded 10 per cent between 1970 and 1980. By 1980, manufacturing had become a major net foreign exchange earner, reducing the dependence on primary exports.

Table 3.1 Malaysia: Gross Domestic Product by Sector, 1955–94 (percentages)

|  | 1955* | 1960* | 1965 | 1970 | 1975 | 1980 | 1985 | 1990 | 1994 |
|---|---|---|---|---|---|---|---|---|---|
| Agriculture | 40.2 | 40.5 | 31.5 | 30.8 | 27.7 | 22.8 | 20.7 | 18.7 | 14.8 |
| Mining | 6.3 | 6.1 | 9.0 | 6.3 | 4.6 | 10.0 | 10.4 | 9.8 | 7.5 |
| Manufacturing | 8.2 | 8.6 | 10.4 | 13.4 | 16.4 | 20.0 | 19.6 | 26.9 | 31.5 |
| Services | 45.3 | 44.8 | 49.1 | 51.3 | 49.5 | 47.2 | 49.3 | 46.1 | 48.8 |

* Peninsular Malaysia only
Sources: Bank Negara Malaysia, Money and Banking in Malaysia, Table 1.2. Ministry of Finance, Malaysia, Economic Report, various issues. Bank Negara Malaysia, Annual Report, various issues

Manufacturing's share of Malaysia's GDP more than doubled from 13 per cent in 1970 to 31.5 per cent in 1994 (see Table 3.1), while its share of total exports increased from a mere 8.5 per cent in 1960 to more than 74 per cent in 1993 (see Table 3.2).

With the new policy emphasis on EOI, the government would rely even more on foreign capital to promote industrialization, since it was wary that growth would otherwise probably contribute more to wealth accumulation by ethnic Chinese (Bowie 1991). Unlike ISI, domestic capitalists had even fewer opportunities to benefit from EOI. Foreign firms in free trade zones mainly used imported equipment and materials for production and were not under any pressure from the government to set up joint-ventures with domestic firms unless they produced for the domestic market. Thus, foreign firms continued to dominate these industries, especially with their control over technology and marketing (Jomo and Edwards 1993: 6–7).

With the NEP, the politically-influential gained access to the manufacturing sector through various means. One way was to get the government to give an economic concession in the form of a licence or lucrative tariff which could be used to form a joint-venture, usually with a foreign company. Another manner was to inject such a licence or contract into a private company and use it for a reverse takeover of a publicly-listed company. A more common form was to secure

Table 3.2 Malaysia: Exports by Major Groups, 1960–93 (percentages)

|  | 1960 | 1965 | 1970 | 1975 | 1980 | 1985 | 1990 | 1993 |
|---|---|---|---|---|---|---|---|---|
| Agriculture | 66.1 | 54.5 | 59.2 | 52.8 | 43.6 | 32.7 | 22.3 | 15.3 |
| Rubber | 55.1 | 38.6 | 33.4 | 21.9 | 16.4 | 7.6 | 3.8 | 1.7 |
| Timber | 5.3 | 9.5 | 16.5 | 12.0 | 14.1 | 10.3 | 8.9 | 6.1 |
| Palm oil | 2.0 | 3.1 | 5.3 | 15.4 | 10.3 | 11.8 | 6.2 | 5.2 |
| Others | 3.7 | 3.3 | 4.0 | 3.5 | 2.8 | 3.0 | 3.4 | 2.3 |
| Minerals | 22.2 | 30.0 | 25.9 | 22.6 | 33.8 | 34.0 | 17.8 | 9.4 |
| Tin | 14.0 | 23.1 | 19.6 | 13.1 | 8.9 | 4.3 | 1.1 | 0.4 |
| Petroleum | 4.0 | 2.3 | 3.9 | 9.3 | 23.8 | 22.9 | 13.4 | 6.6 |
| Liquefied Natural Gas | – | – | – | – | – | 6.0 | 2.8 | 2.1 |
| Others | 4.2 | 4.6 | 2.4 | 0.2 | 1.1 | 0.8 | 0.5 | 0.3 |
| Manufactures | 8.5 | 12.2 | 11.9 | 21.4 | 21.6 | 32.1 | 59.3 | 74.3 |
| Other Exports | 3.2 | 3.3 | 3.0 | 3.2 | 1.0 | 1.2 | 10.6 | 1.0 |
| Total | 100.0 | 100.0 | 100.0 | 100.0 | 100.0 | 100.0 | 100.0 | 100.0 |

Sources: Bank Negara Malaysia, Annual Report, various issues.

heavily discounted stock options in publicly-listed companies when they were required to restructure their share ownership to ensure at least 30 per cent Bumiputera ownership. Another related option was to secure appointments as directors in such companies. Chinese-based manufacturing companies were also looking out for politically well-connected Malays to help secure state concessions.

The need for Chinese (and foreign) capital to establish close links with the Malay political elite became imperative when legislation, such as the controversial Industrial Co-ordination Act (ICA), and monitoring agencies, like the Capital Issues Committee (CIC) and the Foreign Investments Committee (FIC), were established to ensure effective implementation of the NEP. The FIC was responsible for major foreign investment issues, including monitoring, assisting and evaluating the form, extent and conduct of foreign investment, and regulating the acquisition of assets or interests in companies by foreign entities. The Investment Incentives Act was also used by the government to ensure that foreign companies adhered to the NEP guidelines on Bumiputera equity participation and employment. The CIC, set up in 1968, was responsible for advancing the 'indigenization' of corporate stock; in the 1970s, the agency was given more clout. CIC approval was required, for example, before companies obtained public listing and before quoted companies could change their equity structure or the nature of their operations (Low 1985: 88). In 1992, the CIC was replaced by the Securities Commission, which has been more wide-ranging powers.

The ICA was promulgated in 1975 to implement the government's industrialization policies and to ensure the orderly development and growth of manufacturing. The ICA, however, alarmed non-Bumiputera investors, particularly the Chinese, who perceived it as an attempt to advance Malay interests in the manufacturing sector. The ICA gave the government increased authority over the establishment and growth of manufacturing enterprises, and provided the bureaucracy with the means to ensure that the development of the manufacturing sector would be in line with the ethnic redistributive objectives of the NEP. Following the introduction of the ICA, there was a marked slump in foreign and domestic investments except in the oil industry and the FTZs, which were exempt from the ICA guidelines, presumably encouraging capital flight. According to a Morgan Guaranty estimate, total capital flight during 1976 and 1985 amounted to US$12 billion, more than half attributable to Chinese capital (Khoo 1995: 165).

The ICA's ruling that unexempted companies ensure a minimum of 30 per cent Bumiputera ownership in all their businesses beyond a certain size drew the most protests from the Chinese. The government eventually conceded by amending the ICA, first in 1977, and again on several subsequent occasions. The essential premise of the ICA, however, remained intact; licences would be required from the Ministry of Trade and Industry, except in the case of small firms, and these could be revoked if requirements for Bumiputera ownership and employment were not met.

With implementation of the ICA, Bumiputera participation in government-approved manufacturing projects grew appreciably between 1975 and 1985, when the economy was hit by a recession. With increased regulation, publicly-listed Chinese companies had little choice but to restructure. Some prominent Chinese businessmen like Robert Kuok bypassed the state by diversifying overseas, while others, like Lee Loy Seng, preferred to divest their interests in publicly-quoted companies rather than have joint ownership (see Chapter 4). Both Chinese and foreign companies began to actively solicit business ties with politically-influential Malays willing to lend their names for a price without taking on executive roles after becoming owners and directors of the companies (Bowie 1991: 103–4). Small, predominantly manufacturing, enterprises, which were not privy to such avenues to bypass the state were those most affected by the government's new constraints. During a Malaysian Chinese economic conference organized by the Associated Chinese Chambers of Commerce and Industry of Malaysia (ACCCIM) in 1978, it was stated that Chinese capital was running into problems because of the 'misconceived implementation of regulations and the narrowing access of economic opportunities for the Chinese through Government edicts and directives' (quoted in Gomez 1994: 189). Of this period, Tan Koon Swan, then a prominent businessman and a future president of the MCA, would later acknowledge: '. . . in response to the ICA, the Chinese Chamber of Commerce had urged the Chinese to boycott new investment, and we were watching many Chinese professional people beginning to move out of the country' (quoted in *Far Eastern Economic Review* 10 May 1984).

In this economic environment, some MCA leaders, led by Tan Koon Swan, began propounding the ethic of self-help through a 'corporatization movement'. The movement was also seen by these leaders as a means to muster support amongst the Chinese and to increase the MCA's influence in the then newly-formed Barisan

Nasional coalition. The corporatization movement entailed structural change to Chinese businesses to enable them to better cope with growing state intervention in the economy. The most significant of these reforms necessitated increased cooperation between small-scale and family-based Chinese businesses and revamps of their management techniques (see Gale 1985; Yeoh 1989; Gomez 1994: 189–217).

There was a strong political dimension to the corporatization movement. The idea that the Chinese combine their resources to form a large company that would enter new industries to promote Chinese economic interests had been first mooted in 1966 by Tan Siew Sin, then the MCA president and himself a leading owner of corporate equity. UMNO members had then begun putting pressure on the state to intervene in their favor in the economy. This had already led to the establishment of MARA in 1965, Bank Bumiputra in 1966 and later Pernas in 1969. Siew Sin's call was directed primarily at the Chinese business elite.

This was not the first time that Siew Sin's family had been involved in a move to mobilize Chinese capital in the face of an economic environment hostile to the interests of Chinese capital. In the 1930s, during the economic depression, Siew Sin's family had helped initiate a move to bring about the merger of three banks to form a large Chinese banking enterprise, the Oversea-Chinese Banking Corporation (OCBC).[2] However, Siew Sin procrastinated in creating a new large Chinese enterprise owned by Chinese capitalists. The establishment of such a company then could have caused problems for businesses owned by other Chinese capitalists, who were the major financiers of the MCA. Some problems had already emerged among the major owners of OCBC in the late 1950s over the way the bank should develop, suggesting that Chinese business leaders could have problems working together in a common business enterprise.

It was Lee San Choon, the then MCA youth leader, who would act. The business organization created by the MCA in 1968 was not a company, but a co-operative, Koperatif Serbaguna (M) Bhd (KSM). This co-operative was established primarily to cater to the needs of poor and lower middle class Chinese, not big Chinese capitalists. Unlike most other leading members of the MCA, including Siew Sin, who had bourgeois backgrounds, San Choon was of lower middle class origin and had not obtained tertiary education. The son of an unlicensed dentist, San Choon had his early education in a Chinese-medium school, and completed secondary education at the Johore English School. He held a minor position in the government's Social

Welfare Department, then worked as a clerk in a textile factory. The Chinese business elite were cautious of San Choon, and provided little or no support for his attempts to promote KSM as a means to mobilize Chinese capital. These businessmen did not trust the egalitarian structure of ownership and decision-making of a co-operative and were concerned that this would affect business operations and their control over KSM (Gomez 1991: 52).

Despite some initial reservations, Siew Sin began to provide more support for the KSM after 1969. Following the MCA's dismal performance in the 1969 general election, the party decided to withdraw its members from the Cabinet,[3] only to return to the fold a short time later. Siew Sin discovered that his decision to leave the Cabinet had cost his party much support among the Chinese business community. Chinese businessmen were now hesitant to place too much trust in a party leader who was willing to jeopardize the MCA's influence and capacity to protect and promote Chinese business interests by withdrawing from the government. In a step towards regaining their confidence, especially after the NEP-endorsed establishment of public enterprises, Siew Sin tried to actively promote the theme of the need for the Chinese to protect their economic interests. However, this process was hampered by a bitter feud in the party, which effectively split the MCA in the early 1970s.[4] Siew Sin survived the factionalism with the support secured for him by San Choon through his control of KSM. In 1974, Siew Sin stepped down as MCA president in favor of San Choon.

By the early 1970s, as the Chinese community became increasingly concerned over the state's growing intervention in the economy, they were more open to the idea that a party-backed business organization could play a role in protecting their interests. In 1975, the KSM co-operative established an investment holding company, Multi-Purpose Holdings Bhd (MPHB), to expand its interests in the corporate sector. In 1977, San Choon secured the services of Tan Koon Swan, another Chinese businessman with a working class background, to lead KSM and MPHB.

Koon Swan's father was hawker and his mother a construction worker. After completing his secondary education, Koon Swan joined the National Electricity Board in Kuala Lumpur as a clerk at the age of 17. Four years later, he joined the Income Tax Department where he spent six years before accepting an appointment as a tax adviser to Esso (M) Bhd. In 1970, Koon Swan left Esso to become the general manager of Genting Bhd, controlled by Lim Goh Tong. Here, Koon

Swan made a name for himself as a corporate maverick and was considered responsible for the growth and public-listing of Genting. During his tenure at Genting, Koon Swan sold the shares he had acquired in the company for a huge profit in 1973 and used the funds to obtain control of Sungei Way Dredging Company Bhd, later renamed Supreme Corporation. This company became his publicly-listed vehicle, which Koon Swan used well to build up a diversified business group. In 1977, he left Genting to become general manager of KSM and managing director of MPHB. Before joining KSM and MPHB in 1976, Koon Swan attended a business course at Harvard University; that short stint in the United States seems to have had a profound impact on the strategy he would use to develop MPHB and his own listed company, Supreme Corporation (*Malaysian Business* November 1976; *New Straits Times* 22 August 1986; Gomez 1994: 234). Koon Swan only joined the MCA in 1977, after taking up his appointments in these MCA-linked enterprises. His rise in the MCA was swift, due to the patronage of San Choon and his early success in developing KSM and MPHB. By 1982, Koon Swan was one of six MCA vice-presidents, and in 1985, just eight years after joining the party, he was elected president after an intense and protracted effort which deeply divided the party.

The main leaders of the corporatization movement were politicians-cum-businessmen Koon Swan and Lee Loy Seng, the first chairman of MPHB.[5] Both had their reservations over the growing impact of the NEP on the economy, but probably held differing views on how to tackle the situation. Koon Swan, the more vocal of the two on the NEP, was popular among the Chinese for being more outspoken than other MCA leaders. In 1984, the *Far Eastern Economic Review*'s (10 May 1984) profile of Koon Swan said: '(W)hile being careful never to depart from overall support for the ruling National Front coalition, he expressed surprisingly direct reservations about the pace and direction of the New Economic Policy.' The *Far Eastern Economic Review* (15 May 1984) quoted Koon Swan as stating in parliament: 'In the eradication of imbalances inherited from the past, we must not create another imbalance.'

This attempt by the MCA to get the Chinese to pool their economic resources was not a new phenomenon. Chinese, particularly the sub-ethnic communities, had previously engaged in such efforts to deal with a colonial state that was not supportive of their economic interests. One outcome of this was the incorporation of clan-based banks, the largest of which was the Hokkien-based

OCBC. The following study of Hokkiens in the banking sector indicates some probable reasons for the inability of sub-ethnic Chinese communities to co-operate in the management of large corporations, raising questions about the limits and efficacy of trust among Chinese business communities.

The Hokkien Chinese in the Banking Sector

In the late 1800s, Chinese began to mobilize their resources to establish banks to meet the community's needs and to counter British control of the finance sector. In 1903, almost half a century after British banks had started operating in the country, the first Chinese bank, the Kwong Yik Banking Corporation Ltd, was incorporated in Singapore. Between 1903 and 1932, 15 banks would be incorporated in Malaya and Singapore. The other banks established in this period included the Four Seas Communications Bank (formerly the Sze Hai Tong Banking & Insurance Company Ltd) (in 1907), the Chinese Commercial Bank (1912), the Ho Hong Bank (1917), the Oversea Chinese Bank (1919), the Lee Wah Bank (1920), the United Overseas Bank (1935) and the Ban Hin Lee Bank (1935) (Lim 1969: 233; Lee 1988; Brown 1994: 160–61).[6] These banks were clan-based. The Kwong Yik Bank and the Lee Wah Bank were established by Cantonese, the Four Seas Communications Bank was Teochew-led, while the Ho Hong Bank, the Oversea Chinese Bank, the Chinese Commercial Bank and the Ban Hin Lee Bank were all Hokkien banks.

From 1929, local companies began to feel the impact of the Great Depression. In particular, Singaporean companies, tied by then in to international trading markets, were badly affected. Eventually, many Chinese banks were also hit by the recessionary economic conditions. This led to the merger of three Hokkien banks, Ho Hong Bank, the Oversea Chinese Bank and the Chinese Commercial Bank, to form the Oversea-Chinese Banking Corporation Ltd (OCBC) in 1932. Yeap Chor Ee, who had founded the Ban Hin Lee Bank – it started operations in 1918 but was only incorporated as a limited company in Penang in 1935 – was also one of the original shareholders of the OCBC (Lee 1988).[7] Many of the other original shareholders of the OCBC were from the Straits Settlements and had vast interests in the rubber plantation sector which had been badly affected by the Depression (Huff 1994: 232–4). The rubber baron who owned Lee Rubber, Lee Kong Chian, reportedly a champion of Hokkien interests in Singapore, is reputed to have played a major role in bringing about this merger (see *The Star* 31 May 1983). Less than a decade after its incorporation, the OCBC had emerged as the largest Chinese bank outside China. Almost three-quarters of the total assets of Chinese banks in the Straits Settlements were owned by the OCBC, which had also incorporated 18 branches throughout Southeast Asia and in China (Huff 1994: 230).

Although the three-bank merger which led to the incorporation of the OCBC was a Hokkien-led initiative, a number of Babas from Malacca were among the bank's original shareholders.[8] Among them was Chan Kang Swi, a prominent rubber planter who had helped establish the Ho Hong Bank (Lee and Chow 1997: 4). The most prominent Malacca Baba who was a founding shareholder of OCBC was Tan Cheng Lock, who had vast rubber plantation holdings in the state; his family was also represented on the bank's board of directors (Tan 1982: 196). Cheng Lock and his son, Siew Sin, would later become founding leaders of the MCA. The links between the Tan family and the OCBC group are still strong. The OCBC group presently owns a 16.03 per cent stake in the Tan family's publicly-listed company, the United Malacca Rubber Estates Bhd, incorporated in 1910. In 1993, United Malacca Rubber Estates acquired 20 per cent of Pacific Bank Bhd, a quoted financial institution which has its roots in the Batu Pahat Bank Ltd, incorporated in 1919. In 1963, the OCBC incorporated the Pacific Bank to take over the Batu Pahat Bank. United Malacca Rubber Estates is the largest shareholder of Pacific Bank, with a 22 per cent stake (*KLSE Annual Companies Handbook* 21 (1 and 3), 1996: 471–7; 293–303). At the end of December 1996, Pacific Bank was reported to be involved in the takeover and merger of the banking operations of the OCBC group in Malaysia. The Pacific Bank was also to take over the Malaysian insurance operations of another company in the OCBC group, the Great Eastern Life Assurance Company (see *The Edge* 23 December 1996). The Pacific Bank wholly owns an insurance company, Pacific Insurance Bhd.

Apart from the Ban Hin Lee Bank and the Pacific Bank, owned by families of businessmen who had helped incorporate OCBC, some of the leading Chinese banks later incorporated in Malaysia – Malayan Banking Bhd, Public Bank Bhd and MUI Bank Bhd – were led by men who had been in the employ of the OCBC. The three men who founded these three banks left the OCBC in the 1960s following a feud between some of the latter's main shareholders.

Malayan Banking Bhd (Maybank) was established in 1960 by Khoo Teck Puat, whose father, Khoo Yang Tin, had been a founding shareholder of OCBC. Khoo Teck Puat joined the OCBC in 1933 as a clerk after completing his secondary education in Singapore. Khoo served at the OCBC for 26 years before leaving in 1959; during this period, he had risen to the position of deputy general manager. Khoo's reasons for leaving the OCBC have been shrouded in controversy. One suggested reason was his inability to secure a seat on the OCBC's board of directors although he had developed a significant stake in the bank. Khoo was apparently also at odds with OCBC chairman Tan Chin Tuan over the bank's mode of development (see *Insight* May 1983; *The Star* 19 May 1983). Both Tan and Khoo shared a common desire to build up a local bank that could break the stranglehold of foreign banks in Singapore and Malaya; however, they both had different visions of how this was to be done. While Khoo was keen to expand OCBC's network of branches further into Malaya, Tan exercised more caution. Indeed, under Tan's chairmanship, OCBC had come under attack for being too cautious and prudent (*Insight* May 1983).

Among the other original founders of Maybank were some leading Chinese capitalists: Goh Tjoei Kok, a Singaporean industrialist and estate owner who went on to found the Tat Lee Bank (one of Singapore's largest banks) in the 1970s, and Loke Wan Tho, the son of the prominent tin miner, Loke Yew. Although Khoo claimed that his reason for setting up a new bank in Malaysia, rather than Singapore, was because, 'I felt it was wrong to compete with a bank I've worked for more than 25 years,' Maybank quickly emerged as a threat to OCBC's plans to develop the largest local banking group in the peninsula. Within the first five years of its incorporation, Maybank had opened more than a hundred branches in Malaysia, 22 in Singapore, and had achieved the distinction of being the first Malaysian bank to open a branch in England (*Insight* May 1983).

Khoo recognized that the foreign banks which controlled the sector had concentrated their banking activities in the major cities in the peninsula, primarily servicing the larger enterprises. According to Khoo, 'virtually no attempt had been made to make banking facilities available to smaller potential customers, especially in rural areas and in smaller towns. There was an urgent need to fill those gaps' (*Insight* May 1983). By 1966, while Maybank had managed to establish 104 branches in Malaysia, the OCBC's network had less than 30. That year, Maybank's deposit base was in excess of RM540 million, equivalent to that of the OCBC, which had had a 30-year head start (*The Star* 30 May 1983).

In 1966, however, allegations of mismanagement of the bank's funds by Khoo precipitated a run on Maybank, necessitating government intervention. Khoo alleged that a smear campaign had been perpetrated against him by other members of the board (see *Insight* May 1983). Khoo was forced to step down as chief executive of Maybank, but remained a director and shareholder until 1976. Maybank eventually came under the control of the government; currently, its majority shareholder is the state-controlled trust agency, PNB.

Two of Khoo's protégés, Khoo Kay Peng and Teh Hong Piow, also left Maybank during this period. Khoo Kay Peng took up an appointment at the newly-established Bank Bumiputra, then under the control of Razaleigh Hamzah, and later went on to develop MUI Bank Bhd in the 1970s. Another director of Bank Bumiputra then was Robert Kuok. In 1993, however, Khoo Kay Peng had to divest his entire equity in MUI Bank to another Hokkien from Singapore, Quek Leng Chan of the Hong Leong group. The sale of MUI Bank was apparently a move by Khoo to ingratiate himself with UMNO leaders. Khoo had backed Razaleigh Hamzah who had moved into the opposition, after his narrow defeat in the UMNO 1987 party presidency contest. Khoo and Quek had reportedly been very close friends, but had fallen out when they both made takeover bids on a publicly-listed company, Central Sugars Bhd, in 1980 (see *The Star* 9 June 1980). Khoo secured control over Central Sugars (now known as MUI Properties), but his relationship with Quek had been strained. MUI Bank was renamed the Hong Leong Bank.[9]

Teh Hong Piow established Public Bank, currently the largest Chinese bank in Malaysia. He remains the only one of the OCBC 'old boy' network who still retains control of the bank he established. Public Bank was incorporated on 30 December 1965, started operations on 6 August 1966, and secured public-listing on 6 April 1967 (*KLSE Annual Companies Handbook* 21 (4), 1996: 628–9). The first chairman of Public Bank was Nik Ahmad Kamil, an UMNO member who had served as *Mentri Besar* (Chief Minister) of Kelantan, Speaker of the *Dewan Rakyat* (House of Representatives) and Malaysian ambassador to the United Nations, the United States, Australia and the United Kingdom (Tan 1982: 282). Along with Public Bank, Teh incorporated a finance company, Public Finance Bhd, which was publicly-listed on 21 December 1966 (*KLSE Annual Companies Handbook* 21 (4), 1996: 634–5).

Teh was born in Singapore in 1930 to a poor family. His father had migrated from China at the age of 15, worked as salesman and then become a small-scale trader. At the age of 20, after completing his secondary education, Teh joined the OCBC as a clerk to support his family; he rose quickly to become a sub-accountant. In 1960, he joined Maybank as one of its senior executives. In 1964, Teh was appointed Maybank general manager. However, Teh was also affected by the feud within Maybank. At the young age of 35, he applied for and secured a banking licence and became the youngest managing director in full control of a domestic bank (*Investors' Digest* May 1987; *Malaysian Business* 1 August 1987). The award of this licence to Teh was significant as government leaders were then under increasing pressure from UMNO members to ensure more distribution of wealth to Malays, implying that the Chinese were receiving too many concessions from the state. Bank Bumiputra was established in the same year as Public Bank. Another Chinese bank which began operating in 1966 was the D&C Bank, controlled by H.S. Lee. Teh has never disclosed how he managed to secure the banking licence though he has admitted, 'Getting a banking licence in those days wasn't easy. But with the help of friends and connections, we managed to secure one' (quoted in *Malaysian Business* 1 August 1987).

Although Teh used Public Bank's profits to diversify, moving into property development – the bank's original RM2 million capital base was reportedly secured through the profits he had made from property development (see *Far Eastern Economic Review* 3 October 1991) – this diversification phase soon ceased. Teh would later say: 'I came to the realization that it was not wise to go into different types of business enterprises just for the sake of diversification. I believe that in order to do well, one should concentrate on the business which one knows best' (*The Star* 24/10/85). In this regard, Teh was different from Khoo Teck Puat. Of his plans for Maybank, Khoo has said:

> I saw it as a logical holding company for a whole range of financial institutions and services – including a finance company and a building society, a property group, insurance and broking operations, and using the holding company for a wide range of industrial, rubber and tin and other major Malayan and Singaporean concerns (*Insight* May 1983)

Interestingly, this was the pattern of growth of the OCBC group. Khoo Kay Peng, who developed MUI Bank, also followed the pattern described by Khoo Teck Puat (see case study in this chapter).

Like Maybank, Public Bank grew rapidly. Between 1966 and 1996, Public Bank's paid-up capital increased from a mere RM12.750 million to a phenomenal RM826.097 million (*KLSE Annual Companies Handbook* 21 (4), 1996: 628–9). By 1996, Public Bank had 155 branches, including one in Hong Kong, Sri Lanka and Laos as well as a representative office in China and Myanmar. The bank is planning to expand its involvement in Southeast Asia, moving into Thailand, the Philippines and Indonesia. Public Bank started as a 32-staff operation; by the early 1990s, the group had approximately 4500 employees (*Malaysian Business* 1 September 1991 and 1 August 1996). Its publicly-listed finance arm, Public Finance, has 72 branches and is one of the country's leading finance companies. In its 30-year history, the Public Bank group has never declared a loss, even during the mid-1980s economic recession.

Public Bank's growth strategy has been described by one senior bank official: 'Our primary market is small-to-medium businesses, those involved in trade and manufacturing, or cottage industries. About one third of our customers are large corporate clients, and the other two thirds small-to-medium-sized businesses' (quoted in *Far Eastern Economic Review* 3 October 1991). Having established some success in the Malaysian market, Public Bank has turned its attention abroad. In Vietnam, Public Bank is trying to create a niche among ethnic Chinese there, and when Public Bank took over JCG Finance Company Ltd in Hong Kong, it catered primarily to small Chinese businesses and the colony's 74,000-strong Filipino community (*Far Eastern Economic Review* 3 October 1991).

In Malaysia, apart from banking and finance, Public Bank is involved in leasing and factoring, stockbroking and futures trading, trustee services, offshore banking and unit trust services. Among its main overseas acquisitions is the Hong Kong-based JCG Finance, which is also involved in the securities industry. Public Bank (Labuan) Ltd was established to move into offshore banking. Public Bank (Labuan) was used to acquire a 40 per cent stake in Bancorp Holdings in New Zealand, a merchant and investment banking group. Public Bank has a 55 per cent stake in the Singapore-based PB International Factors (*Malaysian Business* 1 September 1991; see also Figure 3.1).

After securing the licence to establish a bank, Teh appears to have been rather independent of ties with the Malay political elite. There is no evidence of major business ties between Teh and well-connected Malay businessmen, nor are there any prominent Bumiputeras on the

## Chinese Business, The NEP and Accommodation

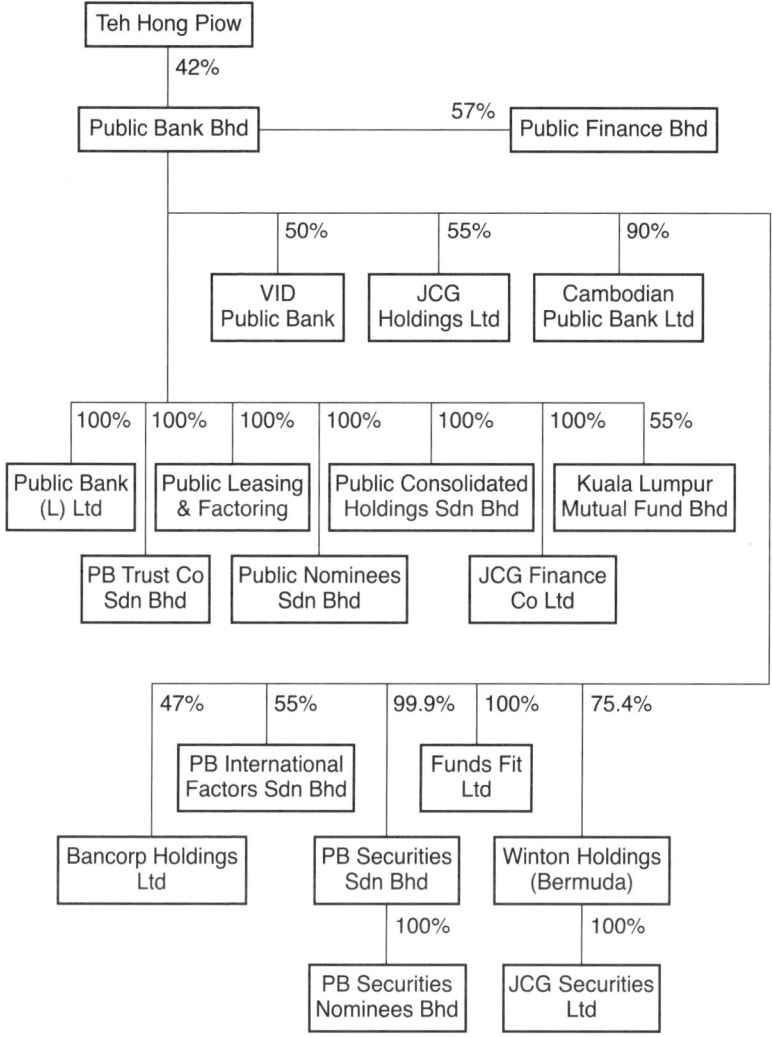

*Figure 3.1* Public Bank Bhd: Simplified Corporate Structure, 1995–96
Sources: KLSE Annual Companies Handbook 21 (4), 1996: 628–39; *Malaysian Business* 1/9/91

board of directors of Public Bank. This suggests, that by conforming with the NEP regulations and steering clear of controversy, Teh has managed to retain control of Public Bank.

The merger that led to the incorporation of the OCBC, and its emergence as a major banking force and as a corporation with significant interests in other sectors of the economy, demonstrated some Hokkiens' capacity to pool their resources, as well as protect and develop their economic interests in Singapore and Malaya. However, the problems that arose in the late 1950s between shareholders over the mode of bank development and its style of management led to friction. In the case of Maybank, although Khoo Teck Puat had been responsible for the growth of the bank, he had to share ownership of the bank with other prominent Chinese. Disputes among these shareholders, in part, contributed to Khoo Teck Puat's removal from the Maybank management. In the case of MUI Bank and Public Bank, however, one individual had majority ownership and control over each of these banks. Both Khoo Kay Peng and Teh Hong Piow had also begun to work more closely with well-connected Malays. As mentioned earlier, Public Bank's first chairman was UMNO politician Nik Ahmad Kamil. Apart from Razaleigh Hamzah, Khoo Kay Peng was also closely associated with Mohammad Noah Omar, the father-in-law of two former Prime Ministers, Abdul Razak and Hussein Onn. Noah had been a long-standing chairman of MUI. Khoo Kay Peng only divested his stake in MUI Bank after he realized that he would not be able to expand the bank's operations due to increasing regulation of the sector and his inability to secure approval from the state to open more branches (see case study). Public Bank has managed to grow as Teh has made it a point to conform to and implement state policies. The fact that Public Bank has concentrated its activities in the financial sector appears to be another reason why the bank has managed to do well. Public Bank, like OCBC, has a reputation in the Malaysian market for being conservative and prudent (see *Malaysian Business* 1 August 1996). This point has also been stressed by Teh:

> We have continuously been able to contain our incidence of non-performing loans as well as being effective in our loan recovery. Thus, as at December 31, 1995, non-performing loans represented only 1.7 per cent of the gross loans and advances. This is well below the industry average of 5.1 per cent (quoted in *Malaysian Business* 1 August 1996).

This pattern of breaking away and establishing their own enterprises was suggestive of a trend among Chinese to venture out on their own, especially when they felt they had acquired enough experience in a particular field to fend for themselves. Another factor that must be highlighted is that allegations of impropriety on the part of controlling shareholders have contributed to the eventual takeover of banks. Khoo Teck Puat came under a cloud over alleged abuses of power for vested interests which led to the run on Maybank. Such allegations were used to remove him from Maybank's board of directors. In the case of Khoo Kay Peng, his takeover of MUI Bank was shrouded in controversy when it was later disclosed that it had contributed to the scandal involving the Singapore-based publicly-listed company, Pan-Electric Industries Ltd, in the mid-1980s.[10] Public Bank, on the other hand, has been largely untainted by any major controversy.[11]

Multi-Purpose Holdings

A key aspect of the corporatization movement was the incorporation by the MCA of a major investment holding company, Multi-Purpose Holdings Bhd (MPHB), to pool Chinese resources to protect and advance Chinese business interests. MPHB, incorporated in 1975, was controlled by the MCA-backed co-operative KSM, and promoted by the MCA as the 'people's company' (see *New Straits Times* 10 June 1981).

MPHB and KSM were only two of approximately 50 investment holding companies and co-operatives that emerged during the corporatization movement. Many clan-based enterprises were also established, but most of them, like KSM and MPHB, were also controlled by various MCA leaders. For example, Ka Yin Holdings Sdn Bhd, controlled by the Hakka-based Federation of Ka Yin Associations, was headed by two key promoters of the corporatization movement, Lee Loy Seng and Choo Ching Hwa, both then directors of MPHB. Lee controlled the KL-Kepong group and was a former MCA senator, while Choo had served as treasurer-general of the MCA. Hok Lian Holdings Sdn Bhd was incorporated by the Hokkien Association in 1981 and led by Lee Yan Lian, the president of the ACCCIM in the early 1980s. The Keng Chew Selangor Society, a Hainanese organization which incorporated Grand Ocean Development Bhd, was linked to Koon Swan and his brother, Tan Loon Swan (Gale 1985: 107–9; Yeoh 1987: 122–3).

The implementation of the ICA and its repercussions for Chinese businesses justified the MCA's corporatization drive and the promotion of MPHB. Koon Swan was specific about his intentions with MPHB: 'We aim to show Chinese businessmen what big corporations can do . . . . The fastest way to grow is through the acquisition of badly-run companies, or companies with the basic infrastructure but which lack the manpower and resources to enable them to grow.' And on how these acquisitions could be funded, Koon Swan explained MPHB would go for a 'continuous increase in capital through rights issues, etc' (all quoted in *New Straits Times* 8 March 1981).

The pattern of growth suggested by Koon Swan seems to have been inspired by what was happening in the American and British corporate sectors. During the late 1970s and early 1980s, as the American economy struggled with numerous economic problems, including a recession, an oil crisis and competition from Japan, government deregulation initiatives spawned significant developments in the corporate sector, giving new meaning to acquisitions, takeovers and mergers as a form of business development. Koon Swan and Daim Zainuddin, another prominent businessman-turned-politician, both of whom had attended a short business management course at Harvard University in the mid-1970s, appeared to have been influenced by this merger and acquisition style of business growth.[12] In Malaysia, first from the late 1970s, and later, after a recession in the mid-1980s and the subsequent deregulation measures introduced by (then Finance Minister) Daim, a merger and acquisition mania appeared to drive the bull markets of these periods. This conglomerate-style acquisition drive characterized the pattern of growth of companies controlled by Daim and Koon Swan. This not only included companies owned in their personal capacity, but also the business groups controlled by UMNO and MCA which they led (see Gomez 1994). These two men appeared to have had enormous impacts on the local corporate scene. Their example of how the stock market could be used as a means to raise money to fund acquisition of companies seemed to have had a profound impact on the business style of many leading corporate figures, particularly those who emerged in the 1970s.[13]

The development of Supreme Corporation Bhd, Koon Swan's own publicly-listed investment holding company, is indicative of his business style. Koon Swan acquired his stake in Supreme Corp when he sold off his interests in Genting Bhd, where he had been employed between 1970 and 1977, when he was appointed by the MCA to lead KSM and MPHB. In 1974, while still employed by Genting, Koon Swan took over Supreme Corp. In 1976, Koon Swan also acquired a stake in Shin Min Daily News (M) Sdn Bhd, which published a leading Chinese newspaper, *Shin Min Daily News*. In 1980, Koon Swan acquired a controlling interest in Straits Echo Press Sdn Bhd, which published the English tabloid, *The Echo*. Another shareholder of Straits Echo Press was Utusan Melayu Press Bhd, publisher of the leading Malay newspaper, *Utusan Melayu*. The majority shareholder of Utusan Melayu Press was UMNO, while the company was led by one of the party's vice presidents, Ghafar Baba. Following Utusan Melayu Press' acquisition of Straits Echo Press equity, Ghafar was appointed chairman of the company. Koon Swan's attempt to become a media baron in Malaysia ran aground when both Straits Echo Press and Shin Min Daily News ran into serious financial problems in the early 1980s. Utusan Melayu Press' stake in Straits Echo Press was sold to Shin Min Daily News which, in turn, was acquired by the UMNO-controlled, publicly-listed newspaper publisher the New Straits Times Press Bhd, in 1985; Straits Echo Press eventually went into receivership (*Far Eastern Economic Review* 26 May 1983). Koon Swan's ownership of these two newspapers reflected his close association with some UMNO leaders. In fact, according to one source, the cash-rich New Straits Times Press was used to acquire Shin Min Daily News in an attempt bail-out Koon Swan – and Utusan Melayu Press – from the financial quagmire he found himself in (cited in Gomez 1990: 62). At that time, the New Straits Times Press was under the control of Daim Zainuddin through UMNO's holding company, Fleet Group.

Eventually, Koon Swan's attempt to develop his main publicly-listed company, Supreme Corp, was also not very successful. From 1978, Supreme Corp acquired an interest in property development companies (Soga Sdn Bhd, Grand Ocean Development Sdn Bhd, Bukit Ritan Realty Sdn Bhd), plantation companies (Johore Oil Palm Plantations Sdn Bhd and Mega Chemicals – first renamed Supreme Plantations Industries and then Everpeace Corporation), an insurance company (QBE Supreme Insurance Sdn Bhd), four companies in the Keng Soon Finance group (renamed Supreme Finance), the Textile Corporation of Malaysia Bhd (renamed Grand United Holdings), which was itself involved in a complex merger with Supreme Corp, and Singapore-based Sigma Metal. These companies, in turn, were involved in a number of cross dealings, including an acquisition into the Singapore-based Pan-Electric Industries (Pan-El). Supreme Corp acquired a huge interest in property, securing land tracts on most states in the west coast of the peninsula, and emerging as the second largest property group after MPHB's listed property company Bandar Raya Developments Bhd. In its conglomerate pattern of growth, many of Supreme Corp's deals – and that of the Malaysian and Singaporean publicly-listed companies in the group, Grand United Holdings, Everpeace Corp, Sigma Metal and Pan-El – involved reverse takeovers, mergers and share-swaps (see *Business Times* 27 November 1985). Inevitably, even before the Pan-El crisis erupted, Koon Swan had run into criticism that he was mixing his private business deals with those of MPHB. Following the Pan-El scandal, trading of Supreme Corp's shares was suspended on the KLSE in December 1985. Supreme Corp was eventually taken over by William Cheng's Lion Corp group and renamed Lion Land Bhd.

Like Supreme Corp, within a few years of its launching in May 1977, MPHB had developed into a huge business empire that embraced, *inter alia*, property developer Bandar Raya Developments Bhd, Malaysian French Bank Bhd (renamed Multi-Purpose Bank), the highly profitable gaming concern Magnum Corporation Bhd and the erstwhile plantation company Dunlop Estates Bhd (renamed Sarawak Enterprise Corporation in 1996). By 1981, even before securing listing on the KLSE, MPHB had more than 27,000 shareholders, almost 72 per cent of whom were Chinese, leading Koon Swan to claim that it was 'owned probably by the largest number of shareholders compared to other public-listed companies in Malaysia' (*Business Times* 19 June 1981). MPHB commenced operations in 1977 with a paid-up capital of just RM30 million; by 1984, the company's paid-up capital had increased twenty-five fold, to RM751.028 million (*KLSE Annual Companies Handbook* 21 (4), 1996: 487–8).

MPHB's phenomenal growth within a short span of time, primarily through an aggressive acquisition drive of some key companies in most sectors of the economy, appeared to convince the Chinese that the MCA had found the means to check the rapid gravitation of corporate power to the UMNO-dominated state (see Gale 1985; Yeoh 1989; Gomez 1994: 189–217). During the 1982 general election, when the MCA recorded one of its best performances ever in a general election, the party won 24 of the 28 parliamentary seats it contested, partly due to the impact that the MPHB had made on the Chinese. Thus, it also appeared that the MCA, through the corporatization movement, had managed to secure the support of more Chinese transcending class and clan divisions.[14]

MPHB's acquisition binge from 1977 involved a number of controversial deals. One corporate takeover involving MPHB revealed a lot about ethnic politics in Malaysia. In November 1981, MPHB acquired from Chang Ming Thien a 40 per cent stake in the United Malayan Banking Corporation Bhd (UMBC), an unlisted bank. UMBC, incorporated by Chang in 1960, had grown rapidly to emerge as the fourth largest bank – in terms of assets, deposits and loans – in the country in 1975, even ahead of the OCBC (Tan 1982: 159–92).[15] In 1976, UMBC ran into problems when it was disclosed that the bank had issued loans to companies owned by its directors, in particular Chang's listed hotel and property development concern, Faber Merlin (M) Bhd, without ensuring that proper lending procedures had been followed (see *Far Eastern Economic Review* 20 February 1976). These revelations led to a run on the bank. Subsequently, the government-owned trust agency, Pernas, acquired a 30 per cent stake in UMBC, later increasing its stake in the bank by a further 10 per cent through a rights issue. Although MPHB's acquisition of UMBC was approved by government authorities, including the Ministry of Finance, some UMNO members, fearful that Pernas would lose executive control over UMBC, argued that the MPHB-UMBC deal contravened the principles of the NEP. The controversy necessitated the intervention of Prime Minister Mahathir Mohamad, and was only resolved after it was agreed that Pernas and MPHB would be co-shareholders, each with a 41 per cent stake in UMBC. When MPHB later learnt that another government agency, Petronas, had acquired a nine per cent stake in UMBC, it decided, in 1984, to dispose of its interest in the bank in exchange for a majority 51 per cent stake in Malaysian French Bank Bhd, a much smaller financial institution, then under the control of Daim Zainuddin. (*Asian Wall Street Journal* 24 August 1984).[16] This was MPHB's second business deal involving Daim; in 1982, MPHB had also sold to Daim its stake in the property development concern, United Estate Projects Bhd (UEP, later renamed Sime UEP Properties Bhd).

A few months after the MPHB-UMBC controversy, another dispute emerged between some UMNO members and the MCA over MPHB's participation in a deal involving a company owned by another Malay leader, UMNO vice-president Ghafar Baba, who would be appointed deputy prime minister in 1986. At that time, Ghafar was involved with Koon Swan in their control of Straits Echo Press. In late 1981, MPHB tried to work with Ghafar's publicly-listed company, Pegi (M) Bhd, to take over the then British-controlled

Dunlop Estates Bhd and secure a stake in the latter's holding company, Dunlop Holdings Ltd. In the event, Ghafar had to back down from the deal when some UMNO members protested that Bumiputeras would not get controlling interests in the two companies. MPHB went on to secure a massive 88 per cent stake in Dunlop Estates (Gomez 1994: 204–5)

The MPHB-UMBC and MPHB-Dunlop Estates controversies revealed how even impartial Malay politicians, who were not too perturbed by MPHB's growth, found that they were forced to take a strong pro-Malay business position in the matter. Inevitably, this strengthened the ethnic politicization of the corporate sector, exacerbating the communal nature of business patterns. Ironically, the UMBC-MPHB and MPHB-Dunlop Estates deals showed that some of MPHB's major corporate transactions involved business cooperation between it (through Koon Swan) and two leading UMNO figures, Daim and Ghafar. Koon Swan had business deals with Daim involving MPHB's swap of UMBC for the Malaysian French Bank and the sale of UEP. Daim had used his control over the New Straits Times Press (through UMNO's Fleet Group) to acquire Koon Swan's stake in Shin Min Daily News. Although MPHB's attempt to work with Ghafar's Pegi fell through, Koon Swan had joint control over the Straits Echo Press with the former UMNO leader.

From 1983, however, following some poor investment ventures, particularly in a trading and shipping company in Hong Kong,[17] MPHB began to declare losses. In 1985, MPHB declared a phenomenal loss of RM191.9 million. The following year, the RM228.4 million loss declared by MPHB was even more substantial, still the largest ever loss recorded by a company in Malaysia! During 1985 and 1986, MPHB also had to write off almost RM420 million worth of investments (*New Straits Times* 6 May 1987).

MPHB's problems were exacerbated when, just months after securing the presidency of the MCA, Tan Koon Swan was arrested in Singapore in 1985 following the collapse of the Singaporean company, Pan-El. The Pan-El crisis was caused by a series of huge loans secured by the company to support some major business deals. Most of these deals involved cross-investments in companies controlled by Koon Swan who had an indirect stake in Pan-El. Although Pan-El owed foreign banks approximately US$225 million at the end of 1985, the company had also committed itself to buying another US$50 million in forward contracts. When creditors began calling in these loans in the middle of 1985, Pan-El defaulted, which led to the suspension of trading of the company's shares. Pan-El was eventually placed under receivership (Clad 1989: 132). It was later disclosed that Koon Swan had channeled RM23 million of MPHB funds into Pan-El in a desperate, but futile, attempt to rescue the Singaporean company. The money was lost when Pan-El was liquidated (*Asian Wall Street Journal* 16 February 1987).[18] Koon Swan stepped down as managing director of MPHB in February 1986, and subsequently, served prison sentences in both Singapore and Malaysia for fraud involving the funds of MPHB and Pan-El.

The MCA was further embarrassed when the deposit-taking co-operatives (DTCs) scandal broke out in August 1986. The scale of the DTC scandal was enormous, affecting the lives of about 588,000, mainly Chinese, Malaysians who had deposits amounting to nearly RM1.4 billion in 24 deposit-taking co-operatives, most of which had been established as part of the corporatization movement. Among the co-operatives implicated in the DTC was the MCA's KSM, the co-operative that had control over MPHB.[19]

In 1987, after the Pan-El and DTC scandals, and the jail sentences imposed on its president Koon Swan, the MCA promised never to mix politics with business. MPHB's entire board of directors, including chairman Lee San Choon, the former MCA president, resigned. The MCA convinced two prominent Chinese businessmen, Robert Kuok and Lee Loy Seng, to take up appointments as directors of MPHB to help revive the company.[20] At the end of 1987, MPHB declared a loss of RM27.66 million, a dramatic improvement from the previous year's figure of RM228.4 million. By mid-1988, when Kuok and Lee resigned from the board, MPHB had recorded a profit of RM17.07 million, and in the following year, a number of takeover bids were being made on the company (*New Straits Times* 22 August 1988).

The first MPHB takeover offer, a RM1.13 billion bid by Quek Leng Chan's Hong Leong group in April 1989, was stymied by the MCA, which declared the bid 'hostile' and not in the interests of the Chinese (*The Star* 17 April 1989). The reason for the MCA's antagonism towards this takeover was its belief that the ultimate beneficiary would be an UMNO-related company. This was because, along with the takeover bid, the Hong Leong group also announced that Hume Industries (M) Bhd, the publicly-quoted member of the group making the bid for MPHB, had obtained a RM500 million supplies contract from an UMNO-controlled company, United Engineers (M) Bhd (UEM). This fed speculation that there would eventually be a tie-up between UEM and Hume. In the event, UEM's majority shareholder, the Renong group, acquired a 23.8 per cent stake in Hume (Gomez 1994: 124–30). The Hong Leong takeover of MPHB fell through, but not before the MCA threatened to leave the Barisan Nasional if the deal was approved.

A month later, in May 1989, Kamunting Corporation Bhd, a minor publicly-listed company – MPHB had a market capitalization 15 times that of Kamunting – controlled by T.K. Lim and his family acquired a 29 per cent stake in MPHB. Interestingly, Lim's family had close business links with the family of Daim Zainuddin. Kamunting was a small, near moribund tin-mining company until August 1987 when 71 per cent of its equity was acquired by Seri Angkasa Sdn Bhd from government-controlled and publicly-listed Malaysia Mining Corporation Bhd (MMC). Prior to this, Seri Angkasa had been the controversial recipient of a privatized interchange on the outskirts of Kuala Lumpur. Apart from the Lim family, Seri Angkasa's other shareholder, with a 35 per cent stake, was Sri Alu Sdn Bhd, owned by Daim's brother, Abdul Wahab Zainuddin (Gomez 1994: 213). Soon after acquiring MPHB, Lim quickly involved the company in a number of cross-holdings (see Figure 3.2). The interlocking stock ownership that emerged between Kamunting and MPHB was a means for the Lim family to secure control over MPHB, thus virtually pre-empting the possibility of a hostile takeover (see Gomez 1994).

If the corporatization movement was primarily an attempt to bring about structural reforms in the operations of Chinese businesses, particularly the small- and medium-scale enterprises (SMEs), it was a failure. There is also little evidence that the owners of many SMEs provided much support to the movement, or that they had much trust in the MCA to protect their interests. Even after the MCA leadership had been taken over by San Choon, and then Koon Swan, both of whom had modest backgrounds, there is no evidence that this was enough to convince the owners of Chinese SMEs that they could rely on this new breed of leaders to protect and develop their economic interests.

Apart from MPHB, none of the companies established during the corporatization movement, including the investment holding companies incorporated by the ACCCIM and the clan-based organizations, emerged as major investment holding companies. Although the ACCCIM represented the interests of more than 20,000 SMEs and individuals, and managed to establish an investment holding

## Chinese Business, The NEP and Accommodation

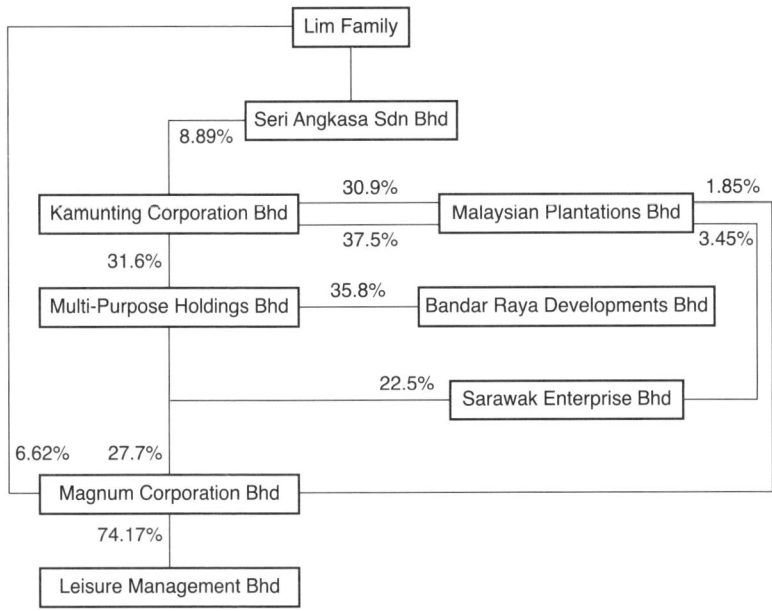

Figure 3.2 Interlocking Stockownership in the Multi-Purpose Holding Group, 1995–96

Sources: KLSE Annual Companies Handbook 21 Book 1 (pp. 183–7; 462–6), Book 3 (pp. 195–9; 311–17), Book 4 (pp. 437–41; 487–93); Malaysian Business 16 November 1996

company, Unico Holdings Bhd, its impact on the economy has been modest (Heng 1992: 1136–42).

The failure of the corporatization movement has been attributed to the inability of the companies in the movement to secure the support of Malay patrons (see, for example, Heng 1992). This widespread perception was probably fed by well-publicized media reports of rather acrimonious attacks made by some UMNO leaders on some of MPHB's major deals. Many aspiring UMNO politicians found it expedient to criticize MPHB to portray themselves as protectors of the Malay community and champions of the NEP. There is, however, much evidence that during MPHB's early development, some of its major corporate deals, particularly those involving UEP, UMBC and Dunlop Estates, entailed collaboration with some of Malaysia's leading Malay politicians, particularly Daim and Ghafar. Some of these deals had also been approved by official regulatory authorities. Moreover, the manner of growth of some of the companies that emerged with the corporatization movement indicated that state patronage was not always necessary. Koon Swan's vast control over the corporate sector through MPHB and Supreme Corp was developed without many concessions from the state. Rather, through his effective use of the stock market for mergers and acquisitions, Koon Swan developed huge corporate bases for both MPHB and Supreme Corp. Koon Swan thus managed to used the stock market to bypass the state as a means of expansion.

If MPHB's style of operation had followed that of the government's trust agency, in particular, PNB, i.e. to acquire and hold investments on behalf of the Chinese – this was, after all, one of the company's original plans – its impact on the economy might have turned out differently. Instead, many of the companies acquired by MPHB were involved in various corporate maneuvers, some of which had a detrimental impact on the group. Moreover, Koon Swan tended to mix his personal business interests with those of MPHB. The Pan-El scandal, for example, affected both MPHB and Supreme Corp, while abuses of power by MCA leaders over the cooperatives under their control contributed to the DTCs scandal. This suggests that apart from some poor investment decisions, corruption had an adverse impact on the corporatization movement. In this regard, the rapid initial rise of MPHB can be compared to the way banks like Maybank and UMBC had become major financial concerns within a short span of time before allegations of impropriety in the management of these banks led to their eventual takeover by the state.

The Chinese companies wanting to take over MPHB – Kamunting and the Hong Leong group – underlines the fact that the large Chinese companies had nothing to do with the corporatization movement. Rather, both Chinese enterprises had established business links with the Malay political elite. It appears that the demise of the corporatization movement was also due to minimal support provided by the large Chinese enterprises. Many Chinese businessmen who had supported the MCA prior to the 1970s were uncomfortable with the new party leadership, which had been taken over by men with more modest class backgrounds. Moreover, given the appreciable decline of the MCA's influence in the Barisan Nasional, it did not appear that it would be able to protect their economic interests in government. A number of the large Chinese enterprises had begun to accommodate the public enterprises during the 1970s to gain access to state patronage. There was also some fear among these Chinese capitalists of the impact that the MPHB would have on their own companies and business ventures. Many owners of large Chinese enterprises were also not willing to relinquish control of the companies they had created to form a huge Chinese conglomerate that could act as a counter force to an interventionist state.

Case studies of William Cheng, Khoo Kay Peng and Vincent Tan Chee Yioun, three businessmen who emerged during the two NEP decades, will reflect further differences in approaches taken by Chinese businessmen when developing their corporate base, the relevance or forms of intra-ethnic business ties and the importance of developing links with well-connected or influential Malays.

| William Cheng and Lion Corporation Bhd | **CASE STUDY** |
|---|---|

William Cheng Heng Jem, a Teochew, was born in Singapore in 1943. Through his main publicly-listed flagship, Lion Corporation Bhd, Cheng had control over six other publicly-listed companies, Amsteel Corporation Bhd, Angkasa Marketing Bhd, Amalgamated Containers Bhd, Chocolate Products Bhd, Lion Land Bhd and Posim Bhd. In 1992, the total market capitalization of his listed companies was estimated at RM5.2 billion (*Malaysian Business* 16 August 1993). Cheng's formal education is believed to be up to lower secondary level. By the age of 16, he was already involved in his family's iron foundry company, Teck Chiang Foundry Co, founded in Singapore in 1939 by his father, Cheng Chwee Huat. After his father's death, Cheng inherited the company's Malaysian operations, and his brother, Cheng Theng Kee, the Singapore-based business (*Malaysian Business* 16 August 1993). Cheng's big break came in the mid-1970s when he obtained a licence to set up Amalgamated Steel Mills Bhd (later renamed Amsteel Corporation).

The roots of Cheng's flagship, Lion Corp, can be traced back to his father's company, Teck Chiang Foundry Co. In an attempt at diversification in the 1950s, Tuck Heng Manufactory Ltd and Teck Chiang Manufactory Ltd were incorporated in Singapore to manufacture rubber compounds for tyre retreading and furniture products. In 1968, Lion Metal Manufacturing Sdn Bhd was incorporated to manufacture steel slotted angles, panels and shelves. The three companies merged in 1973 to form Lion (Teck Chiang) Sdn Bhd; the company name was changed to Lion Corp in 1981 and it was listed on the KLSE in 1982. Since then, the Lion group has diversified extensively, and currently has more than one hundred subsidiaries and associate companies involved in steel, motor, tyres, container, chocolate and confectionery products manufacturing, retailing, distribution and trading, construction and property development, finance, insurance and stockbroking, and agri-products and plantations; the Lion Corp group's primary business, however, is still the steel industry.

The share capital of Lion Corp, an investment holding company, is not very large, amounting to RM121.605 million in 1996, though this was substantially more than its capitalization of RM74 million in 1985. Lion Corp's improved performance in terms of turnover and pre-tax profits during the past decade has been significant. Although Lion Corp registered a turnover of just RM43.62 million and a pre-tax profit of RM12.93 million in 1985, these figures had increased appreciably by 1995, with the company recording an almost tenfold increase in turnover of RM374.38 million and a pre-tax profit of RM80.76 million (see Table 3.3). Nine of the ten largest shareholders of Lion Corp are nominee companies, which makes it difficult to determine the shareholding structure of the company. Cheng, however, is deemed to have a total indirect stake in Lion Corp of 59.17 per cent. Mirzan Mahathir, the eldest son of Prime Minister Mahathir and a director of Lion Corp, has an indirect 25.76 per cent stake in the company. Amsteel, a company controlled by Lion Corp, has an 18.24 per cent stake in the company, indicating an interlocking stock ownership pattern (Cheong 1992: 24–7: *Business Times* 26 April 1991; *KLSE Annual Companies Handbook* 21 (2), 1996: 153–7).

Lion Corp owns 26.10 per cent of Amsteel. Incorporated in October 1974 as Kinta Steel Sdn Bhd, Amsteel was taken over by Lion Corp in 1976. In 1978, one year after the government's Lembaga Tabung Angkatan Tentera (LTAT, or Armed Forces Provident Fund) acquired a 20 per cent stake in Amsteel, the company obtained a licence and pioneer status from the government to produce steel wire rods. Amsteel went on to produce its own steel billets. By the early 1980s, Amsteel was responsible for supplying almost 90 per cent of Malaysia's steel wire rod requirements. Amsteel's first rolling mill commenced operations in 1981; the company went public in 1982 (*KLSE Annual Companies Handbook* 21 (2), 1996: 106–7; *New Straits Times* 13 October 1981).

Amsteel's finance arm is Asia Commercial Finance Bhd, while its stockbroking activities are run through Klang Securities Sdn Bhd. In August 1985, Amsteel acquired a 49 per cent stake in Suzuki

Table 3.3 Lion Corp Bhd: Share Capital, Turnover and Profit Margins, 1985–95 (RM million)

|               | 1985  | 1987  | 1989   | 1991   | 1993   | 1995   |
| ------------- | ----- | ----- | ------ | ------ | ------ | ------ |
| Paid-Up Capital | 74.00 | 74.00 | 89.65  | 120.72 | 121.01 | 121.41 |
| Turnover      | 43.62 | 81.68 | 121.36 | 172.27 | 309.61 | 374.38 |
| Pre-Tax Profit | 12.93 | 13.56 | 12.85  | 36.14  | 37.87  | 80.76  |

Source: Business Times 26 April 1991; KLSE Annual Companies Handbook 21 (2), 1996: 157.

Assemblers (M) Sdn Bhd (SAM), which has had the franchise to assemble and sell Suzuki motorcycles in Malaysia; this launched Amsteel's entry into the motorcycle assembly industry. Another 11 per cent stake in SAM was held by Cheng's associate company, Saranan Maju Sdn Bhd, while the remaining 40 per cent equity was held by LTAT; by 1987, however, Amsteel had acquired 100 per cent control of SAM. In 1987, Amsteel also entered into a joint-venture with then government-owned Heavy Industries Corporation of Malaysia Bhd (HICOM) and Suzuki Motors Co. Ltd of Japan to manufacture Suzuki motorcycle engines locally through HICOM-Suzuki Manufacturing (M) Sdn Bhd. By 1991, SAM's share of the local market for motorcycles was approximately 28 per cent. In 1987, Amsteel also secured the franchise for the assembly and distribution of Suzuki motor vehicles and vans, held through Lion Suzuki. In 1991, SAM and Lion Suzuki were injected into Angkasa Marketing before the latter was floated on the KLSE. Angkasa Marketing is the marketing arm of Amsteel.

Angkasa Marketing, incorporated on 25 August 1978, became a wholly-owned subsidiary of Amsteel in January 1979 and was publicly-listed in 1982. Amsteel had a 61.58 per cent stake in Angkasa Marketing in 1996, while Cheng's direct and indirect stake in Angkasa Marketing was 63.20 per cent. LTAT had a 4.27 per cent stake in the company (*KLSE Annual Companies Handbook* 21 (2), 1996: 1–5). Amsteel's board of directors indicates that the only Bumiputera of prominence was its chairman, the former army chief, Zain Hashim, also chairman of Angkasa Marketing (Cheong 1992: 14–29).

Another publicly-listed company controlled by Amsteel is Lion Land Bhd, formerly known as Supreme Corporation Bhd, previously controlled by Tan Koon Swan. Supreme Corp was originally involved in tin mining before venturing into property development under

Tan's control. The company was enmeshed in the Pan-El scandal in the mid-1980s, which led to Supreme Corp's KLSE suspension in December 1985. Supreme Corp remained suspended until December 1991, when it implemented a shares-for-assets swap involving the acquisition of properties from Lion Development (Penang) Sdn Bhd, owned by Cheng. Following the takeover, the company was renamed Lion Land Bhd (*KLSE Annual Companies Handbook* 21 (2), 1996: 488–98). The company is now primarily involved in property development and computers. In 1993, in an attempt to venture into China, Lion Land acquired a 20 per cent stake in Lion Asia Investment Pte Ltd. In 1994, following a convoluted restructuring exercise which resulted in crossholdings of companies in the Lion group, Lion Land moved into the steel manufacturing industry when it acquired Amsteel's subsidiary, Steelcorp Sdn Bhd. Steelcorp was the holding company of Sabah Gas Industries Sdn Bhd, which makes hot-briquette iron in Labuan, Sabah, and owns a steel mill in Klang. Steelcorp's subsidiary, Amsteel Mills Sdn Bhd, in turn, purchased the steel business of Amsteel, while Amsteel acquired 58.8 per cent of Lion Land. This eventually contributed significantly towards making Lion Land a profitable concern. In the process, Amsteel managed to improve its gearing ratio while reducing the amount of taxes to be paid by its profitable steel business by 10 per cent. In 1995, Lion Land diversified into the timber and education sectors when it acquired an 80 per cent interest in Sabah Forest Industries Sdn Bhd and the total equity of Sepang Education Center Sdn Bhd. In December 1995, Amsteel Corp had a 47.39 per stake in Lion Land, while Angkasa Marketing's equity in the company amounted to 2.13 per cent. The chairman of Lion Land is former Deputy Prime Minister Musa Hitam (*KLSE Annual Companies Handbook* 21 (2), 1996: 488–90).

Chocolate Products, incorporated in March 1970, manufactures and distributes chocolate-related products and confectionery, the most popular of which is the 'Vochelle' brand of chocolates. In 1991, Chocolate Products took over biscuits manufacturer United Brands Industries Sdn Bhd, which manufactures chocolate wafers, sweets and other confectionery. Lion Corp first acquired an interest in Chocolate Products in 1990, but in 1995, the latter's control over Chocolate Products was consolidated through a shares-for-assets swap. Chocolate Products acquired the entire equity of a number of companies owned by Amsteel – Natvest Sdn Bhd, which owns the Subang Parade Shopping Complex near Kuala Lumpur, Megavest

Sdn Bhd, which owns two industrial parks in Malacca and Sabah, and Amashipbreakers Sdn Bhd, which owns a shopping complex in Malacca. These acquisitions moved Chocolate Products into property investment and management, and allowed Amsteel to liquidate assets for cash to reduce its borrowings and secure working capital while allowing the Lion Corp group to retain control of these important investments. Chocolate Products, which had been in the red, was expected to improve its profitability with the acquisition of these companies. Cheng has an indirect stake of 74.66 per cent in Chocolate Products (*KLSE Annual Companies Handbook* 21 (3), 1996: 10–15).

Natvest, incorporated on 27 May 1986, is principally involved in property management and restaurants. Natvest has a stake in five companies involved in beer brewing in China – Hubei Lion Brewery (60 per cent equity), Hubei Jinlongquan Brewery Co Ltd (60 per cent), Hunan Lion Brewery So Ltd (55 per cent), Ningbo Lion Brewery Co Ltd (55 per cent) and Zhuzhou Lian Brewery Co Ltd (55 per cent). Natvest's other investments in China have been through its interests in Beijing Parkson Light Industry Development Co Ltd, Beijing Vochelle Foodstuff Co Ltd and Dong Feng Lion Tyre Co Ltd. Among the directors of Natvest, apart from Cheng, are Cheng Yang Liang (a Singaporean), Zain Hashim and Yahya Talib.[21]

Another company controlled by the Lion Corp group, which is publicly-listed on the KLSE's Second Board, is Posim Bhd, a trading concern incorporated in March 1982. Posim is primarily involved in the distribution of an assortment of building and construction materials, including cement, steel bars and wall, floor and roof tiles. Its subsidiaries are involved in the import and distribution of industrial machines and equipment, manufacturing and distribution of motor accessories, and lubricants. Posim also has a 20 per cent stake in Kinabalu Motor Assembly Sdn Bhd which is involved in assembly of the Isuzu brand of motor vehicles. Cheng's indirect stake in Posim amounted to 46.44 per cent. In January 1996, Posim was used by the Lion Corp group to acquire an 80 per cent stake in Sabah Forest Industries Sdn Bhd (SFI), a company involved in timber extraction and paper manufacturing which had been privatized by the Sabah state government in July 1995.[22] This 80 per cent stake in SFI was held by Avenel Sdn Bhd, in which different companies in the group had a stake. In the process, Posim also undertook to settle debts amounting to a massive RM820 million incurred by SFI. Despite these debts, SFI has timber concession rights to 288,623ha of land for a 99 year period and, at the time of its acquisition, operated a paper mill which processed about 70 per cent of printing and writing paper requirements in Malaysia (*KLSE Annual Companies Handbook* 21 (2), 1996: 687–92).

Another key business of the Lion Corp group is its retail activity which commenced business in 1986 when Amsteel took control of the financially troubled Yuyi chain of stores through Natvest.[23] Amsteel further consolidated its interests in this sector when it acquired another financially troubled concern, the Emporium Holdings group, which owned the largest departmental and supermarket retailing chain in Malaysia. The Emporium Holdings group was founded by two brothers, Lim Tow Seng and Lim Tow Yong in 1961. Taking over a large network of retail networks, Amsteel revamped these outlets under the 'Parkson' name. By 1991, the Parkson group had an annual turnover of approximately RM500 million per annum. Other companies in the retail industry owned by Amsteel include the 'Hop-In' chain of 24-hour convenience stores and Ozly Shoe Sdn Bhd (acquired in 1988), which manufactures a broad range of leisure and rubber shoes.

Amsteel has a 73.10 per cent stake in Lion Asia Ltd, which is listed on the Hong Kong stock exchange and was acquired in September 1993 as a vehicle for the group's business ventures into China. Lion Asia has a 49 per cent interest in Changchun Motorbike Co Ltd and Changchun Motorbike and Engine Co Ltd, which are involved in the manufacture of motorcycles including engines and parts (*KLSE Annual Companies Handbook* 21 (2), 1996: 99–110). Angkasa Marketing also has activities in China, through the acquisition of two Singaporean companies, Lion Rubber Industries Ltd and Willet Investment Ltd, which have investments in tyre and motorcycle manufacturing operations in China. In 1995, it was estimated that the Lion Group had invested almost RM400 million in China. This, reportedly, made Cheng the second largest Malaysian investor in China after Robert Kuok (see *The Edge* 27 March 1995).

Cheng also has business ventures with Taiwanese companies. One publicly-listed company under the Lion Corp group, Amalgamated Containers Bhd, commenced business in 1988 as a joint-venture between Amsteel and the Taiwanese dry cargo container manufacturer, Chun Yuan Steel Industry Co Ltd; almost 90 per cent of its products are manufactured for export. When Amalgamated Containers went public in 1992, its original capital base of approximately RM5.7 million had increased almost ninefold to RM47.8 million, much of it through a shares-for-assets swap and a rights issue. The following year, in 1993, Amalgamated Containers' capitalization almost doubled to RM74.53 million in another shares-for-assets swap when Bright Steel Sdn Bhd,[24] a steel and iron products manufacturer and distributor, was injected into the company. Following the acquisition of Bright Steel, Amalgamated Containers' turnover and pre-tax profit improved appreciably, by 32.5 per cent and 23.7 per cent respectively. In February 1996, Amalgamated Containers used its wholly-owned subsidiary, Omali Corporation Sdn Bhd, to acquire approximately 53 per cent of Metal Containers Ltd, a company listed on the Singapore stock exchange and involved in the manufacture and sale of metal and plastic containers, computer printers and electronic products. Amsteel is the largest single shareholder of equity in Amalgamated Containers with a 13.82 per cent stake, while LTAT is the second largest with a 9.07 per cent; the Taiwanese interest in Amalgamated Containers, through Chun Yuan Steel Industry, is 8.66 per cent. Lion Corp has a direct three per cent stake in the company while Cheng's indirect ownership of Amalgamated Containers amounts to around 46 per cent (*KLSE Annual Companies Handbook* 21 (2), 1996: 76–9).

The Lion group has been described as being 'over-diversified,' with the suggestion that the group has lost its focus on its core business (see *Malaysian Business* 16 August 1993). The group has, however, concentrated on manufacturing, which contributes considerably to the group's turnover and profits (see Table 3.4). Its expansion overseas, particularly its takeover of companies in Singapore and its involvement in joint-ventures in China, has primarily involved businesses related to the metal or motor vehicle industries. In 1995, the Lion Corp group also established Lion Sankyu Tekko Sdn Bhd, a joint-venture with two major Japanese companies, Tokyo Boeiki Incorporated and Sankyu Incorporated, to manufacture steel frames.[25] Similarly, the group's ventures with Taiwanese companies have also involved manufacturing. There is some level of vertical integration in its manufacturing activities. For example, after securing the franchise to distribute Suzuki motor vehicles, Cheng moved into manufacturing component parts and established assembly plants locally. It is, however, obvious from this case study that Cheng's group of companies is involved in a myriad activities that indicate a conglomerate style of growth (see Figure 3.3).

In terms of stock ownership, Cheng has ensured some cross-holdings, probably to protect his interests. Given these crossshold-

*Table 3.4* Lion Corp Bhd: Sectoral Breakdown in Terms of Turnover and Pre-Tax Profits, 1995 (RM million)

| Sector | Turnover | Pre-Tax Profit |
|---|---|---|
| Construction & Engineering | 66.4 | 5.6 |
| Manufacturing | 124.9 | 8.0 |
| Motor | 139.5 | 9.0 |
| Telecommunications | 9.1 | (0.8) |
| Financial Services | 9.2 | 7.1 |
| Investment & Others | 25.3 | 0.2 |

Source: *KLSE Annual Companies Handbook* 21 (2), 1996: 158

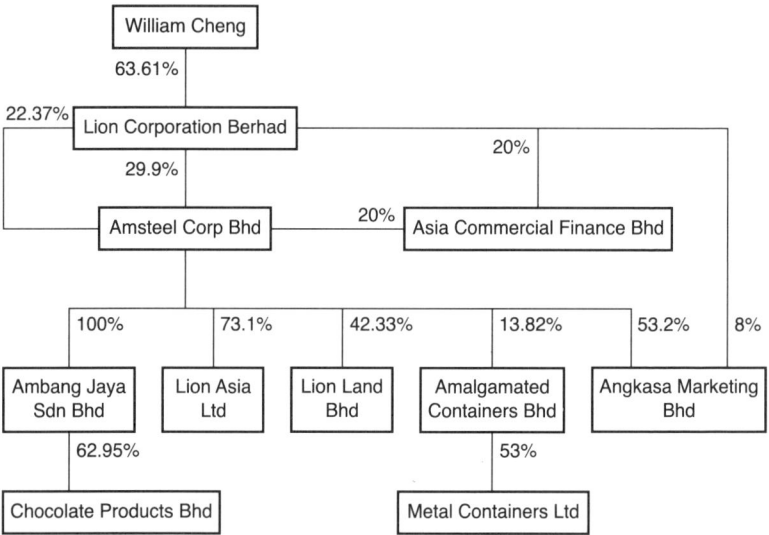

*Figure 3.3* Lion Corp Bhd: Simplified Corporate Structure, 1995–96
Source: *Malaysian Business* 16/8/93

ings, there have been efforts to cross-subsidize businesses among the companies in the Lion group. This has led to a high level of intra-group transactions, with lucrative business opportunities passed around to make their publicly-listed companies look more profitable.

Cheng is not closely associated with any particular UMNO leader and has obtained one major economic privilege from the government, a license and pioneer status to manufacture steel, which he secured in

1978 after he had restructured Amsteel to ensure Bumiputera equity participation, as required by the NEP. This license proved to be the stepping stone for the group's expansion. It should be pointed out that Mirzan Mahathir obtained his stake in Lion Corp from the government and not by linking up with Cheng. Thus, the nature of relations between the two men is obscure. Mirzan has recently emerged as a prominent corporate figure, particularly involved in logistics, but there have been no major business ties between the other companies controlled by the two men. However, Cheng has some influential Bumiputeras sitting as directors of some of his companies; Musa Hitam and Zain Hashim are two notable examples.

The equity in his main publicly-listed companies is tightly held, particularly of the cash cow in the Lion group, Amsteel (see Figure 3.3). There has been some deft maneuvering of assets among the publicly-listed companies in the Lion group to ensure control, reduce taxation and enhance the profitability of some of its concerns. The expansion of this group has involved a number of shares-for-assets swaps, facilitated by rights issues to increase capitalization and consolidate control; this was the case, for example, with Chocolate Products (involving Natvest), Angkasa Marketing (involving Suzuki Assemblers, Lion Suzuki Marketing and Lion Suzuki Motor) and Amalgamated Containers (involving Bright Steel).

Cheng is married to Hong Kong actress Chelsea Chan and has three young daughters (ibid.). Through his numerous holding companies, like William Cheng Sdn Bhd, Cheng has a direct 35.10 per cent stake in his main listed company, Lion Corp, which suggests that the group's equity is held personally by him. Cheng has, however, employed managers to run his diverse operations, and shown a preference for more professional management. Key decisions involving the group's activities are probably his sole prerogative.

---

Khoo Kay Peng and MUI Bhd **CASE STUDY**

Khoo Kay Peng, a Hokkien, was born in Batu Pahat, Johore in 1938. The son of a branch manager of the Singapore-based Oversea-Chinese Banking Corporation (OCBC), Khoo completed his secondary education at the age of 18 and started out as a clerk at

OCBC's headquarters in Singapore. He returned to Malaysia in 1960 to take up a managerial appointment at Malayan Banking Bhd, which had just been established by Khoo Teck Puat, whom Khoo Kay Peng had worked with at OCBC. Khoo left Malayan Banking in 1966 to become general manager of the newly-formed government-owned bank, Bank Bumiputra Bhd, then under the chairmanship of Razaleigh Hamzah, who went on to become Finance Minister from 1976 to 1984. Another prominent Chinese appointed by the government as director of Bank Bumiputra was Robert Kuok. Khoo was eventually appointed a director of Bank Bumiputra, but resigned in 1976, following his takeover of Malayan United Industries Bhd (MUI), a small, ailing, publicly-listed toothbrush, carton boxes and enamelware manufacturing concern.[26] Khoo was also appointed chairman of Magnum Corporation Bhd in 1977. In that year, the MCA-controlled co-operative, KSM, had acquired a stake in the gaming company. In 1980, Khoo was appointed a director of Malayan Banking, which had come under government control following a run on the bank (*New Straits Times* 21 November 1985; *Business Times* 24 March 1989). Khoo's appointment at Bank Bumiputra was reportedly due to Finance Minister Razaleigh's influence. Other prominent politicians with whom Khoo had close ties included former MCA president Tan Koon Swan. During his tenure at Bank Bumiputra, Khoo also seems to have cultivated a relationship with Robert Kuok, who has featured in a number of his subsequent business ventures.

Using MUI as his flagship, Khoo quickly involved the company in a myriad of takeovers, share-swaps, cross-holdings and an assortment of business activities. Among the two most important early acquisitions by MUI were Tong Bee Finance (M) Bhd and publicly-listed Central Sugars Bhd. MUI acquired Tong Bee Finance, a small finance company, in 1976, and renamed it MUI Finance. MUI acquired a controlling 56.6 per cent equity in Central Sugars in 1980 following a struggle with the Hong Leong group controlled by Quek Leng Chan.

Prior to this battle for control of Central Sugars by Quek and Khoo, *Malaysian Business* (16 March 1993) noted that 'the two had been "business twins" which no rival could contemplate separating. The Central Sugars saga apparently spoilt this relationship.' Central Sugars was then one of Malaysia's two sugar refiners. The other sugar refining company was owned by Robert Kuok, with whom Khoo had established intimate business ties. Central Sugars was acquired from

Multi-Purpose Holdings, then controlled by Khoo's close friend, Tan Koon Swan. MUI quickly increased its stake in Central Sugars to 77.4 per cent, part of which was paid for with new MUI shares (*The Star* 25 March 1980 and 14 July 1980). Central Sugars – first renamed Malayan United Manufacturing (MUM) and later MUI Properties – also owned a 40 per cent stake in another publicly-listed company, Pan Malaysia Cement Works (PMCW), which, in turn, had a 50 per cent interest in Associated Pan Malaysia Cement Sdn Bhd (APMC), one of the largest local producers of cement, and a 62 per cent stake in another listed concern, Pan Malaysia Rubber Industries Bhd (PMRI), a manufacturing and trading company (*The Star* 9 June 1980; *New Straits Times* 24 November 1980).

Despite MUI's interests in manufacturing, Khoo was keen to secure control of a bank. In July 1980, MUI acquired a 21 per cent stake in Southern Bank Bhd, then Malaysia's 11th largest bank in terms of assets. Southern Bank was then controlled by Penang-based Saw Choo Theng and his family. The Southern Bank equity was acquired from the MCA's private investment holding company, Huaren Holdings Sdn Bhd, and paid for through the issue of new MUI shares (*The Star* 14 Juyly 1980). Although MUI managed to increase its equity in Southern Bank to 32.69 per cent – this was reduced to 23 per cent following a special Bumiputera issue – making it the bank's largest shareholder, MUI failed to gain control of the bank. Other shareholders of the bank then included Loh Boon Siew and Lim Goh Tong (*Business Times* 14 July 1980).

In early 1982, MUI tried to put together a major banking merger involving its takeover of a small Sarawak-based bank, Kwong Lee Bank Bhd, and then merging its banking activities with the D&C Bank Bhd, then controlled by Alex Lee[27] and his family with Syed Kechik Syed Mohamed.[28] The merger fell through, but MUI still gained a controlling 50.32 per cent interest in the Kwong Lee Bank through a share-swap. Among other shareholders of the Kwong Lee Bank were the Lam family, who had founded the bank and the Singapore-based OCBC group. MUI eventually increased its stake in the Kwong Lee Bank to almost 82 per cent (*Business Times* 8 December 1982). After the Kwong Lee Bank takeover in December 1982, MUI divested its entire equity in Southern Bank to Killinghall Tin (M) Bhd for cash.[29] In the process, MUI made a capital gain of RM25.11 million for its brief investment in Southern Bank (*New Straits Times* 8 December 1982). Kwong Lee Bank was renamed the MUI Bank.

Between 1976 and 1980, MUI diversified rapidly. In financial services, MUI acquired a stake in a stockbroking firm and established an insurance company through a joint-venture with an American-based company, United Continental Insurance Bhd. In the property sector, MUI acquired an interest in companies located in Malaysia and abroad, particularly in Hong Kong. For example, through a shares-for-assets swap, MUI acquired the East Ocean Centre in Hong Kong from Li Ka Shing's Cheung Kong group. MUI also ventured into the hotel sector in the 1980s when, through a shares-for-assets swap, MUI acquired two hotel companies incorporated in Singapore, Hotel Malaysia Ltd and Ming Court Hotel Ltd, from Khoo's former associate in OCBC and Malayan Banking, Khoo Teck Puat; MUI built on this to establish the Ming Court chain of hotels (*Business Times* 23 February 1981 and 1 September 1981). By 1981, MUI was a well diversified conglomerate with interests in banking, finance and insurance (MUI Bank, MUI Finance and United Continental Insurance), hotels (Ming Court), trading (PMRI and Cement Marketing), properties and manufacturing (PMCW, APMC and PMRI). Since most of MUI's takeovers were facilitated by share-swaps as well as bonus and rights issues, the company's share capital grew a massive ten fold between 1976 and 1980, from a mere RM6.4 million to RM64.2 million (see Table 3.5).

Professional managers were brought in by Khoo to manage these newly acquired assets. MUI Finance, for example, was second from the bottom in the league of finance companies when it was acquired in 1976, but by 1983, it was among the top five in terms of assets; at the end of 1982, MUI Finance's assets had exceeded RM320 million. When taken over in 1976, MUI Finance had only two branches and was registering pre-tax profits of around RM220,000; by the end of 1982, it had 10 branches and its pre-tax profits had risen to about

*Table 3.5* MUI Bhd: Share Capital, Turnover and Profit Margins, 1978–95 (RM million)

|  | 1979 | 1980 | 1981 | 1982 | 1984 | 1986 | 1987 | 1988 | 1990 | 1995 |
|---|---|---|---|---|---|---|---|---|---|---|
| Paid-Up Capital | 6.41 | 64.23 | 296.48 | 341.18 | 341.28 | 341.28 | 341.28 | 341.28 | 648.44 | 1296.88 |
| Turnover | n.a | 271.98 | 383.91 | 305.12 | 300.85 | 429.24 | 312.76 | n.a | n.a | 907.47 |
| Pre-Tax Profit | 1.61 | 22.13 | 59.25 | 64.17 | 91.05 | 53.848 | 4.15 | 24.68 | 62.81 | 174.99 |

Sources: *KLSE Annual Companies Handbook* 21 (3), 1996: 133–39; *Malaysian Business* 16/2/84

RM8 million. After taking over MUI Bank, a new and sound management team led by professional bankers was employed; development planning and opening of branches were given priority (*Business Times* 4 April 1983). After acquiring the Ming Court in Singapore, MUI expanded its hotel business in Malaysia, taking over hotels in the tourist hotspots of Port Dickson and Penang, and building a major new hotel in the heart of the national capital; by 1983, the Ming Court group had become one of the biggest hotel chains in the country. The hotel chain quickly expanded overseas, with hotels in the United States, Canada, Australia and Hong Kong. With the booming construction industry of the early 1980s, demand for cement increased, boosting the development of MUI's cement manufacturing activities (*Business Times* 5 April 1983). Its sugar refining business, however, began to decline. In 1983, MUI sold off its sugar refining mill (*Malaysian Business* 16 February 1984). By 1985, with assets totaling RM4.2 billion, MUI had emerged as Malaysia's top company in terms of assets, even eclipsing the Malaysian multi-national company Sime Darby Bhd, which was a distant second with RM3.4 billion worth of assets. The third largest company was the MCA-controlled Multi-Purpose Holdings, with assets totaling RM2.3 billion (*Business Times* 24 March 1989). During the late 1970s and early 1980s, the MUI Group also registered a significant increase in profits (see Table 3.5).

MUI's meteoric rise in Malaysia's corporate sector was primarily effected through controversial equity swaps. Khoo's business was growing at the same time that the corporatization movement, led by the MCA, was taking off. MUI experienced a similar pattern of growth as Multi-Purpose Holdings. As in the case of Multi-Purpose Holdings, MUI's rapid growth was achieved through a highly aggressive spate of acquisitions and reverse takeovers, which inevitably led to a problem of high gearing ratio. Both Multi-Purpose Holdings and MUI became market favorites and caught the imagination of Malaysia's small investors, especially the Chinese, many of whom believed that the means to growth was through acquisitions (*Far Eastern Economic Review* 6 March 1991). By 1981, MUI's stock price had escalated so dramatically that its market capitalization topped the RM1 billion mark (*Malaysian Business* 16 February 1984). However, as one report noted, MUI's growth was largely built through shares-for-assets swaps, enabling Khoo to conserve his resources while issuing paper in return for real assets (see *Far Eastern Economic Review* 6 March 1981).

During this period of MUI's rapid growth, between the mid-1970s and early 1980s, Khoo also worked with a number of prominent Malay politicians, besides his close ties with Chinese politicians. MUI's chairman was Mohamed Noah Omar, the father-in-law of former Prime Ministers Abdul Razak Hussein and Hussein Onn. The chairman of MUI Bank in the early 1980s was Tunku Osman Tuanku Temenggong Ahmad, a member of the Johore royal house. In 1981, when MUI made a special share issue for Bumiputeras, the UMNO co-operative, Koperasi Usaha Bersatu Bhd (KUB) was among those to acquire an interest in the company (*Business Times* 7 May 1982). Another prominent director and shareholder of a MUI group subsidiary, MUI Continental Insurance Bhd, is Abu Talib Othman, the former Attorney-General, who is also director of a number of other Chinese-controlled companies.

MUI had tried to work with other politically influential Malay politicians-cum-businessmen, such as Syed Kechik during the proposed merger between MUI Bank and the D&C Bank. When the merger was on the drawing board, Syed Kechik was quoted as saying that this would lead to a 'meaningful partnership with Khoo Kay Peng so that it achieves the objectives of the government to make the NEP a success, and to reflect the true spirit of cooperation between Bumiputera and non-Bumiputera businessmen' (ibid.).[30] D&C Bank's other major shareholders were H.S. Lee and his son, Alex Lee. The main aspects of the deal involved a share-swap, with new MUI shares offered to the shareholders of D&C Bank and MUI Bank, and the merger of the two banks; following the deal, the Lee family and Syed Kechik would each obtain substantial interests in MUI (*Business Times* 7/5/82).[31] The deal eventually fell through when the Malaysian authorities changed the terms of the share-swap. MUI, however, went ahead with the takeover of the Kwong Lee Bank and, as mentioned, renamed it MUI Bank.

Such a pattern of growth was, however, not without its problems and adverse repercussions. This became evident in 1984 when MUI became enmeshed in one of Malaysia's worst business scandals, after a share-swap involving MUI's takeover of the MUI Bank. The scandal involved the Singapore-based Pan-El. It was alleged that the MUI shares issued in the share-swap for MUI Bank equity had been bought by Peter Tham, a stockbroker and chief executive of Pan-El, who had been introduced to MUI Bank vendors by Khoo. When the price of the MUI shares fell appreciably, Tham suffered huge losses. Tham went into forward transactions to try to bail himself out, but this resulted in further losses and the collapse of Pan-El with debts of around S$400 million. The collapse of the company led to the temporary closure of the Singapore and Kuala Lumpur stock exchanges. Tham was eventually sentenced to a eight-year jail term in Singapore in October 1986 (*Asiaweek* 9 June 1989). The scandal also implicated another of Khoo's close associates, Tan Koon Swan, who was also charged with abusing his influence over Multi-Purpose Holdings to channel RM23 million from Multi-Purpose Holdings into Pan-El, in which he had an indirect stake (Gomez 1994: 209). The prolonged investigation and persistent allegations of Khoo's involvement in this scandal negatively affected his business interests in Malaysia. These allegation were serious. The *Far Eastern Economic Review* (6 June 1989) quotes the Singaporean authorities as stating that Khoo 'had benefited from Peter Tham's illegal activities. This had caused losses to the Pan-El Group of Companies in the region of S$36 million.'

In 1987, Khoo began liquidating much of his equity in MUI to close associates, apparently to arrest the further decline of the MUI group due to his problems with Pan-El. During that year, Robert Kuok acquired around 14 per cent of Khoo's interest in MUI. By 1989, around 15 per cent of Khoo's interests in MUI had reportedly been taken over by Tan Chin Nam and his publicly-listed company, IGB Corporation Bhd (see *Asiaweek* 9 June 1989). Eventually, Khoo was left with only around 10 per cent of MUI's equity; he had originally owned around 30 per cent of the company's stock. However, MUI, in turn, was used to acquire a 5.4 per cent stake in IGB; whereas later, PMCW was disclosed as holding a 9.26 per cent stake in MUI, indicating an interesting interlocking ownership arrangement to enable Khoo to retain control over MUI (see *Asiaweek* 9 June 1989; *Far Eastern Economic Review* 6 June 1989; *Business Times* 19 May 1989; *New Straits Times* 11 July 1990). Kuok also played a visible role in trying to help out Koon Swan after he was charged for offences relating to the Pan-El scandal. Kuok was also brought in by the MCA to rescue Multi-Purpose Holdings. Although Khoo was never charged with any criminal offense involving Pan-El, he paid the liquidators of the company S$36 million in 1989. Khoo was believed to have liquidated much of his interests in MUI to friends to help raise the funds to pay Pan-El's liquidators (see *Far Eastern Economic Review* 6 June 1989).

Tainted by the Pan-El scandal, and badly affected by the economic recession in the mid-1980s, it was hardly surprising that MUI's phenomenal growth – through acquisitions – stalled following the market crash in 1987, with its stock price falling significantly. From the mid-1980s until the early 1990s, MUI appeared to be concentrating on consolidating its myriad business activities. During this period, in 1988, Khoo and Kuok were considering merging their business activities in Malaysia. This did not materialize, but for a short while – between 1989 and 1991 – MUI established cross-holdings with IGB Corp which, in turn, bought into Vincent Tan Chee Yioun's rapidly developing conglomerate, the Berjaya Group Bhd; reports of a merger of these three groups abounded (see, for example, *Asian Wall Street Journal* 6 November 1989; *Asiaweek* 19 January 1990). This attempted merger disintegrated into a messy dispute, culminating in a MUI takeover attempt by Berjaya Group, which was countered by an attempt by Khoo to buy control of the Berjaya Group (see the case study below on Vincent Tan).

Given Khoo's problems in Malaysia and Singapore, there was much speculation that MUI would concentrate on developing its investments overseas, in spite of the improved economic situation domestically.[32] In fact, during the late 1980s and early 1990s, MUI acquired a 31 per cent stake in Heritage USA, a large theme park and resort company, and attempted several takeovers of media companies in England and Hong Kong; most of these investments were in the hotel and property sectors in North America, Europe and the ASEAN region (see *Malaysian Business* 16 May 1991; *Business Times* 19 May 1989). In China, MUI (China) Ltd was incorporated primarily to venture into property development and hotels in Shenzen. In Vietnam, MUI is venturing into cement-related activities, particularly the production of ready-mixed concrete (*New Straits Times* 5 April 1993). This has been attributed to the fact that 'MUI had little opportunity to expand at home in recent years as it fended off several takeover attempts' (*Asian Wall Street Journal* 8 December 1993).

In November 1993, MUI sold MUI Bank and MUI Finance to the Hong Leong group for RM1.1 billion. Hong Leong renamed MUI Bank the Hong Leong Bank and listed it on the KLSE while MUI Finance was sold to Ahmad Sebi, who is supposedly linked to Finance Minister Anwar Ibrahim. Khoo was willing to sell MUI Bank and MUI Finance although these companies accounted for a great proportion of the MUI group's total profits. In 1986, MUI's banking and finance division accounted for 92.3 per cent of the group's profits. In 1992, the year before MUI Bank and MUI Finance were sold to the Hong Leong group, these two companies collectively contributed 82 per cent of the MUI group's total pre-tax profit (*Malaysian Business* 16 June 1993). However, as far back as 1991, there were reports that some influential politicians wanted to see control over MUI Bank change hands (see *Malaysian Business* 1 October 1991). It was also obvious that MUI Bank had problems securing approval to expand, particularly to open new branches. For example, between 1990 and 1993, MUI Bank was only given approval to open one additional branch, while other banks, such as Malayan Banking and the Chinese-owned Public Bank, were allowed to open between ten to twenty new branches annually during the same period (*Malaysian Business* 16 June 1993). With the banking sector heavily regulated, there was increasing pressure from the government that small banks merge to create larger, more viable financial concerns. MUI also had to contend with problems due to its links with Pan-El (*Malaysian Business* 16 May 1991).

By 1993, however, MUI appeared back on the acquisition trail. In that year, MUI swapped three Ming Court hotels for a 60.8 per cent stake in the enlarged share capital of publicly-listed Metrojaya Bhd, a department store chain and property holding company (*Malaysian Business* 16 June 1993). MUI also invested considerable funds in expanding its cement operations, acquiring a construction company, MUI Hikari Construction Sdn Bhd, and on property development (*Malaysian Business* 1 October 1994; *The Star* 20 November 1994). The MUI group also moved into education, buying an interest in Curtin University in Australia and a stake in MSC-Syme Business School, which runs a twinning program with Australia's Monash University, and establishing the MSC Premier College, which runs twinning programs with a number of overseas universities (*The Star* 2 August 1994; *The Edge* 13 March 1995) (see also Table 3.6).

The MUI group also underwent a major restructuring exercise in 1994 and 1995. MUI sold its property companies to Malayan United Manufacturing (MUM), renaming the company MUI Properties. In August 1995, MUI Properties divested to MUI its entire 35 per cent stake in PMCW. MUI eventually declared a 57.62 per cent stake in PMCW which, in turn, has a substantial interest in Pan Malaysian Industries (PMI, formerly PMRI) (*The Star* 2 August 1994). In 1994, PMCW sold its 14.22 per cent stake in MUI to PMI through a share-swap, giving it a 32.98 per cent stake in MUI. By October 1995, PMI had a 44.03 per cent stake in MUI (*KLSE Annual Companies Handbooks* 1 and 3, 1996: 109-26 and 133-9). Following this restructuring, PMI emerged as Khoo's main listed holding company, with MUI under the control of PMI. Through extensive interlocking stock ownership among these publicly-listed companies, Khoo locked control over these companies, forestalling the possibility of a hostile takeover.

Despite these acquisitions, new business developments and restructuring of companies in the MUI group in Malaysia, part of the RM1.1 billion obtained from the sale of MUI Bank and MUI Finance was used to acquire two Hong Kong companies – 53 per cent of Morning Star Holdings, a hotel and travel services company publicly-listed on the Hong Kong Stock Exchange (from the Indonesian-based and Chinese controlled Lippo Group) and a 30 per cent stake in Kerry Financial Services, controlled by Kuok (*Asian Wall Street Journal* 8 December 1993). In 1994, MUI bought into another Hong Kong-based company linked to Kuok, South China Morning Post (Holdings) Ltd (SCMP), a listed concern that publishes the English newspaper, the *South China Morning Post*. SCMP, reportedly the most profitable listed publishing group in Asia, also owned a substantial stake in Post Publishing Co Ltd, a Bangkok-based company which publishes the influential English language newspaper, the *Bangkok Post*. In April 1994, MUI first acquired a 15.1 per cent stake in SCMP from Rupert Murdoch's News Corp Ltd; in the following month, MUI acquired another five per cent stake in SCMP from Singapore Press Holdings Ltd, giving MUI a 20.58 per cent stake in the company. Robert Kuok owned another 34.9 per cent stake in SCMP, also acquired from Murdoch's News

*Table 3.6* MUI Bhd: Sectoral Breakdown in Terms of Turnover and Pre-Tax Profits, 1995 (RM million)

| Sector | Turnover | Pre-Tax Profit |
| --- | --- | --- |
| Financial, leasing & insurance | 55.5 | 12.7 |
| Hotel & catering | 31.6 | 2.7 |
| Properties | 26.0 | 12.3 |
| Education services | 13.9 | 3.7 |
| Manufacturing & trading | 615.8 | 110.4 |
| Media & communications | 104.5 | 65.9 |
| Travel & tours | 43.1 | 1.4 |
| Others | 17.1 | (34.0) |

Source: *KLSE Annual Companies Handbook* 21 (3), 1996: 139

Corp (*The Star* 19 May 1994). MUI also acquired a 39.4 per cent stake in Shangri-La Properties Inc, a Manila-based company in which the Kuok group has much equity (*Malaysian Business* 1 October 1994).

Khoo's interests in the MUI group are primarily held through his holding companies, KKP Enterprise Sdn Bhd, KKP Holdings Sdn Bhd and Soo Lay Holdings Sdn Bhd (see Figure 3.4). According to company records, KKP Holdings, an investment holding company, was incorporated on 2 September 1977 and is almost wholly owned

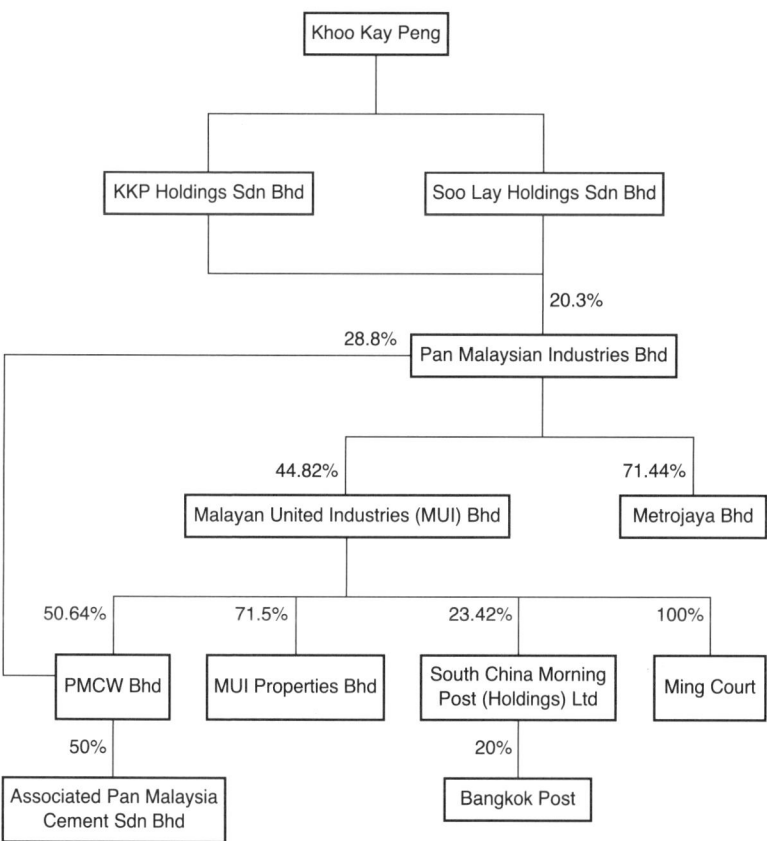

*Figure 3.4* MUI Bhd: Simplified Corporate Structure, 1995–96

Sources: *KLSE Annual Companies Handbook* 21 (1), 1996: 109–21; *KLSE Annual Companies Handbook* 21 (3), 1996: 133–7, 340–5

by Khoo. KKP Enterprise, an investment holding company, was incorporated on 26 January 1984 and has a paid-up capital of RM1 million, owned almost equally by Soo Lay Holdings and KKP Holdings. Soo Lay Holdings, also an investment holding company, was incorporated on 13 December 1976 and its shareholders in 1994 were Khoo (109,990,000) and Pauline Chai Siew Phin (10,000 shares). Chai is also a director of KKP Enterprise. Given the extensive crossholdings in the MUI Group, it is difficult to precisely quantify Khoo's total interests in his company. None of Khoo's children are directors sitting on the boards of the listed companies in the MUI group. The companies remain under a professional management team, although senior managers in the MUI group admit that Khoo remains primarily responsible for key decisions on company operations (see *The Edge* 13 March 1995).

---

Vincent Tan Chee Yioun and Berjaya Group Bhd         **CASE STUDY**

Vincent Tan was born in Batu Pahat, Johore in 1952, the fourth child – in a family of six brothers and a sister – of a small-scale transportation company owner. Tan wanted to pursue a law degree after completing his secondary education, but since his father's business had floundered, he went to work as a clerk at United Malayan Banking Corporation Bhd (UMBC). Tan also worked part time selling insurance for American International Assurance (AIA), and did so well that he became an agency manager at a relatively young age. He then also ventured into some small-scale trading business. Tan came to prominence in 1982 when, at the age of 30, he acquired the Malaysian franchise for the McDonald's fast-food chain. Tan managed to secure the franchise after managing to persuade McDonald's executives to bypass other more established concerns vying for the licence. Tan's franchise is held through Golden Arches Restaurants Sdn Bhd, in which McDonald's owns a 49 per cent stake and Tan 26 per cent; the remaining 25 per cent equity is held by Mohd Shah Kadir, the son of a former UMNO minister, Abdul Kadir Yusof, who also served as chairman of Golden Arches Restaurants. By the mid-1990s, McDonald's had around 60 outlets in Malaysia, and Tan is believed to ask for and gets a million ringgit from a franchise holder for the opening of each new outlet (*Malaysian*

*Business* 1 January 1992 and 16 December 1993; *Asian Wall Street Journal* 6 November 1989; *Asiaweek* 22 June 1994).

In 1983, a year after securing the McDonald's franchise, through a private investment holding company, Nautilus Corporation Sdn Bhd, Tan led a group which bought a 37.8 per cent stake in Berjaya Kawat Bhd, then a small, publicly-listed steel-wire manufacturer; the company's name was changed to Berjaya Corporation (*New Straits Times* 4 May 1984). In early 1984, Azman Hashim, of the Arab Malaysian group, joined Berjaya Corporation's board of directors when he bought out the interests of Tan's Bumiputera partners in Nautilus.[33] In the following year, however, Azman divested his interests in Berjaya Corporation. Mohd Shah Kadir, Tan's business partner in the McDonald's franchise, acquired an interest in Nautilus, probably to comply with the Bumiputera equity-ownership requirements of the NEP.

With Berjaya Corporation under Tan's control, the company was used to acquire companies in various businesses. In March 1985, Berjaya Corporation acquired a 48 per cent stake in Regnis (M) Sdn Bhd, the company incorporated to handle the Malaysian operations of the American-based Singer Sewing Machine Co. The deal was financed by a 5-for-1 rights issue, raising Berjaya Corporation's paid-up capital from RM14.3 million to RM85.6 million. Tan's franchises for two American-based products – the McDonald's fast-food chain and Singer-brand merchandise – would contribute much to developing his local corporate base.[34]

In 1986, Berjaya Corporation also acquired a leasing company (Prime Credit Leasing Sdn Bhd) and an insurance company (United Prime Insurance (M) Sdn Bhd) (*Euromoney* August 1988). In May 1986, Berjaya Corporation acquired a 22 per cent stake in another quoted company, Palmco Holdings Bhd, involved it in a crossholding exercise, but divested it a year later for a loss of almost RM2 million (*The Star* 13 July 1987). In 1987, Berjaya Corporation acquired a 28 per cent interest in South Pacific Textile Industries Bhd (SPTI), made a general offer for this textile company and eventually ended up holding 71 per cent of the company's equity; SPTI had operations in Fiji, Mauritius, Jamaica and Puerto Rico (*The Star* 18 October 1988). Tan has, however, not been successful in all his takeover bids during the early 1980s. Between 1984 and 1985, Tan's attempted takeover of two locally quoted companies, General Lumber Bhd (now Land & General) and Cold Storage Bhd, fell through (*Malaysian Business* 16 June 1990). Cold Storage was then under the control of newly-appointed Finance Minister Daim Zainuddin.[35]

Of these myriad acquisitions, Tan's most important purchase involved his private holding company, B&B Enterprise Sdn Bhd, being awarded the right to acquire 70 per cent of the government's gaming entity Sports Toto Bhd in 1985, ostensibly as part of the government's privatization policy. This lottery operator, incorporated by the government in 1969 to generate funds for the government's sports budget, was then fully owned by the government's holding company, the Ministry of Finance Inc., under the jurisdiction of then Finance Minister Daim. Since the sale of the Sports Toto was not open to bidding, its privatization came under severe criticism (see *Far Eastern Economic Review* 31 August 1989). Among the shareholders of B&B Enterprise were Tan's brother, Danny Tan Chee Sing, and Mohd Shah Kadir, Tan's partner in McDonald's and a co-shareholder of Nautilus.

Soon after acquiring the 70 per cent stake in Sport Toto, B&B Enterprise sold 10 per cent to Melewar Corporation Bhd, controlled by Tunku Abdullah, the younger brother of the ruler of the state of Negri Sembilan (and now of Malaysia) and a close associate of Prime Minister Mahathir. To help Tan acquire his shares in Sports Toto, a RM19 million loan was arranged by Arab-Malaysian Merchant Bank Bhd, controlled by Azman Hashim, who had briefly held an interest in Berjaya Corporation. The collateral for the loan was the Sports Toto shares, together with personal guarantees from Tan and his associates in B&B Enterprise. Another guarantor was Ahmad Sebi Ahmad Bakar, who would take up, and hold, for a short while, a minor stake in Berjaya Corp (*Investors' Digest* February 1989). Ahmad Sebi was then managing director of the private television network, TV3, then owned by UMNO through its holding company, Fleet Group Sdn Bhd, which was under the control of Daim Zainuddin (*The Star* 12 July 1987).[36] In 1989, Berjaya Corp acquired a 17 per cent stake in TV3, and then divested it to the Johore State Economic Development Corporation for a RM17 million profit (*Malaysian Business* 16 June 1990; *The Star* 28 May 1991). In the 1990s, Ahmad Sebi would appear again in a number of deals involving Vincent Tan's companies.

When the Sports Toto shares were publicly-listed in July 1987 at an offer price of RM2, its closing price on the first day of trading on the KLSE was RM9.55, almost five times its offer price! B&B Enterprise's stake in the company was reduced to 45 per cent, while Melewar owned 7.5 per cent, and the government retained 30 per cent equity (*The Star* 12 May 1988). A month later, in August 1987, Tan swapped his stake in Sports Toto for a substantial stake in

Berjaya Corp. The eight Berjaya Corp shares for one Sports Toto share-swap increased his stake in Berjaya Corp significantly. As expected, Sports Toto has become a major cash-cow in the Berjaya Group. In 1985, before its privatization, Sports Toto's sales from its betting operations totaled RM76 million; by 1993, total sales had increased 780 per cent, to RM670 million (*Asiamoney* June 1994).

In June 1988, about a year after Tan secured control of Sports Toto, he swapped his Berjaya Corp shares for a controlling stake in loss-making, publicly-listed Raleigh Bhd, which had been Daim's flagship company before his ministerial appointment to the Treasury. By September 1986, after Prime Minister Mahathir directed that all his cabinet ministers divest their corporate holdings, Daim was believed to have been looking for a buyer for his equity in Raleigh. Tan later acquired the Raleigh stake from Daim's associates, who were believed to be holding the company's equity in trust for the minister (*Asiaweek* 19 January 1990). One month before the share-swap, in another controversial deal, the government sold the remaining 30 per cent stake in Sports Toto to Raleigh in May 1988. To finance these acquisitions, Raleigh declared a then unprecedented 7-for-2 rights issue (*The Star* 20 september 1988). Raleigh was renamed Berjaya Group, Berjaya Corp was renamed Berjaya Industrial Bhd, and Sports Toto was renamed Berjaya Leisure Bhd.[37]

In 1993, Tan was again the beneficiary of a major privatized contract when Indah Water Konsortium Sdn Bhd, a consortium led by his Berjaya Group, was awarded the privatized RM6 billion sewerage contract which entailed the planning and construction of new systems, besides the refurbishing and upgrading of existing sewerage systems for a concession period of twenty-eight years (Cheong 1995: 236–9). Having no experience in sewerage, Berjaya Group was expected to rely heavily on its main partner in Indah Water, Northwest Water Ltd, the leading British water treatment company.

Protests against the award of the contract came from many quarters, including UMNO members, even though non-Bumiputeras still had very limited access then to privatization opportunities. As protests mounted in UMNO, in December 1994, Indah Water was bought over through a share-swap for the price of RM450 million, or RM15 per share, by Prime Utilities Bhd (formerly Berjaya South Island). The chairman of Prime Utilities is Ahmad Sebi Abu Bakar who has a 12.5 per cent stake in the company, while Berjaya Group has an indirect 18.46 per cent stake in Prime Utilities (*KLSE Annual Companies Handbook* 21 (1), 1996: 19–24). Ahmad Sebi appears to be one of Tan's closest business associates. In 1995, Ahmad Sebi would also acquire a 12.52 per cent stake in Intiplus Bhd, a publicly-listed investment holding company primarily involved in financial services that Tan had secured control of in 1994 (Cheong 1995: 83–90). Tan secured control of Intiplus by injecting into it four companies involved in financial services owned by Berjaya Group – Berjaya General Insurance Sdn Bhd, Berjaya Prudential Assurance Bhd, Inter-Pacific Capital Sdn Bhd and Prime Credit Leasing Sdn Bhd. As in the case of most other takeovers involving Tan, 367.368 million new Intiplus shares were issued to acquire these four companies from Berjaya Group. Tan holds an indirect 55 per cent stake in Intiplus, which was renamed Berjaya Capital Bhd in July 1996 (Cheong 1995: 83–90; *KLSE Annual Companies Handbook* 21 (2), 1996: 383–8). Tan (through Berjaya Group) and Ahmad Sebi (through Advance Synergy Bhd) have a joint interest in the merchant bank, Perdana Merchant Bankers Bhd. Ahmad Sebi is the chairman of publicly-listed Advance Synergy, in which he has a controlling 12.25 per cent (*KLSE Annual Companies Handbook* 21 (4), 1996: 119–21, 287–8).

The manner in which Tan has managed to secure control over Berjaya Group and his access to two major privatized projects – Sports Toto and the sewerage contract – during a period when Chinese businessmen have not been privy to much such patronage has raised questions about his relationship to influential politicians. Moreover, Vincent Tan was also given a license to establish an English newspaper, *The Sun*, and was allowed to hold a 20 per cent stake in Star Publications Bhd, which publishes another major leading English newspaper, *The Star*. Tan also owned 17 per cent of TV3, while the company was still the only private television network.

Malaysian media licences are tightly controlled by the state. Almost all leading electronic and print media companies are owned or controlled by businessmen closely associated with leaders of the Barisan Nasional (see Gomez 1990: 178). Licenses issued to media companies have to be renewed on a yearly basis, and can be retracted – or suspended – at will by the government. This helps ensure that owners of media companies are careful not to fall foul of the ruling elite. In 1995, Mutiara Telecommunications Sdn Bhd, a private company owned by Tan, was awarded a license to launch Malaysia's fourth mobile telecommunication service (*Malaysian Business* 1 June 1995).

## Chinese Business, The NEP and Accommodation

Since the 1980s, when Berjaya Group was emerging as one of the country's most active corporate raiders, acquiring and selling stakes in several major publicly-listed companies, Tan has been involved in a number of business deals involving other politically well-connected Bumiputeras, including Wan Azmi Wan Hamzah who controls the Land & General group, Sulaimen Manan, who controls Taiping Consolidated Bhd, and Tengku Adnan Tengku Mansor, a former UMNO supreme council member and the deputy chairman of Berjaya Singer. When Tan divested his 20 per cent interest in Star Publications, part of this equity was sold to Adnan, who owns also almost five per cent of Berjaya Group stock (*The Star* 9 September 1994). Adnan is also the deputy chairman of Dunham-Bush (M) Bhd (formerly Topgroup Holdings Bhd), which is listed on the KLSE's second board; Tan has an indirect 70.39 per cent stake in this manufacturer of air-conditioning and refrigeration products (*KLSE Annual Companies Handbook* 21 (4), 1996: 1039–46). Tan has also had business ties with companies owned by members of the Negri Sembilan royalty. When Tan acquired Sports Toto, he initially had to share part ownership of the company with Tunku Abdullah, the brother of the Negri Sembilan ruler. Berjaya Group has a 65 per cent stake in Singer Furniture (M) Sdn Bhd; the remaining 35 per cent equity in this furniture manufacturing company is owned by Antah Holdings, the business group owned by the children of the Negri Sembilan ruler (*Malaysian Business* 1 January 1990). As mentioned, Tan's closest business associate is probably Ahmad Sebi, with whom he has an interest in publicly-listed Prime Utilities and Berjaya Capital, and in the merchant bank, Perdana Merchant Bankers Bhd; both men also had an interest in Berjaya Industrial when Tan first acquired control of the company (Gomez and Jomo 1997: 152–9; *KLSE Annual Companies Handbook* 21 (4), 1996: 119–21, 287–8).

Besides Vincent Tan's close ties with the UMNO elite, members of the Negri Sembilan royal house and well-connected Malay businessmen, he was involved in a 1989 attempt to develop what one magazine termed a 'super conglomerate,' involving Khoo Kay Peng's MUI group and Tan Chin Nam of IGB Corporation Bhd (see *Malaysian Business* 1 October 1991). MUI and IGB had already established interlocking ties in 1987. Tan Chin Nam was believed to be the prime mover behind this endeavor to involve Berjaya Group in the interlocking links between IGB Corp and MUI. This move to establish a 'a three-way Malaysian Chinese alliance,' as *Asiaweek* (19 January 1990) described it, was also seen by one local analyst as 'a possible collective defence among the three, largely Chinese-dominated, conglomerates against hostile Malay takeover' (quoted in *Malaysian Business* 16 May 1991). Khoo was then out of favor with UMNO leaders for supporting former party vice-president Razaleigh, who had mounted a challenge for the UMNO presidency in 1987.

Tan Chin Nam had emerged during the late 1960s as a major figure in property development. Tan Chin Nam's main publicly-listed company, IGB Corp, was incorporated in November 1964 as Ipoh Garden Sdn Bhd, and was primarily involved in housing development in Ipoh, the capital of the state of Perak. During the mid-1970s, Tan Chin Nam expanded his operations to most other major cities on the west coast of the peninsula. By the 1980s, the IGB Corp group had developed a vertically integrated operation, having moved into construction, the manufacture and supply of building materials, and consultancy services for construction projects. Currently, Tan Chin Nam has control over three other publicly-listed companies: Tan & Tan Developments Bhd, incorporated in 1972, and which has pioneered condominium development; Ipmuda Bhd, established in 1975 to function as the trading arm of IGB Corp; and IJM Corporation Bhd (formerly known as IJM Engineering & Construction Sdn Bhd), incorporated in 1983 to function as the holding company of IGB Corp, but currently involved in construction, quarrying, plantation and education. The IGB Corp group also has extensive business interests abroad, including in the United States, Australia, Europe (United Kingdom and Italy), Latin America (Chile and Argentina), South Asia (Pakistan and Bangladesh), East Asia (Hong Kong and China) and Southeast Asia (Singapore and Vietnam) (*KLSE Annual Companies Handbook* 21 (3), 1996: 159–67; 21 (4): 413–18, 715–21, 814–21). Among these four publicly-listed companies, the most prominent Bumiputera associated with the company is the former Attorney-General, Abu Talib Othman, who is a director of IGB Corp and Tan & Tan Developments. This is indicative of Tan Chin Nam's limited links with the Malay political elite.

Thus, when the rather independent Tan Chin Nam (who had emerged during the 1960s), the politically out-of-favor Khoo Kay Peng (who had come to prominence in the 1970s), and the Daim-linked Vincent Tan (who only became a major corporate figure in the mid-1980s) began discussions to forge an alliance among the companies they controlled, it was most unexpected. There was, however, huge business potential in such an alliance for all three groups given IGB's influence in the property sector locally and abroad, MUI's reputation in financial services, and Berjaya Group's strength in consumer product manufacturing and gaming. The interlocking achieved by the three companies would have opened up possibilities for massive acquisition drives, though it was also suggested that the alliance was primarily to facilitate the business expansion of these three groups abroad (see *Asiaweek* 19 January 1990). Moreover, during the period leading up to the proposed alliance, Khoo and Vincent Tan were known to have been badly affected by the mid-1980s recession as many of their acquisitions were believed to have been leveraged buy-outs. Vincent Tan was reported to have amassed almost RM200 million in personal debt amidst a welter of transactions leading to the takeover and transformation of Berjaya Group into a conglomerate (see *Asian Wall Street Journal* 6 November 1989). Another report claimed that Tan Chin Nam's companies had bought shares of companies in the Berjaya Group to help ease Vincent Tan's debt burden (see *Asiaweek* 19 September 1990). Khoo was apparently in similarly dire straits. The MUI group's reputation had been badly tarnished by the Pan-El scandal, and Khoo had also been affected by the stock market crash in late 1987. Between 1987 and 1988, Khoo had begun liquidating much of his equity in MUI to close associates. As mentioned, around five per cent of his interests in MUI was taken over by Tan Chin Nam, while Robert Kuok acquired another 14 per cent of Khoo's interest in MUI. Kuok's company's had also acquired almost 30 per cent of Pan Malaysia Rubber Industries Bhd (later renamed Pan Malaysian Industries), an associate listed company in the MUI group. Khoo had vacated the chairmanship of Pan Malaysian Industries in favor of Teo Joo Kim, a director of Kuok Singapore Ltd. Khoo had also reportedly asked Kuok to sit on the board of MUI. In fact, for some time in 1988, there was much market speculation that Khoo and Kuok were considering merging the business activities of their MUI and Perlis Plantations groups to 'form a giant enterprise' (see *New Straits Times* 1 February 1988). However, the Perlis Plantations-MUI merger did not materialize.

Despite this, when the MUI-Berjaya Group-IGB Corp alliance was proposed the following year, it is probable that Kuok was still a majority shareholder of MUI. Kuok's ties with Tan Chin Nam and Khoo are long-standing and well known. Kuok had been involved with Tan Chin Nam in several property deals in the 1970s and the two men have reportedly maintained close ties since (see *Far Eastern Economic Review* 7 February 1991; see also *Asiaweek* 9 June 1989).[38]

Kuok's business ties with Vincent Tan were, however, rather obscure. According to *Business Week* (11 November 1991), Vincent Tan and Kuok are 'friends' and both men had been collectively involved in business ventures, especially in property development projects abroad. More importantly, Kuok, like Vincent Tan, had also been associated with Daim Zainuddin in a few major business deals (see Chapter 2). Kuok also openly called for Chinese to work together. Kuok himself has the strongest reputation among Malaysian Chinese businessmen in terms of working with other Chinese of the diaspora (see Chapters 1 and 2).

There is much evidence that Tan Chin Nam was the most active of the three in trying to push through the proposed tripartite alliance. When the alliance was proposed, an IGB Corp executive was quoted as stating: 'Malaysian companies are by and large still too small. You need to pool resources to go abroad' (*Asiaweek* 19 January 1990). When the MUI-Berjaya Group-IGB Corp alliance was first consolidated through a convoluted, interlocking crossholding structure in 1989, only the IGB Corp had a stake in both MUI and the Berjaya Group. IGB Corp and Tan Chin Nam (through other companies) had already been buying into MUI since 1987, to help Khoo. By 1989, around 15 per cent of Khoo's interests in MUI was under Tan Chin Nam's control. Meanwhile, Khoo had acquired almost 13 per cent of IGB Corp's equity (see *Asiaweek* 9 June 1989; *Business Times* 24 March 1989; *Malaysian Business* 16 May 1991). Between 1987 and 1989, the other major shareholders of MUI, besides Khoo were Kuok and the gaming concern, Magnum Corporation Bhd, of the Multi-Purpose Holdings group with a 5.32 per cent stake (*Business Times* 24 March 1989).[39] In fact, when Kuok acquired almost 14 per cent of MUI's equity from Khoo in 1987, the latter's stake in MUI had been reduced from around 30 per cent to 10 per cent (*Business Times* 19 May 1989). By 1991, Kuok was still believed to hold at least eight per cent of MUI equity (see *Malaysian Business* 16 September 1991). IGB Corp also acquired a 20 per cent stake in Berjaya Group and an 8.5 per cent stake in Berjaya Industrial (*Malaysian Business* 16 May 1991). The combined assets of the three groups would have amounted to a massive RM8 billion and their activities would have meant that the new group would have had interests in almost every sector of the economy.

This proposed alliance did not go far, however, although there was one major deal involving Tan Chin Nam and Vincent Tan. In 1989, Vincent Tan took on the Hong Kong-based Semi-Tech Microelectronics (Far East) Ltd, owned by casino magnate Stanley Ho and James Ting, for control of the US-based Singer Sewing Machine Company Inc. (SSMC), a publicly-listed investment holding company which owns the franchise for Singer-brand sewing machines and other consumer goods. SSMC had established manufacturing operations in Asia, Latin America and Europe and a well-developed world-wide distribution network. If Semi-Tech Microelectronics secured control of SSMC, Berjaya Group's control of the Singer franchise in Malaysia, held through Regnis (M) Bhd, was under threat. Tan Chin Nam's IGB Corp helped Vincent Tan in his bid to take over SSMC (see *Business Times* 29 December 1989; *Asiaweek* 19 January 1990). Ho and Ting eventually managed to retain control of SSMC only after reaching a compromise with Tan. Berjaya Group obtained SSMC's equity in Singer Furniture (M) Bhd and a 49 per cent stake in Regnis; royalty payments to Singer were cut from three per cent to 1.75 per cent, while Regnis' right to sell Singer consumer brands in Malaysia was guaranteed. Tan later secured a RM5 million profit after divesting some of his equity in Regnis, and acquired a 20 per cent stake in Semi-Tech Microelectronics (see *Far Eastern Economic Review* 31 August 1989; *Asian Wall Street Journal* 6 November 1989; *Malaysian Business* 1 January 1990).

Apart from this attempted takeover of SSMC involving Vincent Tan and Tan Chin Nam, there were no other major business deals involving these three companies. Instead, at the end of 1990, problems developed among them, and a messy confrontation ensued, first between Khoo and Tan Chin Nam, and then, between Khoo and Vincent Tan. In fact, market speculation later emerged that Tan Chin Nam would back a takeover attempt of MUI by Vincent Tan (see *Malaysian Business* 16 May 1991). Disagreements had stemmed from a number of issues, including involvement in a major property development project in Australia initiated by the IGB Corp, and MUI's apparent 'conservatism.' While IGB Corp and Berjaya Group were relatively highly geared, MUI, which had little debt and huge cash reserves, was still the most cautious of the trio when considering business ventures (see *Asian Wall Street Journal* 4 July 1990; *Malaysian Business* 16 May 1991 and 1 October 1991).

After the proposed alliance fell apart, IGB Corp had sold its entire stake in Berjaya Industrial, and trimmed its stake in the Berjaya Group to less than five per cent by late 1990. IGB Corp also gradually began down-sizing its stake in MUI. When IGB Corp, unsuccessfully, tried to force Khoo to buy back the almost 13 per cent of MUI equity that it owned, the relationship between Tan Chin Nam and Khoo soured. Meanwhile, Vincent Tan attempted a takeover of MUI, at one stage in late 1991, acquiring almost 31 per cent of MUI's equity, just short of the 33.3 per cent figure, which would have necessitated making a general offer for the rest of the MUI shares. Vincent Tan's interests in MUI were held through Berjaya Industrial (10.8 per cent) and Berjaya Leisure (20 per cent) (*Business Times* 29 October 1991).

One indication of the seriousness of this takeover attempt was that though Vincent Tan would gain control of a bank, he would have to relinquish his stake in his cash cow, the gaming operation, Sports Toto. Vincent Tan's ownership of Sports Toto had been crucial to the development of his corporate holdings. Indeed, all the businessmen who have secured gaming licences have managed to develop huge corporate empires within relatively short periods of time, including Lim Goh Tong (Genting Bhd) and T. Ananda Krishnan (Tanjong plc).[40] Since the MUI group owned a bank, once Berjaya Group acquired the MUI equity, it would have been required, under Malaysia's banking regulations, to divest its interests in its gaming operation (*Business Times* 29 October 1991).[41] Apart from this, a loan of around RM400 million had been taken by companies in the Berjaya Group to buy the MUI equity, substantially increasing the group's gearing ratio and burdening it with huge interest payments (*Malaysian Business* 16 December 1993).[42]

Khoo retaliated by rebuilding his interests in MUI. By 1991, he reportedly had 32.4 per cent ownership of MUI. Khoo also used MUI's listed manufacturing arm, Malayan United Manufacturing (MUM, now MUI Properties), in which MUI had a 69 per cent stake, to mount a takeover of Berjaya Group, at one stage even making a general offer for the Berjaya Group (*Far Eastern Economic Review* 19 September 1991; *Malaysian Business* 16 December 1991). Other companies in the MUI group were used to acquire a stake in MUI to develop a crossholding pattern that would consolidate Khoo's control over MUI. Two of these companies, Pan Malaysia Cement Works Bhd and Pan Malaysian Industries Bhd, collectively held about 15 per cent of MUI stock (*Asian Wall Street Journal* 22 June 1991). It was suggested that Khoo also sold some of his interests in MUI to 'friendly parties' to raise funds to buy more MUI shares in the open market (see *Malaysian Business* 16/9/91). The battle between Vincent Tan and Khoo reached an impasse when Tan announced that he had 51 per cent control of Berjaya Group. To fend off Khoo's takeover bid, Tan had built up his stake in Berjaya Group from 32.8 per cent to 51.03 per cent by buying out his co-directors' interests in the company; Tan then also made a general offer for Berjaya Group (*Malaysian Business* 1 October 1991; 16 June 1993). The stand-off remained unresolved until the middle of 1993. In May 1993, almost two years after the feud had started, Vincent Tan divested his interests in MUI, but not before making sure that his investment in MUI had yielded a gain of RM30 million (*Malaysian Business* 16 June 1993).

Kuok does not figure in the controversy that emerged between Vincent Tan, Tan Chin Nam and Khoo. During the public battle between Vincent Tan and Khoo, the latter's allies would inform the press that Khoo had the support of Kuok who was believed to still own at least eight per cent of MUI equity (see *Malaysian Business* 16/9/91). Kuok would later develop his ties with Khoo in Hong Kong, where both men would jointly own a stake in the media publishing company, South China Morning Post Holdings (see Chapter 2 and the case study of MUI). Khoo would also acquire a 30 per cent stake in Kerry Financial Services Ltd, a company controlled by Kuok's family based in Hong Kong (*Asian Wall Street Journal* 8 December 1993).

Vincent Tan was reportedly working with an UMNO politician, Ishak Ismail – closely associated with Deputy Prime Minister Anwar – who had acquired a 3.5 per cent stake in MUI (*Asian Wall Street Journal* 22 July 1991). Ishak had apparently teamed up with Vincent Tan to help facilitate the MUI takeover (see *Far Eastern Economic Review* 15 August 1991 and 19 September 1991). Ishak's 3.5 per cent stake in MUI, held through an obscure private company, Sanorex Sdn Bhd, was acquired from Tan Chin Nam's IGB Corp (*Asian Wall Street Journal* 22 July 1991). Sanorex later sold its 3.5 per cent stake in MUI to Vincent Tan (*Malaysian Business* 16 June 1993). *Far Eastern Economic Review* (19 September 1991) reported that Vincent Tan's attempted takeover of MUI 'allegedly had the support of the ruling party officials [and] was rumored to be a payback for Khoo's backing of opposition leader Tengku Razaleigh Hamzah in last October's general election.'[43] There may be some truth in these reports as Malaysia's Banking and Financial Institutions Act (BAFIA) stipulates that Bank Negara Malaysia, the central bank, has to approve any bid by individuals to acquire more than five per cent equity of a financial institution; permission has to be granted by the Finance Minister to acquire more than 20 per cent interest in a financial institution. Since MUI wholly owned a bank, MUI Bank, and a finance company, MUI Finance, this suggests that Tan had secured permission from the Finance Minister to build up his stake in MUI (*Malaysian Business* 16 September 1991).[44] The development of Vincent Tan's major business ventures points to a number of significant facts. First, in his style of business, the use of rights issues and reverse takeovers figures prominently, reflecting a form of business that had become popular among some of the country's leading capitalists from the late 1970s. Second, Tan's successful development of the Berjaya Group within just a decade was primarily due to his ability to co-operate with influential Malay businessmen. Third, Tan's failed attempts at working with Chinese businessmen have not helped to promote intra-ethnic business co-operation. Due to these reasons, Vincent Tan's image as an independent businessman has been persistently questioned by market analysts, and his manner of developing his corporate base has been subject to much criticism.

Berjaya Group is expanding its gaming operations abroad. The company has interests in gaming in South America, and has established a base in the United States by acquiring a 40 per cent stake in the publicly-quoted International Totalizator System (*New Straits Times* 7 December 1993; *Asiaweek* 8 September 1994). Through Hong Kong-based Berjaya Universal Casino, a company involved in the development and management of casino projects, Berjaya Group has opened casino resorts in Mauritius, Seychelles and Argentina. Berjaya Group also announced its intention to invest US$100 million in China, primarily in the gaming sector, by establishing computerized lottery outlets in six cities and moving into horse-track betting. Other ventures in China include involvement in leisure projects, including developing golf courses and amusement parks (see *New Straits Times* 7/12/93; *Far Eastern Economic Review* 1 April 1993; *Euromoney* June 1994).

From the mid-1980s, through Berjaya Textiles, Tan was also actively involved in the textile industry, developing a huge presence in Malaysia – through acquisition of other textile companies – and abroad. Tan has, however, been divesting his interests in this sector, arguing that '(t)extiles is tough,' and attributing this to rising labor costs in Malaysia (quoted in *Asiaweek* 22 June 1994). In December 1993, Berjaya Textiles was sold to Tiong Hiew King, the owner of one of Sarawak's leading timber companies, Rimbunan Hijau Sdn Bhd. Berjaya Textiles was renamed Jaya Tiasa Holdings Bhd – it is listed among the top 40 Chinese-controlled companies in Table 1.2 –

and is now involved in plywood and veener manufacturing. Tan, however, used Berjaya Industrial to acquire Berjaya Textiles' subsidiaries before divesting the shell company to Tiong (*Malaysian Business* 16 December 1993; Cheong 1995: 91–5). This meant that Tan had helped Tiong's company secure immediate public-listed status. Tan, interestingly, has moved into the timber industry, investing US$60 million in a timber project in the Solomons (see *Asiaweek* 22 June 1994).

Although Tan has extensive business ventures abroad, there is little evidence that he has established close ties with other Chinese. There are reports that he had been involved in some ventures with Robert Kuok, but unlike Khoo Kay Peng, who jointly controls companies with Kuok, Tan does not appear to have developed similar business ties. Rather, Tan has been involved in well-publicized feuds with other Chinese. Apart from the MUI controversy, Tan also had a long public feud with T.K. Lim of the Kamunting-Multi-Purpose Holdings group. Both Berjaya Group and Kamunting had stakes in Magnum Corp, and Lim and Tan clashed over the sale of Magnum Corp's interest in a property development concern, Sri Damansara Sdn Bhd, to Land & General Bhd, owned by Wan Azmi. Tan built up his stake in Magnum to 32.5 per cent, just short of the 33.3 per cent mark, which would have required a mandatory general offer for the rest of the Magnum equity. Tan divested his entire Magnum equity to Dunlop Estates (now Sarawak Enterprises), then majority owned by Multi-Purpose Holdings; in the process, Tan made a capital gain of RM43.8 million (Gomez 1994: 219–20).[45]

The main business tie-up that Tan appears to have forged with ethnic Chinese outside Malaysia was with Hong Kong-based Stanley Ho and James Ting, even though Tan had been involved in a takeover battle with both men over the US-based SSMC. Berjaya Group has a 20 per cent stake in Semi-Tech Microelectronics, in which Ho and Ting have control. In 1989, Berjaya Group and a subsidiary of SSMC formed a joint-venture to set up a plant in Malaysia to manufacture Singer sewing machines (*New Straits Times* 11 August 1989). Although Tan made a profit from his brief investment in Magnum and SSMC, when asked in an interview in 1993, 'What has been your greatest regret?,' he would respond: 'Not getting Magnum was probably the second biggest. My biggest regret was losing the Singer world-wide empire to James Ting of Semi-Tech Global Ltd, Hong Kong. Do you know, if we had been successful, we would be in 120 countries?' (quoted in *Malaysian Business* 16 December 1993)

Vincent Tan also appears to still have a good relationship with Tan Chin Nam. In September 1993, Jasa Megah Industries (JMI) Bhd, a publicly-listed controlled by Tan Chin Nam was sold to Thong Kok Cheong and Thong Kok Kee, both reportedly close associates of Vincent Tan; Kok Kee is a director of Berjaya Group. In December 1994, JMI acquired a leisure company owned by Vincent Tan, Tropicana Golf and Country Resort Bhd; the company was acquired for RM208.79 million, paid for with the issue of 52.196 million new JMI shares (Cheong 1995: 176–9).[46] The chairman and chief executive officer of JMI is Tan's brother, Danny Tan Chee Sing, who is also the largest single shareholder of the company with an 18.83 per cent stake (*KLSE Annual Companies Handbook* 21 (4), 1996: 735–9).[47]

In 1993, Tan was estimated to own assets worth RM1 billion (see *Malaysian Business* 16 December 1993). The Berjaya Group of companies is estimated to comprise around 200 firms involved in a diverse range of businesses (see Table 3.7). In Malaysia, the group has approximately 16,500 employees. All the top ten shareholders of Berjaya Group are nominee companies, thus making it difficult to quantify Vincent Tan's total interest in the company. Tan is officially listed as having a 34 per cent stake in the Berjaya Group, of which 18.5 per cent is a direct stake and 15.5 per cent indirect. Tan's brother, Danny Tan Chee Sing holds another 2.4 per cent in the company (*KLSE Annual Companies Handbook* 21 (2), 1996: 282–8). Vincent Tan's total equity ownership in the Berjaya Group is

*Table 3.7* Berjaya Group Bhd: Sectoral Breakdown in Terms of Turnover and Pre-Tax Profits, 1995 (RM million)

| Sector | Turnover | Pre-Tax Profit |
| --- | --- | --- |
| Marketing of Consumer Durables | 1127.2 | 63.8 |
| Manufacturing | 224.9 | 2.5 |
| Leisure: Gaming | 1021.2 | 149.8 |
| Others | 217.1 | (32.2) |
| Financial services: | | |
| General insurance | 138.8 | 27.9 |
| Life insurance | 174.4 | 19.0 |
| Securities dealing & trading | 203.0 | 122.6 |
| Hire purchase, lease & loan financing | 11.2 | 4.3 |
| Property investment & development | 177.0 | 44.2 |
| Investment & others | 0.5 | (130.1) |

*Source:* KLSE Annual Companies Handbook 21 (2), 1996: 291

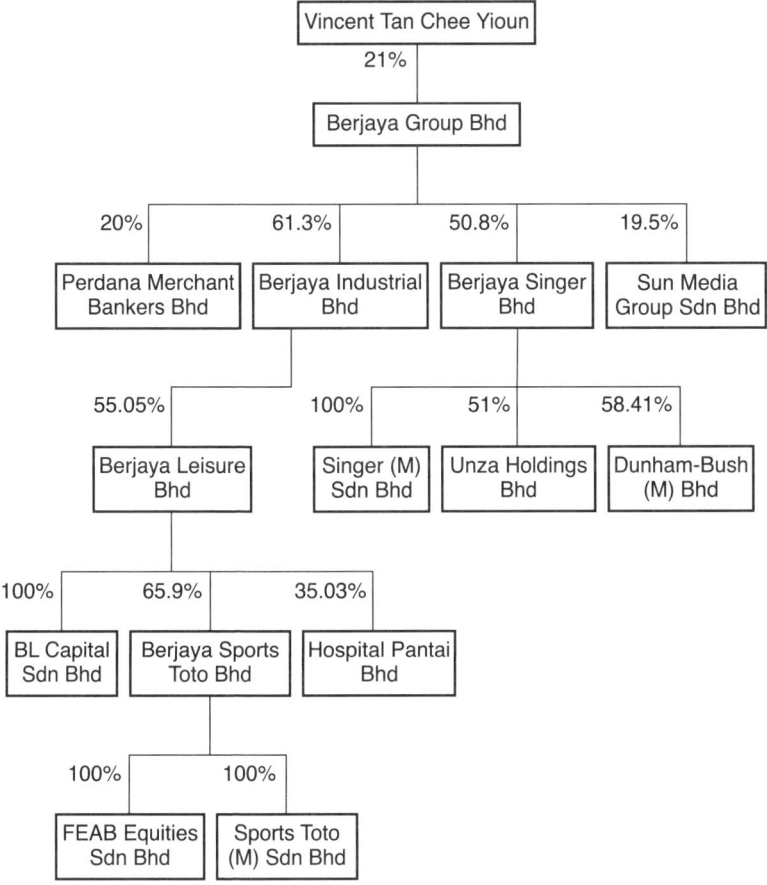

*Figure 3.5* Berjaya Group Bhd: Simplified Corporate Structure, 1995–96
Sources: *KLSE Annual Companies Handbook* 21 (1–4): 1

probably much higher. During the height of his battle with Khoo Kay Peng, Tan built up his interest in the Berjaya Group to 51 per cent (see *Malaysian Business* 1 October 1991). Though Tan may have since divested some of this stock to friendly parties, the huge number of nominee companies used to hold Berjaya Group shares has made it difficult to determine the actual extent of corporate equity ownership by particular individuals in Malaysia.

## Conclusion

Although Cheng, Khoo and Tan were all from middle class backgrounds, they were only educated up to secondary level. While Khoo's father was a bank employee, Tan's and Cheng's families had backgrounds in business; however, only Cheng inherited part of his family's business, which facilitated the early development of his corporate base. Tan and Khoo started out as bank employees before venturing into business. Khoo, in particular, spent a long period in the employ of a number of key banks, including OCBC, Maybank and Bank Bumiputra, before taking over and developing the MUI group, particularly its finance companies MUI Bank and MUI Finance. Tan moved into a series of small-scale business activities before securing the McDonald's franchise.

Although Cheng secured a licence to develop his business in steel, there is little evidence that he was closely associated with well-connected businessmen or politicians. Khoo and Tan's business groups, on the other hand, seem to be quite politicized in the sense that these two men have close ties with politicians. Khoo was linked with the soon-to-be Finance Minister, Razaleigh Hamzah, then chairman of Bank Bumiputra, where Khoo had been employed in a managerial capacity and was later appointed a director. Khoo would also be appointed a director of government-owned Malayan Banking. MUI's shareholders in the early 1980s included the UMNO co-operative, KUB. Khoo was also closely associated with the MCA, in particular with its former president, Tan Koon Swan. MUI acquired two companies from MCA companies – Central Sugars (from Multi-Purpose Holdings) and Southern Bank (from the party's private investment holding company, Huaren Holdings). Khoo was also a director of Magnum, controlled by Multi-Purpose Holdings. During Razaleigh's spell with the opposition, Khoo is believed to have had problems with the UMNO leadership. It has taken Khoo some time to re-cultivate ties with the UMNO elite, but this has meant relinquishing MUI group's most profitable enterprise, the MUI Bank. The study on Khoo reveals that while there are potentially lucrative returns to be secured for Chinese businessmen working with well-connected Malays, these businessmen are also susceptible to problems if their patrons in power were to fall from grace.

In all Vincent Tan's early business ventures, he was associated with men with links to UMNO. In the McDonald's franchise, for instance, Tan was involved with a former UMNO minister and his son, Mohd

Shah Kadir. In Berjaya Kawat (now Berjaya Industrial), Tan was associated with Azman Hashim (once an UMNO trustee) and the politically well-connected Ahmad Sebi. Tan's original partner in Sports Toto was Tunku Abdullah, a former UMNO MP. Raleigh (now Berjaya Group), Tan's holding company, was Daim's main publicly-listed company before his ministerial appointment. Tan has also secured two major privatized projects and various licences from the government. He, however, does not seem to have any links with the MCA.

In terms of business style, while businessmen like Kuok, Lim and Loh built up companies from scratch, Cheng, Khoo and Tan have built up large, well-diversified groups through a myriad of shares-for-assets swaps, takeovers and reverse takeovers. Crossholdings were implemented in all three groups, probably to protect their corporate base. These crossholdings have led to a high level of intra-group transactions, with profitable business opportunities passed around to make their publicly-listed companies more profitable. This has also enabled them to cross-subsidize business among the companies in these three groups. Tan, however, has shown the greatest proclivity for building up equity in a particular company, holding on to it for a protracted period before divesting it for a huge profit; during this process, there is little involvement by the Berjaya Group in the management of these companies. The best examples include the Berjaya Group's acquisitions in MUI, TV3, Magnum, Star Publications and the US-based SSMC. In contrast, Khoo and Cheng have been involved in the management and restructuring of most of the companies acquired by the MUI and Lion groups (with the possible exception, of course, of MUI's acquisition of IGB Corp and Berjaya Group).

In all three groups, conglomerate styles of growth were practised, with all three men venturing into practically any business field promising profitable returns. Only Cheng, however, has developed a reputation in a particular field – the steel industry. In fact, only the Lion Corp group has shown evidence of developing vertically integrated manufacturing capacity in its primary business, steel manufacturing, and in the auto assembly industry (manufacture of component parts and assembly of motor vehicles). Though the MUI group's main activity was in banking and finance, Khoo eventually had to relinquish his interests in this sector. Since then, the MUI group does not appear to have a primary focus, though its involvement in property development is growing. There have also been significant horizontal takeovers in the hotel sector, which has expanded the MUI group's interests in this sector, both in Malaysia and abroad. MUI's current ventures abroad are in publishing, property development and hotels, while properties, hotels, retailing and manufacturing are its primary activities in the Malaysian corporate sector. Despite MUI's long involvement in the cement industry, this does not appear to be the primary focus of the group, though there were plans to expand its operations in line with increasing demand. The Berjaya Group is so diversified that it does not appear to have a core business.

Yet, in 1997, in *Asiaweek*'s (21 November 1997) compilation of Asia's top one thousand companies in terms of sales, among Malaysia's Chinese-controlled companies that made the list, the Berjaya Group achieved the highest ranking, recording total sales of US$2526.6 million. This figure was well above the other ethnic Chinese companies that made the list: Robert Kuok's Perlis Plantations (US$2333.5 million) and Federal Flour Mills (US$1473.5 million), Cheng's Amsteel Corporation Bhd (US$2295.7 million). Other Chinese companies just outside the top one thousand companies were the late Loh Boon Siew's Oriental Holdings Bhd (US$1250.4 million), T.K. Lim's Magnum Corp (US$1110.4 million) and Lim Goh Tong's Genting Bhd (US$1031.7 million) (ibid.). However, if the sales figures of Perlis Plantations and Federal Flour Mills are combined, Kuok would achieve a much higher ranking. If profit as a percentage of sales is taken as the criterion for determining performance, Tan's ranking among all these Chinese companies would fall to last place! Genting would take top place with 22 per cent, followed by Oriental Holdings (12.5 per cent), Magnum Corp (10.2 per cent), Federal Flour Mills (3.1 per cent), Perlis Plantations (3 per cent), Amsteel Corp (2.2 per cent) and Berjaya Group (1.3 per cent) (ibid.).

Berjaya Group's high sales figure is not primarily attributable to the nature of its gaming operations; the contributions of consumer durables and manufacturing activities have also been significant (see Table 3.7), with Tan's control of the Singer franchise significant here. The Berjaya Group also has an interest in companies involved in the manufacture of a number of other products: Dunham-Bush (M) Bhd has an integrated air-conditioning and refrigerating manufacturing operation, with interests in Singapore, Hong Kong and China. The group still produces and exports bicycles, one of the original activities of Berjaya Group, and manufactures electronic and telecommunication products (*Asiamoney* June 1994). This suggests that the Berjaya Group has a productive manufacturing base which has contributed to the group's total revenue (see Table 3.7). In this regard, the sales volume registered by Amsteel Corp is a good indication of the productive capacity achieved by the company's steel and motor assembly business.

It is, however, noteworthy that the contribution of gaming to Berjaya Group's total revenue is lower than that of marketing consumer durables (see Table 3.7). Of the companies listed by *Asiaweek* (21 November 1991), two of the top three with the highest profits as a percentage of sales – Genting and Magnum – are in gaming. In fact, by 1994, although Sports Toto had been privatized for almost ten years, and the volume of its lottery sales had increased appreciably, the company had captured only 20 per cent of this market. Magnum had 44 per cent of the market, while the Pan Malaysian Pools lottery, run by T. Ananda Krishnan's publicly-listed Tanjong plc, had 29 per cent, even though it had only been set up in 1989. Yet, Sports Toto has 721 sales outlets, while Magnum has 500 and Tanjong just over 300 (*Asiaweek* 22 June 1994; see also Gomez and Jomo 1997: 159–65).

Given the extensive crossholdings in these three groups, and since a large number of nominee companies figure in the list of their largest shareholders, it is difficult to exactly quantify the total equity owned by Cheng, Khoo and Tan. Although all three groups are conglomerates comprising a large number of predominantly small and medium-sized companies (in terms of capitalization), and Cheng, Khoo and Tan all depend on professional managers to oversee their diverse business interests, authority over key policy decisions is in the hands of a single individual in all three groups. Cheng and Khoo use a number of family holding companies to control their interests, while Tan appears to have developed a more intricate holding pattern through companies in the group which are ultimately controlled by Berjaya Group.

Intra-ethnic business linkages do not appear to have been important for Cheng and Tan. In spite of numerous ventures in China, there is no evidence that the Lion group has worked closely with other Chinese companies in Malaysia or in other countries in the region. Tan has some deals with Tan Chin Nam, but most of his business deals involving other Chinese businessmen, particularly Khoo and T.K. Lim, have ended acrimoniously. Khoo jointly owns a number of companies abroad with Robert Kuok. However, apart from Khoo's ties with Kuok, there is no evidence that he has established significant business ownership linkages or long-term joint-ventures with other prominent ethnic Chinese businessmen. Although he has had business deals with Li Ka Shing and the Indonesian-based Lippo Group, these deals have merely involved the acquisition of companies, rather than establishing joint interests in a company.

# Chinese Business, Liberalization and Ascendance

## Liberalization, Authoritarianism and Patronage

In the mid-1980s, the Malaysian economy was so badly affected by a global recession, exacerbated by fiscal and debt crises, that it could not sustain the impressive average growth it had achieved since independence. The economy was plagued by severe declines in commodity prices – oil prices plunged in the early and mid-1980s, the tin market collapsed in 1985 and the prices of rubber, cocoa and palm oil fell. A massive ringgit depreciation, a significant increase in public debt, and inability to stem the decline in private investment also contributed to an appreciable decline in economic growth. In 1985, for the first time since independence, the economy contracted, registering a minus one per cent growth rate.

Declining private investment by Chinese businessmen, upset over the extent of state intervention, exacerbated the economic recession. Chinese businessmen found that with increasing Malay hegemony in the Barisan Nasional, they could not depend on the MCA to protect their interests by influencing policy decisions. By the end of the 1970s, not only were MCA leaders no longer appointed as ministers to the influential Finance and Trade & Industry ministries, barely a quarter of almost two dozen cabinet ministers were non-Bumiputeras.[1] Furthermore, the failure of the corporatization movement suggested that the promotion of Chinese capitalism was problematic and did not have the capacity to draw a wide range of Chinese businesses, especially the older and more established Chinese companies, to mount an effective joint corporate strategy that would sustain their economic interests.

The recession in the mid-1980s led to a turning point in government policy. Influenced by neoliberal Thatcherism and

Reaganomics, Prime Minister Mahathir actively sought to deregulate the economy, promote privatization, augment support for the private sector and increase investment incentives, even going so far as to relax some requirements of the NEP. To encourage foreign and domestic investments, the Promotion of Investments Act (PIA) was enacted in 1986 to provide pioneer status for periods between 5 and 10 years to investments in export-oriented manufacturing. Fiscal incentives offered by the PIA included tax relief on capital expenditure and exemption from import and excise duties and sales tax. To promote domestic private investment, the government relaxed its stringent Bumiputera investment and employee requirements for licensing manufacturing enterprises. After 1986, foreign investors were allowed to own all equity in local corporations provided they exported at least 80 per cent of their manufactured products. Privatization aimed at eradicating inefficiency, weak management and poor financial discipline in the public sector, while 'Malaysia Incorporated' sought to get the public sector to collaborate more effectively with the private sector. These new private sector-oriented initiatives meant severe curtailment of the growth of public enterprises in the economy, with the private sector promoted as the new engine of growth.

The government's liberalization efforts – in addition to a resurgence of export-oriented manufacturing industries, largely under the auspices of foreign, especially East Asian, capital – helped to reinvigorate the economy. The role and contribution of direct foreign investment (DFI) to gross domestic capital formation increased appreciably from 1986. Between 1985 and 1990, DFI increased almost fourfold, from US$695 million to US$2,333 million, before soaring further to US$5,183 million in 1992 (see Table 4.1; Ghazali 1994: 42–3). Among Southeast Asian countries, Malaysia attracted the largest amount of DFI (see Table 4.1). With growth rates of over eight per cent since 1988, virtually full

Table 4.1 DFI Flows to Southeast Asian Countries, 1985–1994 (US$ million)

| Country | 1985 | 1990 | 1991 | 1992 | 1993 | 1994 |
| --- | --- | --- | --- | --- | --- | --- |
| Indonesia | 310 | 1093 | 1482 | 1777 | 2004 | 2109 |
| Philippines | 12 | 530 | 544 | 228 | 763 | 1000 |
| Thailand | 163 | 2444 | 2014 | 2116 | 1726 | 640 |
| Malaysia | 695 | 2333 | 3998 | 5183 | 5006 | 4348 |

Source: World Bank 1996: 28

employment had been achieved, social mobility increased and business opportunities expanded by the mid-1990s.

Changes within the national and regional economy also began to effect policy changes. As labor shortages began to push up wages, the government began to promote more capital-intensive and higher technology ventures in contrast to its previous emphasis on labor-intensive low technology manufacturing. Since the Malaysian economy was beginning to lose its competitiveness in such labor-intensive manufacturing activities, and as a more educated labor force began to emerge, new policies were drawn up to broaden and deepen Malaysia's technological base. Companies were encouraged to acquire and develop such new technology, and to venture abroad to tap the economic potential offered by newly-emerging economies, i.e. in the Indochina region, South Asia, parts of Latin America and Africa and in China.

These liberalization policies, particularly privatization, entailed minimizing the role played by the state in the economy, and were generally well received by the Chinese. Government patronage has, however, still persisted through privatization, although inter-ethnic business co-operation – between Chinese capable of implementing contracts and Malays with access to state patronage – has increased (see Gomez 1997b). In manufacturing, even medium-sized companies began to gain access to state concessions. For example, in the Chinese-dominated state of Penang, Eng Technology Bhd and Loh Kim Teow (LKT) Bhd secured licensed manufacturing warehouse (LMW) status, which provided them with tariff exemptions. In 1995, Prime Minister Mahathir suggested that Malays should learn to speak Chinese in view of its commercial value (*New Straits Times* 15 April 1995). The government seemed to believe that its long neglect of the small- and medium-scale enterprises (SMEs) had been to the detriment of the economy.

In addition to this, non-Bumiputeras have been generally receptive to the cultural liberalization measures instituted by the Prime Minister in the 1990s, especially his promotion of the English language and education, even in tertiary institutions. There has also been a greater tolerance for various forms of non-Malay cultural expression. These moves, however, appear to stem from political expediency. For example, the decision by Mahathir to lift a long-standing ban on the lion dance – he even went on to open a lion dance festival – and liberalize travel restrictions to China came just before the 1990 general election. Again, in late 1994, when a general election appeared imminent, Deputy Prime Minister Anwar Ibrahim made a well-publicized visit to China, where he praised the values and importance of Chinese philosophy. These moves towards economic and cultural liberalization have not been accompanied by significantly greater political and civil liberties for the Chinese. However, Malaysian Chinese seem to have been more concerned with maintaining their economic, educational and cultural rights compared to their political rights (Lee 1980).

The objectives of the post-NEP policies introduced from 1991, such as 'Vision 2020' and the National Development Policy (NDP), which include the attainment of 'an "economically just" society with inter-ethnic economic parity,' have been welcomed by non-Bumiputeras.[2] Furthermore, the explicit commitments of these policies appear ethnically unbiased: the need for Malaysia to achieve 'fully developed country' status by the year 2020, primarily by accelerating industrialization, growth and modernization, and to forge a 'Malaysian nation' which transcends existing ethnic identities and loyalties. Although the process through which the objectives of Vision 2020 can be achieved are vague, the rhetoric behind this grand plan, and the government's economic and cultural liberalization initiatives have attracted the support of non-Bumiputeras who appear content with a Malay leadership whom they believe to be more accommodative of their (non-Malay) interests since it is now more secure, both politically and economically. The emphasis of the government's post-1990 policies on the market – rather than the public sector – to promote growth, the greater official encouragement of SMEs, and the support provided to large local corporations to invest overseas, where the government's influence is even less, have been perceived by the Chinese as a sign of good faith by the government in its commitment to reducing intervention.

The apparent development of inter-ethnic business co-operation and the government's economic and cultural liberalization initiatives have enabled UMNO leaders to benefit in terms of electoral support from the non-Bumiputeras, particularly the urban middle-class Chinese who have seldom supported the Barisan Nasional (see Gomez 1996a). The extent of the swing in Chinese support to the Barisan Nasional can be seen from a comparison of the votes secured by the ruling coalition in Chinese-majority constituencies during the 1990 and 1995 general elections. The Chinese constituted more than 35 per cent of the electorate in 58 of the total 192 parliamentary constituencies in the 1995 general election. In almost 60 per cent of these 58 constituencies, a double-digit percentage point increase in support for the Barisan

## Chinese Business, Liberalization and Ascendance

Nasional was recorded. In 29 of these 58 constituencies, an increase in support of nearly, or more than, 15 percentage points was recorded; in two of these 29 constituencies – in Johore and in Perak – increases were 25 percentage points and 27 percentage points respectively. In seven of eight constituencies in Penang, in ten of eleven in Perak, in four of five in Kuala Lumpur, and in all four in Selangor, where the predominantly Chinese-based opposition party, the DAP, had previously enjoyed huge backing, the Barisan Nasional recorded almost double-digit percentage point increase in support. In the urban areas of Malacca, Negri Sembilan, Kedah and Pahang, Chinese support for the Barisan Nasional increased considerably. Only in one of these 58 constituencies did the Barisan Nasional's support diminish.[3]

Prime Minister Mahathir's overwhelming influence in these liberalization initiatives, particularly the 'Vision 2020' statement and the NDP, cannot be understated. Mahathir, who is convinced he knows what is best for the country, has been known to push policies even in the face of resistance from within his own cabinet. The best example of this was when Mahathir launched his (import-substituting) heavy industrialization policy despite widespread criticism from almost all quarters (see Jomo 1989; Machado 1992). This policy was implemented through incorporation of a government-owned company, Heavy Industries Corporation of Malaysia Bhd (HICOM), which collaborated with foreign, mainly Japanese, companies to develop a variety of industries, ranging from steel and cement production to the manufacture of a national car, the Proton Saga. To finance these initiatives, the government resorted to massive borrowings from abroad, mainly from Japan. In part, this contributed to the enormous rise in accumulated public sector foreign debt between 1980 and 1987, from RM4.9 billion to RM28.5 billion (Malaysia 1986, 1989). For Mahathir, this heavy industrialization drive would diversify the industrial sector and replace declining private investments with increased public investments. Although the Chinese had partly contributed to this decline in private investments, there was not much attempt by the government to involve or encourage Chinese participation in its heavy industrialization drive. The government, claiming that private capitalists would be reluctant to participate in these heavy industry projects in view of the huge capital investments required and their limited technological expertise, bypassed the domestic manufacturing sector. Some observers saw this as yet another instance of a deliberate policy of 'ethnic (Chinese) bypass' (Jomo 1994).

There has been some justification for such criticisms of the government's heavy industrialization policy. In the automobile assembly industry, there were about seven companies involved in the assembly of a wide range of European and Japanese model cars producing about 80,000 cars a year by the early 1980s (*Far Eastern Economic Review* 16 June 1983). The Chinese had a dominant presence in this sector (as the case studies on Loh Boon Siew and William Cheng have already indicated).[4] Apart from this, most Malaysian car sales companies were Chinese-owned. Among the most prominent, apart from Loh's Oriental group, were the Tan Chong group controlled by the Tan family, the Cycle & Carriage group controlled by the Chua family, and the United Motor Works (UMW) group controlled by Eric Chia (Torii 1991: 391–2).

Yet, Chinese experience and involvement in car assembly and sales appear to have been given scant consideration in policy planning when the government launched its national car project. Only a subsidiary of UMW was given a 35 per cent stake in Edaran Otomobil Nasional Bhd (EON), the company established by HICOM in 1985 to handle the sale of the Proton Saga. Mahathir had been a long-standing associate of then UMW chairman, Eric Chia. Both men had served as directors of a major public enterprise, Food Industries of Malaysia (FIMA) Bhd (privatized in 1990). Mahathir had resigned as director of FIMA in 1981 when he took office as Prime Minister (Gomez and Jomo 1997: 102). Mahathir had also expressed his appreciation for Chia's entrepreneurial capacity. In 1979, Mahathir praised Chia as 'one of three Malaysians who had ventured into new fields and succeeded' (*Insight* December 1981). Chia had secured the franchise to distribute Toyota motor vehicles, handled through UMW, which transformed the small company into one registering annual turnovers approaching almost half a billion ringgit (*Insight* December 1981). Chia, however, eventually lost control of UMW in the mid-1980s when the company was badly affected by the recession.[5] The government trust agency, PNB, currently has majority ownership of UMW.

To implement the national car project, the government entered into negotiations with the Japanese firm Mitsubishi. By ignoring the contribution the Chinese could have made to the national car project, the government, in effect, undermined its own bargaining capacity in its negotiations with Mitsubishi, allowing the latter to obtain better terms and conditions for itself in the joint-venture. Mahathir himself would later acknowledge that Malaysia's interests had not been well served by this joint-venture. The Prime Minister complained that Mitsubishi had been slow in transferring technology to its local partners, while continued dependence on the Japanese for parts and materials was increasing trade deficits (*Far Eastern Economic Review* 2 May 1996). Mahathir would even encourage Malaysian businessmen to establish joint-ventures with European car manufacturers to produce new models of the national car. One such project was set up with France's Automobile Citroen, involving the publicly-listed Diversified Resources Bhd, controlled by the late Yahya Ahmad. This venture was successful enough to justify the privatization of HICOM Holdings to Yahya in 1995, giving him a near monopoly over the production and sale of the various national car models.[6]

Mahathir's overwhelming influence in policy-making, for example in the privatization and heavy industries policies, was reflective of the unduly preponderant share of power held by the office of the Prime Minister. Mahathir has tried to justify this concentration of power in decision-making by voicing reservations about the ability of a bloated and inefficient bureaucracy to formulate and implement policy. The establishment of numerous research institutions, or 'think tanks', since the mid-1980s was apparently motivated by Mahathir to undermine the bureaucracy's dominance in policy-making (Noda 1996: 408–9). The most prominent research institutions – the Institute of Strategic and International Studies (ISIS) and the Malaysian Institute of Economic Research (MIER) – conspicuously serve the government. In fact, the post-1990 economic development policies are believed to bear the marks of such advice from outside the bureaucracy proper, particularly from ISIS. Mahathir's determination to take the Malaysian economy to 'fully developed status' as quickly as possible – to his mind, achievable primarily through greater economic efficiency and productivity – and his reluctance to decentralize power has increasingly determined policy formulation and changed the nature of governance.

This call for economic development has also been used by Mahathir to legitimize authoritarianism, specifically by executive dominance over other arms of government. Such authoritarianism, which Mahathir has defended as an 'Asian' form of democracy, is, he says, necessary for preserving inter-racial harmony. This has involved extensive limitations on civil liberties, such as freedom of the press, assembly and expression (see Munro-Kua 1996). Mahathir has also justified such limits on democratic space by arguing that the local political system has evolved, and should evolve, on the basis of values different from those which operate under Western liberal democracy. His 'Asian' form of democracy is principally perceived as an alternative to liberalism, where 'values' are paramount, and the rights of the individual are subordinated, ostensibly to protect the rights of the community. This form of authoritarianism is often justified by cultural relativist arguments. It has been claimed, for example, that historically, Malaysian – and, in particular, Malay – social and political structures have been authoritarian, hierarchical and highly stratified. The dominant Malay political norms value loyalty to the ruler over and above individual freedom and rights, tend to avoid adversarial relations and favor order over conflict.

Despite the increasing concentration of power in the executive arm of the government, there is little evidence of growing tension between the large multi-ethnic middle class that has emerged following the implementation of the NEP and the authoritarian state. Rather, as the 1995 general election results indicated, the Barisan Nasional still commands a high degree of popular support, while a large portion of the middle class credit Malaysia's commendable economic performance, as well as success in reducing poverty, raising real incomes and diminishing wealth disparities among ethnic communities to Mahathir's leadership of an authoritarian state (see Gomez 1996a). Mahathir probably also invokes his administration's success in promoting economic growth to justify his authoritarian style of governance; he has stated, 'nobody cares about human rights so long as you can register annual growth rates of 8.5 per cent' (quoted in *Third World Resurgence* August 1993). Undoubtedly, Mahathir's economic – and cultural – liberalization policies have also helped to stem disaffection, particularly among Chinese.

In spite of the rapid growth of a large Malaysian middle class, there is still only limited inter-ethnic co-operation due to continued ethnic polarization. Moreover, the bulk of the middle class is rather materialistic in orientation and unlikely to want to risk their position by seeking reforms. The limited reformist orientation of the middle class may also be due to the fact that the access of most Bumiputeras to higher education has been facilitated by the award of state scholarships and the enforcement of ethnic quotas. Much of the Bumiputera middle class is either employed by the state or by public enterprises, and views UMNO as the main means for their upward social mobility. Many Bumiputeras still conceive of UMNO and the state as protectors of their political and economic interests.

In tandem with these liberalization initiatives, however, there was another development which was to have a profound impact on Chinese capital. With increasing UMNO hegemony over the state in the late 1980s, Malay politicians could now use their influence over the bureaucracy to help develop a politically well-connected 'new rich' (see Gomez and Jomo 1997: 117–65). This was supposedly the outcome of Mahathir's grand design to create a class of Bumiputera capitalists who would be aided and protected by state concessions until they were capable of competing in the market independent of state patronage. However, these attempts to nurture the growth of Bumiputera capitalists consolidated a system of patronage and contributed to the public perception that the state's active participation in the economy has had a serious impact on the process and pattern of wealth accumulation. Such perceptions were fueled by Mahathir's open – and oft-quoted – sentiment that he saw no reason why there should not be 10 Malay millionaires to every 10 Chinese millionaires. This theme had been elaborated on by the Prime Minister:

> In trying to redress the imbalance, it will be necessary to concentrate your effort on the Malays, to bring out more Malay entrepreneurs and to bring out, and make more Malay millionaires, if you like, so that the number of Malays who are rich equals the number of Chinese who are rich, the number of Malays who are poor equals the number of Chinese who are poor and the number of unemployed Malays equals the number of unemployed Chinese . . . then you can say that parity has been achieved (quoted in *Malaysian Business* 16 October 1986).

Thus, one of the consequences of UMNO hegemony, justified as an objective of the NEP, has been the emergence of businessmen linked to senior UMNO leaders who have come to own a substantial portion of corporate stock due to political patronage. Such patronage has contributed to the meteoric rise of a new breed of well-connected Malay businessmen – particularly those linked to the three most powerful politicians in the country, Prime Minister Mahathir, Deputy Prime Minister Anwar Ibrahim and Government Economic Adviser Daim Zainuddin – who could not have gained anything close to their current wealth without political patronage (see Table 4.2). The business interests of Mahathir's sons and of Anwar's supporters as well as the widespread ownership of corporate stock of Daim's protégés has fueled friction among party leaders for access to state

*Chinese Business in Malaysia*

*Table 4.2* Political Affiliation of Prominent Business Figures who are Shareholders and/or Directors of Publicly-Listed Companies

| Name | Publicly-Listed Company | Background |
|---|---|---|
| Halim Saad | Renong<br>United Engineers (M) (UEM)<br>Kinta Kellas<br>Time Engineering<br>Ho Hup Construction<br>Faber Group<br>FCW Holdings<br>Park May<br>Crest Petroleum | Protégé of Government Economic Advisor and former Finance Minister Daim Zainuddin. Halim admitted publicly in 1988 that he held UMNO's vast corporate holdings in trust for the party. He worked under Daim when the latter was in charge of Peremba, then a government-owned company. |
| Tajudin Ramli | Malaysia Airlines<br>Malaysian Helicopter Services (MHS)<br>Technology Resources Industries (TRI) | Protégé of Daim; worked under him in Peremba. |
| Wan Azmi Wan Hamzah | RJ Reynolds<br>Land & General<br>Rohas-Euco Industries<br>Bell & Order<br>Systematic Education Group | Protégé of Daim; worked under him in Peremba. Has worked with the KL-Kepong group, T.K. Lim's MPHB and some medium-scale Chinese companies. |
| Samsudin Abu Hassan | Granite Industries<br>Austral Amalgamated<br>Dataprep Holdings | Protégé of Daim; worked under him in Peremba. Has had business deals with Ting Pek Khiing and with Teh Soon Seng (through Aokam Perdana). |
| Ahmad Sebi Abu Bakar | Advance Synergy<br>Prime Utilities<br>United Merchant Group<br>Ban Hin Lee Bank | Once protégé of Daim, though now more associated with Deputy Prime Minister and Finance Minister Anwar Ibrahim. Anwar's contemporary at the University of Malaya. Closely associated with Vincent Tan and has deals with the Hong Leong group. |
| Yahya Ahmad (deceased) | HICOM Holdings<br>Diversified Resources<br>Gadek (M)<br>Gadek Capital<br>Edaran Otomobil Nasional (EON)<br>Perusahaan Otomobil Nasional (Proton)<br>Kedah Cement Holdings<br>Cycle & Carriage Bintang<br>Golden Pharos<br>Uniphoenix Corporation | Protégé of Prime Minister Mahathir Mohamad. Anwar's school contemporary. |

## Chinese Business, Liberalization and Ascendance

*Table 4.2* Continued

| Name | Publicly-Listed Company | Background |
|---|---|---|
| Tunku Abdullah | Malaysian Assurance Alliance (MAA) Melewar Corporation George Town Holdings Aokam Perdana Malayan Cement MBf Capital Bhd MBf Holdings Bhd | Former UMNO MP; long-term close associate of Mahathir. Involved with Vincent Tan in privatization of Sports Toto. Worked closely with Loy Hean Heong of the MBf group. |
| Tengku Adnan Mansor | Star Publications Berjaya Group Berjaya Singer Berjaya Industrial EMC Logistics Minho Dunham-Bush (M) Unza Holdings | Former UMNO Supreme Council member. Closely associated with Vincent Tan. |
| Rashid Hussain | Rashid Hussain DCB Bank Kwong Yik Bank | Close to Daim, but also linked closely with Anwar's associates in 1996. Worked with Chua Ma Yu to develop Rashid Hussain. |
| A. Kadir Jasin Nazri Abdullah Mohd Noor Mutalib Khalid Ahmad | New Straits Times (NSTP) TV3 Malaysian Resources Corp Malakoff Commerce Asset Holdings | All associated with Anwar during the takeover of NSTP and TV3 in 1993. Hong Leong group was involved in this takeover through Malaysian Resources Corp. Kadir remains a Daim associate. |
| Amin Shah Omar Shah | PSC Industries Setron (M) Atacorp Holdings Kedah Cement Holdings Daibochi Plastic & Packaging Industry | UMNO member. Daim protégé. |
| Ishak Ismail | KFC Holdings (M) Idris Hydraulic Golden Plus Holdings Ayamas Food Corporation Best World Land Promet Pintaras Jaya Scientex Incorporated Gemtech Resources | UMNO member. Former secretary of Anwar's UMNO division in Penang. |
| Mohd Sarit Yusoh | KFC Holdings (M) Ayamas Food Corporation Golden Plus Holdings Malayawata Steel Khee San Goh Ban Huat Syarikat Kurnia Setia | UMNO member. Former political secretary to Anwar. |

## Chinese Business in Malaysia

*Table 4.2 Continued*

| Name | Publicly-Listed Company | Background |
|---|---|---|
| Abdul Mulok Damit | Pengkalen Industrial Holdings Construction & Supplies House | UMNO MP; associate of Daim. Jointly owns these companies with Joseph Ambrose Lee. |
| Basir Ismail | Cycle & Carriage Ltd Cycle & Carriage Bintang Cold Storage United Plantations Fima Corporation | Close associate of Mahathir. |
| Mohd Noor Yusof | Datuk Keramat Holdings George Town Holdings TV3 | Former political secretary to Mahathir. Had majority ownership of UMBC before divesting the bank to state-controlled Sime Darby. |
| Ahmad Zahid Hamidi | Kretam Holdings | UMNO Youth head; MP; Anwar associate. |
| Kamaruddin Jaffar | Sabah Shipyard Wing Teik Holdings Westmont Industries Inch Kenneth Kajang Rubber plc Mercury Industries | Kelantan UMNO leader; Anwar confidante. Had interest in Setron, now under control of Amin Shah. Associated with Joseph Chong, a Gerakan MP and majority owner of Westmont group, which also includes Wing Teik Holdings. |
| Kamaruddin Mohd Nor | Eastern & Oriental Dialog Group | Kelantan UMNO leader. Anwar confidante. |
| Shuaib Lazim | Ekran George Town Holdings | Close associate of Mahathir and Daim. Former UMNO state assemblyman. Works closely with Ting Pek Khiing. |
| Anuar Othman | Konsortium Perkapalan | Once protégé of Daim. Now associated with Anwar. Worked at Peremba. Former UMNO business trustee. |
| Hassan Abas | Cycle & Carriage Bintang | Protégé of Daim. Worked at Peremba. |
| Shamsuddin Kadir | Sapura Holdings Uniphone Telecommunications | Associated with Mahathir. |
| Azman Hashim | AAMB Holdings Arab-Malaysian Corporation Arab-Malaysian Finance Arab-Malaysian First Property Trust Arab-Malaysian Development South Peninsular Industries | UMNO member. Founding director of Fleet Holdings, UMNO's main investment holding company. |

## Chinese Business, Liberalization and Ascendance

*Table 4.2* Continued

| Name | Publicly-Listed Company | Background |
| --- | --- | --- |
| Ibrahim Mohamed | Uniphoenix Corporation<br>Damansara Realty | Associated with Mahathir. Worked with Brian Chang to develop Promet. |
| Ibrahim Abdul Rahman | Industrial Oxygen Inc. | Former UMNO MP. Anwar's father. |
| Mokhzani Mahathir | Tongkah Holdings<br>Technology Resources Industries (TRI)<br>Parkway Holdings<br>Pantai Hospital<br>UCM Industrial Corporation | Mahathir's second son. |
| Mirzan Mahathir | Mamee-Double Decker<br>Lion Corporation<br>Dataprep Holdings<br>Konsortium Holdings<br>KIG Glass Industrial<br>Sunway Building Technology<br>Worldwide Holdings<br>Artwright Holdings | Mahathir's first son. |
| Mukhriz Mahathir | Reliance Pacific | Mahathir's son. |
| Ahmad Razali Ali | Golden Plus Holdings<br>Timah Langat | Former UMNO Chief Minister of Selangor. Mahathir's brother-in-law. |
| Hashim Mohd Ali | Arab-Malaysian Corp<br>Ajinomoto<br>Konsortium Perkapalan<br>Hong Leong Credit<br>Country Heights Holdings | Mahathir brother-in-law. |
| Saleha Mohd Ali | Leong Hup Holdings<br>Fitters Holdings<br>Hirotako Holdings | Mahathir sister-in-law. |
| Jaffar Mohd Ali | Jastera<br>Cycle & Carriage Bintang | Mahathir brother-in-law. |
| Musa Hitam | Lion Land<br>Bright Packaging Industry | Former Deputy Prime Minister. |
| Ghafar Baba | Union Paper | Former Deputy Prime Minister. |
| Mohd Sofi Ghafar | Taiping Consolidated<br>HLG Capital | Son of fomer Deputy Prime Minister Ghafar Baba. |
| Megat Fairouz Junaidi | Talam Corporation<br>Kanzen<br>FACB | Son of UMNO Minister Megat Junid. |
| Robert Hamzah | KL-Kepong<br>Batu Kawan | Brother of former Finance Minister Razaleigh Hamzah. |

*Chinese Business in Malaysia*

*Table 4.2* Continued

| Name | Publicly-Listed Company | Background |
|---|---|---|
| Abd. Hamid Pawanteh | Amalgamated Industrial Steel<br>HICOM Holdings<br>Consolidated Farms<br>DNP Holdings | Former UMNO Chief Minister of Perlis. |
| Mohd Farid Ariffin | Diperdana Corporation<br>Island & Peninsular<br>Austral Enterprises | Former UMNO Deputy Minister. |
| Ahmad Rithaudden | Kinta Kellas<br>Idris Hydraulic | Former UMNO Minister. |
| Syed Nahar Shahabuddin | Sime UEP Propertites | Former Chief Minister of Kedah. |
| Aishah Ghani | Metrojaya<br>Ganz Technologies | Former head of UMNO's women's wing and cabinet member. |
| Hamzah Abu Samah | Malayan Flour Mills<br>Ho Wah Genting | Former UMNO cabinet member. |
| Mohd Khir Johari | Malayan United Industries (MUI)<br>Leisure Management<br>MUI Properties<br>Magnum Corporation | Former UMNO cabinet member. |
| Abdul Hamid Omar* | Olympia Industries<br>FACB<br>Lien Hoe Corporation | Former Lord President. |
| Abu Talib Othman* | Tan & Tan Developments<br>IGB Corporation<br>Multi-Purpose Holdings<br>Multi-Purpose Bank<br>Rothmans of Pall Mall (M)<br>Sapura Tele-<br>   communications<br>Crest Petroleum | Former Attorney General. |
| Haniff Omar* | Genting<br>Resorts World<br>Park May<br>General Corporation<br>KFC Holdings<br>AMMB Holdings<br>Arab-Malaysian Finance | Former Inspector-General of Police. |
| Sallehuddin Mohamed* | Cycle & Carriage Bintang<br>Malaysia Building Society | Former Chief Secretary of the Government |

* Former members of the bureaucracy or the judiciary.
Sources: *KLSE Annual Companies Handbook* 21 (1–4), 1996.

resources. In the process, the business community has become increasingly fragmented, both structurally and politically.

Politicians from the other political parties in the ruling coalition have also emerged as directors and shareholders of publicly-listed companies. However, their appointments to these posts do not guarantee access to state concessions, but usually help get past bureaucratic red tape. Prominent former MCA leaders who serve as directors of publicly-listed companies include former deputy presidents Lee Kim Sai, who is chairman of Metro Kajang Holdings Bhd, and Richard Ho, who is a director of DMIB Bhd and Malayan Banking. Among the former MCA vice-presidents, Chong Hon Nyan is a director of Asia Pacific Land Bhd and Tractors (M) Holdings Bhd, while Liew Sip Hon is chairman of Wing Teik Holdings Bhd and the Long Huat group. Former MIC vice-president K. Pathmanaban is a director of DMIB and Pembinaan YCS Bhd. Among the former Gerakan leaders, ex-president Lim Chong Eu is chairman of Suiwah Corporation Bhd, while ex-vice president Alex Lee is a director of Amalgamated Industrial Steel Bhd. Even the former MP who left the opposition DAP, Lee Lam Thye, is a director of Arab-Malaysian Corporation Bhd, Sime-UEP Properties Bhd and MBM Resources Bhd. Most of these Chinese and Indian former party leaders are non-executive directors and probably do not play an active role in decision-making. This is suggested by the fact that despite some interlocking directorships among them, there is seldom any business co-operation between the companies concerned.

A number of prominent Malays with backgrounds in politics or the civil service also hold executive and non-executive posts in Chinese-controlled companies which are not among the top one hundred publicly-listed corporations (see Table 1.2). Ex-Deputy Prime Minister Musa Hitam is a director of Lion Land Bhd, while ex-Deputy Prime Minister Ghafar Baba is chairman of Union Paper Bhd. Former Minister Mohd Khir Johari is a director of Leisure Management Bhd (and MUI Bhd and Magnum Corporation Bhd), while Aishah Ghani is a director of Metrojaya Bhd and Ganz Technologies Bhd, which is listed on the second board. The former Attorney General, Abu Talib Othman, is a director of Tan & Tan Developments Bhd, IGB Corporation Bhd and the Multi-Purpose Bank (and Multi-Purpose Holdings Bhd). Former Inspector General of Police Haniff Omar is a director of General Corporation Bhd (apart from Genting Bhd and Resorts World Bhd), while the former Lord President Hamid Omar is a director of Olympia Industries Bhd,

Lien Hoe Corporation Bhd and FACB Bhd. Although all these companies are Chinese-controlled companies, none of these Malays appears to play a significant role in decision-making. Although some are directors of Chinese as well as Malay-controlled companies, there appear to be few business connections between these companies. There is some evidence of business deals between a few of the leading Malay and Chinese businessmen. For example, Wan Azmi Wan Hamzah has had business deals with the Berjaya Group, the Hong Leong group and the KL-Kepong group (see Gomez and Jomo 1997: 138–47). Ahmad Sebi Abu Bakar has been involved in numerous business ventures with Vincent Tan Chee Yioun and the Hong Leong group (see Chapter 3). Samsudin Abu Hassan has worked with Ting Pek Khiing and Teh Soon Seng (of Aokam Perdana Bhd). Three businessmen-cum-politicians closely associated with Deputy Prime Minister Anwar, i.e. Kamaruddin Jaffar, Ishak Ismail and Mohd Sarit Yusoh, have business links with a number of Chinese (and Indian) businessmen. Kamaruddin Jaffar has business ties with Joseph Chong through the Westmont group. Ishak Ismail has worked with Vincent Tan, and with the Lau family in KFC Holdings Bhd. Ishak also controls Best World Land with the Indian businessman Kenneth Eswaran. Mohd Sarit, who has worked with Ishak Ismail and the Lau family in KFC Holdings, is a director of Goh Ban Huat (controlled by the Goh family) and chairman of Khee San Bhd (controlled by the Yan family). There is evidence that some Bumiputera businessmen have established long-term business relations with some smaller Chinese companies. Wan Azmi, through his private holding company, Rohas Sdn Bhd, is thus involved in the production of rubber shoes (Rugayah 1994: 73–90). However, most of these inter-ethnic business links have emerged through common ownership of a publicly-listed company, rather than through collaboration in a productive business venture.

This still limited Malay-Chinese business co-operation has been lamented by senior government leaders. This could be due to limited Chinese confidence in Malay businessmen on the one hand and to Malay insecurity in undertaking business with Chinese on the other. It is also probable that some Malays do not see the need for such business co-operation. A significant number of those politically well-connected businessmen like Halim Saad, Tajudin Ramli, Wan Azmi Wan Hamzah, the late Yahya Ahmad, Ahmad Sebi Abu Bakar, Ishak Ismail and Mirzan Mahathir have ownership and control of publicly-listed companies and play an active role in the development of these companies. Their links with senior politicians give them access to various state resources or state-controlled opportunities which have enabled them to develop huge business empires within a short span of time. These men are supposed to be representative of the dynamic and entrepreneurial Bumiputera business class that Mahathir has sought to create. In fact, although they may share a common patron, there is little evidence of joint business deals between most of these politically well-connected Bumiputera businessmen. For example, although Halim Saad, Tajudin Ramli, Wan Azmi Wan Hamzah and Samsudin Abu Hassan are all considered protégés of Daim Zainuddin and were all employed during the early 1980s by Peremba Bhd, a government-owned property development under Daim's control, there have been no major business joint-ventures among these men.

The emergence of a politically well-connected 'new rich,' which has helped to concentrate power in the hands of the executive, has further diminished the influence of the MCA in government and among Chinese businessmen. By the late 1980s, most prominent Chinese businessmen were beginning to directly relate to prominent Malay politicians in order to benefit from state patronage (see Hara 1991; Heng 1992; Gomez 1994). Chinese funding appears to have become crucial to these politicians because 'money politics' had reached such epidemic proportions in UMNO by the late 1980s that grassroots support had had to be reciprocated with some form of – usually monetary – benefit.

Money politics involves, among other issues, favoritism, conflicts of interest and nepotism in the award of state concessions, securing votes or support during federal, state and party elections by disbursing current or future material benefits usually due to direct and indirect interference by political parties or influential politicians in the corporate sector. This basis of money politics may be termed politicized or 'political business'.[7] The term 'political business' has been used to refer to the various forms of political involvement in business, for example of how UMNO's hegemony over the state has been abused to enable the accumulation of a vast amount of corporate assets ostensibly for the party (see Gomez 1990; 1994). By the mid-1980s, UMNO had developed a huge stake in the media and had interests in the banking, property development, hotels and construction sectors through its holding companies, Fleet Group Sdn Bhd, Hatibudi Sdn Bhd and Waspavest Sdn Bhd (see Gomez 1990). In the mid-1980s, factionalism in UMNO grew over struggles to secure access to lucrative contracts and licences. Criticism was made of an UMNO clique benefiting most from the party's corporate investments, with some members abusing control over party assets for their own vested interests. By the mid-1980s, criticism of the party's involvement in business no longer came only from outside, but also from within the party. This divided UMNO so badly that Mahathir had to move to have the party deregistered and create UMNO Baru (or 'New UMNO') under his control in its place.[8] In the process, most of the old party's corporate assets were channeled into the hands of individual businessmen, particularly Halim Saad, Tajudin Ramli and Samsudin Abu Hassan, all protégés of UMNO treasurer Daim (see Gomez 1994). This led to a change in the form of political business by the early 1990s. Patronage has instead been dispensed through individual UMNO leaders, intensifying money politics practices. The need for politicians to dispense large amounts of money or other percuniary benefits to secure enough grassroots support to ascend the party hierarchy has led to an increasing number of them trying to develop business bases to secure access to funds. With UMNO more deeply factionalized, Chinese businessmen can pick and choose who they court. In turn, many Malay politicians-cum-businessmen seek out Chinese partners to help them implement the contracts they have secured from the state as cheaply as possible to enhance profit margins.

The use of patronage to develop a strong coterie of politically-aligned businessmen and a large grassroots base, and the staggering use of money in party elections, was obvious during the 1993 UMNO party election when Anwar Ibrahim ousted Ghafar Baba as deputy president of the party. It was estimated that between RM200 million and RM300 million was spent for the campaign. During the 1984 UMNO election, when Razaleigh Hamzah challenged Musa Hitam for the post of deputy president, it was believed that a sum of RM20 million was spent during the campaign period (Gomez 1994: 58–9). This phenomenal increase in the use of funds in UMNO elections was indicative of the lengths to which senior party positions were being fought for and secured in order to gain access to increased state resources.[9]

The role played by non-Bumiputera companies in business deals which indirectly favored Anwar in the run-up to the UMNO election was also evident. The most obvious example was the help provided by the Hong Leong group to Anwar's allies to enable them to secure control of the leading newspaper publishing company, the New

Straits Times Press Bhd, and the private television network, TV3. The control by Anwar's allies over these two companies helped them use the media so effectively to undermine Ghafar Baba's campaign that the veteran UMNO leader conceded defeat even before the actual elections at the general assembly. Other businessmen, like Vincent Tan and T. Ananda Krishnan, were also believed to have helped raise funds for Anwar's campaign (see *Aliran* 13 (2) 1993).

The funding of Malay politicians by Chinese businessmen has been reciprocated with the distribution of business opportunities to the latter. For example, the Hong Leong group is believed to have secured control of MUI Bank and MUI Finance in 1993 for its role in Anwar's successful bid for the UMNO deputy presidency (see, for example, *Asian Wall Street Journal* 12 November 1993; *The Straits Times* [Singapore] 1 December 1993). After gaining control of MUI Bank and MUI Finance, the Hong Leong group divested its stake in MUI Finance – and in the Ban Hin Lee Bank – to Ahmad Sebi, reputedly a close ally of Anwar. The growth of such corporate deals among the business and political elite has been seen as evidence of growing business cooperation between Malays and Chinese, which has ironically enabled the Barisan Nasional to mobilize greater political support.

Mahathir has, however, recognized the importance of Chinese – and foreign – capital for sustaining growth and promoting industrialization, necessitating some checks on the activities of rentier capitalists. Mahathir has also shown signs that he will no longer tolerate rentiers who waste the economic opportunities they secure from the state. For Mahathir, the dynamic, entrepreneurial Bumiputera class he wishes to create should develop the capacity to compete and perform in an international business environment. Thus, Mahathir has argued that those who have productively and profitably utilized concessions from the government will stand to benefit more from state patronage. Among those who have benefited in the process are a few Chinese companies, among them YTL Corporation Bhd, controlled by Yeoh Tiong Lay and his son Francis Yeoh, and Ekran Bhd, controlled by Ting Pek Khiing (see case studies below).

There are other reasons why it has become imperative for Mahathir to channel government concessions to the Chinese. From an economic perspective, the Prime Minister sees the opening up of China's economy as offering potentially lucrative business ventures for Malaysian capital. This appears to have also encouraged

Mahathir's call for greater business co-operation between Chinese and Malays.

There is also growing evidence of major divisions among Malays, on class and regional bases. Rural Malays, long the bastion of UMNO support, appear to have become disillusioned with the nature and impact of rapid economic development and modernization on the community. Many rural Malays are of the view that they have benefited little from the government's strong emphasis on urbanization, industrialization and modernization. There also appears to be growing frustration among rural Malays that government policies have exacerbated intra-ethnic social differentiation and economic disparities (see Gomez 1996a). This has enabled the opposition, particularly the Islamic-oriented PAS, to make inroads into the Malay heartland. Intra-class differences among Malays have also emerged, partly reflected in the widening factionalism within UMNO These divisions among the Malays have compelled the Barisan Nasional to project a more multi-racial image and orientation to secure more non-Bumiputera votes. As the results of the 1995 general election results have indicated, this has effectively secured the Barisan Nasional such support.[10]

There obviously are a variety of developments in Malaysian politics and business which are having an impact on the development of Chinese capital. First, the factionalism in UMNO and Mahathir's desire to create a Bumiputera capitalist class seem to be determining how some Chinese businesses seek to cultivate Malay leaders. Second, Mahathir's desire to push Malaysia towards fully developed nation status and his recognition of the potential Chinese contribution to this goal has led to greater liberalization and the inclusion of Chinese capital into the Prime Minister's development aspirations for the country; albeit on his terms. In the process, the Chinese have also benefited from state concessions, while those who have impressed the Prime Minister appear to have been particularly favored. Finally, Chinese businessmen, especially those who have continued to operate rather independently of the state, have recognized that despite the moves towards economic liberalization, it is still necessary to work with well-connected Malays given the reality of elite Malay political dominance. The manner in which Chinese businessmen have responded to this changing situation can be seen in the following brief studies of two major Chinese companies, the Hong Leong group, controlled by Quek Leng Chan, and the KL-Kepong group, controlled by the family of the late Lee Loy Seng. Both groups did not have histories of working with UMNO-linked companies or with well-connected Malays before the late 1980s.

## Chinese Businessmen, Malay Patrons and Inter-Ethnic Cooperation

Quek Leng Chan

The Hong Leong Company was incorporated in Singapore in 1941 by four brothers from Fuzhou province in China who had migrated to the British colony in the 1930s. Hong Leong Co started out as a trading firm, ventured into plantations and manufacturing in the 1950s, then diversified further into property development in the 1960s and into finance in the 1970s. During these four decades, the company expanded its operations to Malaysia, Hong Kong and London (*Far Eastern Economic Review* 5 December 1985). In 1965, Quek Leng Chan, then a fresh law graduate, took charge of company operations in Malaysia.

Quek, through his main holding company, the Hong Leong Co. (M) Bhd and its three publicly-listed flagship companies, Hong Leong Industries Bhd, Hume Industries Bhd and Hong Leong Credit Bhd, developed the group in Malaysia through a series of acquisitions. By the early 1990s, Hume Industries was the largest construction materials manufacturer in the country, and a major shareholder in Nanyang Press Bhd, which publishes a leading Chinese newspaper, the *Nanyang Siang Pau*; Hong Leong Industries Bhd, a manufacturer and trader in ceramic tiles, building materials and assembler of Yamaha motorcycles, had control of OYL Industries Bhd, which in 1992 had an estimated 30 per cent of the local air-conditioner market;[11] and Hong Leong Credit Bhd owned a major finance company, Hong Leong Finance Bhd, a major bank, Hong Leong Bank Bhd (formerly MUI Bank) and the stockbroking company HLG Capital Bhd (formerly Zalik Bhd). These Malaysian companies have, or have had, an interest in a number of other publicly-quoted companies, including Hong Leong Properties Bhd (formerly Bedford Bhd), Malaysian Pacific Industries Bhd, Mycom Bhd and Malaysian Resources Corporation Bhd. Most of the group's overseas assets – in the United Kingdom, Hong Kong, Singapore, the Philippines and China – are held through the Hong Kong-based Guoco Group Ltd (*Far Eastern Economic Review* 22 February 1990; *Business Times* 12 November 1993; *Malaysian Business* 1 March 1994).

Although Quek was well acquainted with former Home Affairs Minister Ghazali Shafie and former Finance Minister Razaleigh Hamzah (see *Aliran* 1993: 13 [12]), there is no evidence that he was privy to state patronage nor that the Hong Leong group worked closely with UMNO-linked companies or well-connected businessmen until the late 1980s to develop his corporate assets in Malaysia. In April 1989, Hume Industries was awarded a RM500 million supplies contract by an UMNO-controlled company, United Engineers (M) Bhd (UEM). Later that year, a private company Jaguh Mutiara Sdn Bhd acquired a 24 per cent stake in Hume Industries. In April 1990, UMNO's investment holding company, Fleet Group Sdn Bhd, acquired Jaguh Mutiara. Fleet Group eventually came under the control of Renong Bhd, a publicly-listed construction company controlled by Halim Saad, a protégé of Daim Zainuddin. In February 1991, Hume Industries acquired a controlling stake in the publicly-listed Chinese newspaper publishing company, Nanyang Press Bhd; this stake was acquired from Land & General Bhd, a quoted property development concern controlled by Wan Azmi Wan Hamzah, another protégé of Daim (Gomez 1994: 86–7).

The Hong Leong group appears to have been developing an especially significant interest in the banking and finance sector, both locally and abroad. In Hong Kong, Hong Leong joined forces with the Kuwait Investment Office (KIO) to acquire the Dao Heng Bank in 1987. In 1989, Hong Leong also secured a controlling interest in another Hong Kong bank, the Hang Lung Bank, which was merged with the Dao Heng Bank; this gave the Hong Leong group the fifth largest bank network in the territory. In 1992, the group bought another bank in Hong Kong, the Overseas Trust Bank. In 1988, the group again teamed up with KIO to acquire a quoted finance company First Capital Corp in Singapore. In Britain, Hong Leong acquired the Benchmark Bank plc, renaming it the Dao Heng Bank (London) plc (*Far Eastern Economic Review* 22 February 1990; *Malaysian Business* 1 March 1994).

In Malaysia, the group's links with UMNO leaders are most manifest in the banking sector. Despite its involvement in finance, credit and stockbroking through Hong Leong Finance, Hong Leong Credit and HLG Capital respectively, for a long time the Hong Leong group had not been able to secure a controlling interest in a bank to consolidate its interests in the financial sector. The group's attempts to secure a banking licence from the government had not been successful. In 1989, Hume Industries' attempted takeover of Multi-

Purpose Holdings Bhd, which had control of the Malaysian French Bank (now the Multi-Purpose Bank), fell through. Although the Hong Leong group had managed to develop a large stake in a minor bank, the Ban Hin Lee Bank, the bank's controlling shareholders, the Penang-based Yeap family, had managed to ensure that Hong Leong could not even secure a seat on the board of directors. Through Hong Leong Credit and HLG Capital, the Hong Leong group held about 25 per cent of the Ban Hin Lee Bank's equity by 1992, following the public-listing of the bank in 1991, when the Yeap family's interests in the bank had been reduced from 70 to 49 per cent (*Malaysian Business* 16 December 1992).

In January 1993, the management buy-out (MBO) of TV3 – then Malaysia's sole private television network – and the major newspaper publishing company, the New Straits Times Press Bhd (NSTP), revealed the growing links between the Hong Leong group and Finance Minister Anwar Ibrahim. There was much speculation in the foreign media and in the more independent Malaysian press that the acquisition of these two important media companies from the UMNO-linked Renong group was to the interest of Anwar, who was then preparing to bid for the UMNO deputy presidency (see *Aliran* 1993: 13 [2]; *Far Eastern Economic Review* 15 July 1993). Through a reverse takeover involving Malaysian Resources Corporation Bhd (MRCB), a minor, ailing publicly-listed company it controlled, the Hong Leong group helped associates of Anwar gain control of the two media companies, which proved crucial for the Finance Minister to secure the UMNO deputy presidency and thus consolidate his position as Prime Minister Mahathir's successor. After Anwar's associates had secured a controlling interest in the MRCB, the Hong Leong group eventually divested its remaining equity in the listed company (Gomez 1994: 134–8).

In November 1993, just after Anwar was elected UMNO deputy president, the Hong Leong group announced – after protracted negotiations since January 1993 – its RM1.1 billion takeover of MUI Bank and its subsidiary, MUI Finance Bhd, from Khoo Kay Peng. Khoo was reportedly 'railroaded into selling the bank' after falling out of favor with senior UMNO leaders for his apparently close relationship with Razaleigh Hamzah (*Asian Wall Street Journal* 12 November 1993). The Hong Leong group not only obtained speedy approval from Anwar's Finance Ministry for the takeover, but was also exempted from complying with Malaysia's banking rules which limit the shareholdings of any individual corporate shareholder of a bank to no more than 20 per cent (ibid.). MUI Bank was subsequently renamed the Hong Leong Bank and was publicly-listed in October 1994.

MUI Finance was renamed United Merchant Finance Bhd, injected into a new investment holding company, the United Merchant Group Bhd (UMG), and listed on the KLSE in August 1994. Offered for sale at RM2.75 per share, each UMG share yielded a premium of RM3.25 when the shares began trading (*The Star* 19 August 1994). However, in an unprecedented move on the KLSE, a day after its listing, 39.2 per cent of UMG's equity was sold by the Hong Leong group to another publicly-listed company, Advance Synergy Bhd, controlled by Ahmad Sebi Abu Bakar, Anwar's contemporary at the University of Malaya (*The Star* 20 August 1994). The Hong Leong group subsequently also divested its interest in the Ban Hin Lee Bank to Ahmad Sebi. Hong Leong Co, however, still has a 5.5 per cent stake in Advance Synergy (*KLSE Annual Companies Handbook* 21 (4), 1996: 119–23).

In response to allegations of close links between the Hong Leong group and Finance Minister Anwar, a senior executive of the group claimed that these ties were 'not political' and that there was 'no harm aligning ourselves to the government' (quoted in *The Straits Times* [Singapore] 1 December 1993). When queried on these apparent links, Anwar insisted that he did not 'favor any group. As long as everything is in order and it benefits the economy, business proposals will be approved' (quoted in ibid.).

In 1994, the Hong Leong group also acquired a merchant bank, through a 29.9 per cent stake in Perdana Merchant Bankers Bhd, in which Advance Synergy has a controlling interest.[12] Through HLG Capital, the group also has a 22 per cent interest in KLOFFE Capital Sdn Bhd, which operates the Kuala Lumpur Options and Financial Futures Exchange (KLOFFE) (*KLSE Annual Companies Handbook* 21 (2) 1996: 371–5). The other shareholders of KLOFFE Capital are all politically well-connected companies, including the New Straits Times Press, the major brokerage company Rashid Hussain Bhd, and the Renong group (Gomez 1994: 130–3). The Hong Leong group's acquisition of the Hong Leong Bank and Perdana Merchant Bankers, and its involvement in the KLOFFE since the early 1990s has enabled it to create an integrated financial network in Malaysia (see Figure 4.1). Quek was also one of very few Chinese businessmen appointed to the Malaysian Business Council (MBC), formed by the Prime Minister in early 1991 to enhance government-private sector

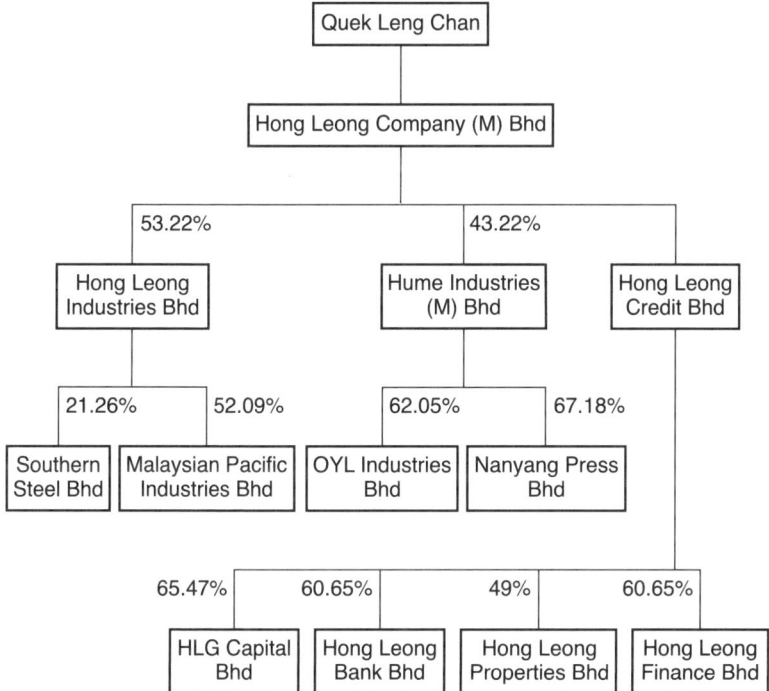

*Figure 4.1* Hong Leong Co. Bhd: Simplified Corporate Structure, 1995–96
Source: KLSE Annual Companies Handbooks 21 (1–4), 1996.

dialogue, indicating the Hong Leong group's importance in the corporate sector (*Malaysian Business* 1 March 1994).

Lee Loy Seng

Lee Loy Seng was born in 1921 in Ipoh, Perak, to a Cantonese family that had been involved in tin-mining for three generations. One of 21 siblings, Lee studied at a Chinese-medium school, and was sent, at the age of 16, to China for tertiary education; he stayed only a year, returning before the outbreak of the Sino-Japanese war. Lee's education was further stalled when the Japanese invaded Malaya during the Second World War. After the war, at the age of 24, Lee spent a year at school, to pick up English. He had planned to go to Australia to study medicine, but was instead required to stay back and help out in the family business. Lee spent the next 15 years working in the tin mining industry (*Malaysian Business* May 1973; *New Straits Times* 20 November 1985).

Lee's involvement in rubber was accidental. In 1955, his family bought a rubber plantation surrounded by tin mines, presuming that the land could be mined for tin (*Malaysian Business* May 1973). The land, however, yielded no tin, and Lee was assigned to manage the estate until it could be divested. Lee soon realized that the shares of rubber companies were undervalued. Most foreign shareholders were divesting their interests in the plantation sector for fear of competition from synthetic rubber and for fear of their prospects in independent Malaya. Lee also realized that it was far cheaper to acquire rubber companies than to buy estate land. Lee's first acquisition was the Parit Perak Rubber Company Ltd, a company controlled by Europeans with a large cash reserve of RM300,000, for which he paid only RM300,000. As Lee puts it: 'I was paying $300,000 to get $300,000 in the bank. And the land for free' (quoted in *New Straits Times* 20 November 1985). Parit Perak's cash reserves were used to buy another plantation company, Glenealy Plantations (M) Bhd, which, together with Parit Perak, was used to acquire Batu Lintang Rubber Company Bhd. In turn, these three companies were used to buy equity in Batu Kawan Estate Bhd. Eventually, Lee went on to also acquire Duff Development Bhd, Ulu Benut Consolidated Rubber Company (M) Bhd and his flagship company, KL-Kepong Bhd. Lee first bought into KL-Kepong in 1969 and kept increasing his equity in the company until he gained control of it in 1972. Through this series of acquisitions, Lee emerged as one of Malaya's largest rubber plantation owner. In 1992, the KL-Kepong group had about 87,000 hectares of plantation land involved in rubber, oil palm and cocoa spread over seven states, Kedah, Perak, Selangor, Negri Sembilan, Johore, Pahang and Sabah (see *Malaysian Business* May 1973; *The Star* 10 August 1982; *New Straits Times* 15 November 1985 and 29 February 1992). Most were acquired between 1957 (when he bought Parit Perak) and the early 1970s (when he completed the takeover of KL-Kepong), i.e. mainly before the NEP, when public enterprises began buying into foreign-owned plantation companies.

Lee's business-style was reflective of how a number of leading Chinese businessmen developed their corporate holdings. Lee strongly believed that the acquisition of companies was crucial: 'In order to grow big, you have to carry out an acquisition exercise' (quoted in *The Star* 9 August 1982). When he was asked: 'Would you, from experience as a planter and a businessman, venture into a field which is entirely different from your own speciality – that is go into an area where you have no knowledge of?', Lee's answer was an emphatic, 'Yes, I would, if the money was good' (quoted in ibid.).

Lee, an MCA member, was appointed chairman of Multi-Purpose Holdings during the party's corporatization drive in the mid-1970s. Multi-Purpose Holdings' early growth pattern was similar to this style of acquiring companies in a varied number of activities. Tan Koon Swan, the managing director of Multi-Purpose Holdings, used a similar business pattern to develop Supreme Corporation Bhd, his personal publicly-listed holding company (see Chapter 3).

However, in the case of the KL-Kepong group, even by 1992, a year before Lee's death, the group's investment outside the plantation sector was minimal, with some involvement in manufacturing, part of which was vertically integrated with the group's main activities, rubber, cocoa and palm oil production. The group was involved in a joint-venture, Palm-Oleo Sdn Bhd, to manufacture fatty acids; the other shareholders were Tan Chin Nam's IGB Corporation Bhd and three Japanese companies. The KL-Kepong group had also set up KL-Kepong Cocoa Products Sdn Bhd to manufacture cocoa butter, powder and related products (*New Straits Times* 29 February 1992). A British-listed manufacturing company, Yule Catto & Co plc, which manufactures rubber threads and latex examination gloves, was also acquired; the KL-Kepong group has a 29 per cent interest in the company.[13] This vertically-integrated growth, much of which had commenced in the beginning of the 1990s, was linked to the decline of the rubber industry and fluctuations in commodity prices affecting the performance of the KL-Kepong group and its future prospects.

In 1992, however, a significant change in KL-Kepong's corporate development pattern was observable when the group began diversification into property development. KL-Kepong entered into a joint-venture to develop a 521-acre plantation site on the outskirts of Kuala Lumpur into a residential, recreational and commercial area; the group's partner in the project was the listed property company, Land & General Bhd, controlled by Wan Azmi Wan Hamzah (*Investors' Digest* January 1992). In this property development project, KL-Kepong sold two of its estates – Kerling and Sungei Jernih – to Clarity Crest Sdn Bhd, a subsidiary of Land & General. KL-Kepong simultaneously acquired a 30 per cent stake in the project to develop this area, which included an adjoining piece of land owned by Land & General (*KLSE Annual Companies Handbook* 21 (3), 1996: 410). This joint-venture was rather significant as Lee had not worked with an influential Malay businessmen in a major project before this. The only noteworthy Bumiputera link that the KL-Kepong group has had was with former Finance Minister, Razaleigh Hamzah, who was director of company in the 1970s; his brother, Robert Hamzah, is still a director of KL-Kepong. Although Lee's son, Lee Oi Hian, had already been appointed the joint managing director of KL-Kepong when the move to work with Wan Azmi was made, the joint-venture appears to suggest a change of policy by the elder Lee as to the mode of the group's future development. As Lee died the following year, it is difficult to confirm this view.

KL-Kepong is currently led by his son Lee Oi Hian. In 1994, two of the KL-Kepong group's plantation companies, Parit Perak and Glenealy, were sold; but, the primary assets of these two companies, its plantation landholdings, were bought back by KL-Kepong. Such an arrangement, essentially selling listed shell companies, resembled a deal effected by Lee Loy Seng in his mid-1980s sale of Batu Lintang and Ulu Benut. Batu Lintang was sold to Sarawak tycoon Wee Boon Ping, who later sold it to Ahmad Sebi Abu Bakar; the company was renamed Advance Synergy. Ulu Benut was renamed Construction and Supplies House Bhd (CASH) and came under the control of the Sabah-based Joseph Ambrose Lee in 1993 (*Malaysian Business* 1 January 1994).[14]

Glenealy was sold by KL-Kepong to the Sarawak-based Yaw family, which has control of the Samling Corporation Sdn Bhd, one of the largest timber companies in the state (Cheong 1995: 56–9). Parit Perak was sold in 1995 to Ishak Ismail, who is closely associated with Deputy Prime Minister Anwar Ibrahim; the company is now an investment holding company, led by Anuar Othman, a Daim protégé. Anuar has an indirect 52 per cent stake in Parit Perak (Cheong 1995: 121–4; *Malaysian Business* 1 January 1994; *KLSE Annual Companies Handbook* 21 (3), 1996: 573–6). Anuar held an interest in Renong Bhd and United Engineers (M) Bhd (UEM), both listed companies under UMNO control. Anuar divested his interests in these two companies in 1994 following a fall-out with Renong's controlling shareholder, Halim Saad (Gomez and Jomo 1997: 50). The KL-Kepong group currently has a much more modest corporate structure, compared to its complex crossholdings in the early 1970s (see Figure 4.2).

There are a number of similarities in the business styles of Lee and Quek. Both men developed huge corporations through a series of

## Chinese Business, Liberalization and Ascendance

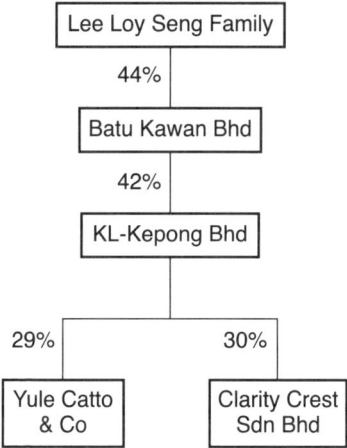

*Figure 4.2* KL-Kepong Bhd: Simplified Corporate Structure, 1995–96
Source: *KLSE Annual Companies Handbook* 21 (3), 1996: 398–404, 409–420.

acquisitions. Quek and Lee have also operated rather independently, coming to prominence during the 1960s and the early 1970s. However, while Lee has pursued horizontal growth for the KL-Kepong group with an emphasis on the plantation sector, Hong Leong Co has had a more diversified growth with involvement in manufacturing, media and finance. While Lee was an MCA member closely associated with the corporatization movement, Quek appears to have kept his distance from Chinese politics, and even attempted a takeover of Multi-Purpose Holdings, a product of the corporatization movement. One probable reason why Quek may not have associated himself with Chinese politicians is that he is from Singapore and had managed to get Malaysian citizenship with the help of Ghazali Shafie. Moreover, there have been reports that Quek has not been popular in the local Chinese business community. For example, one report in the Singapore-based *Business Times* quotes a chief executive of a company who has dealt with Quek thus: 'He (Quek) is often seen as an outcast among the Chinese. To him, everything is commercial. There is no sentiment – it is pure business' (quoted in *Aliran* 1993: 13 [12]).

There was little need for Malay patronage to grow through acquisitions in the immediate post-colonial as well as NEP eras, as evident in the rapid rise of Multi-Purpose Holdings, MUI and

Berjaya Group (see Chapters 2 and 3). However, as some key sectors, especially banking and finance, came under increasing regulation, and as some sectors, such as plantations and mining, began to diminish in importance, changes in styles of operation became imperative. When banking regulations were changed to limit majority ownership, and Quek's long-held ambition to secure control over a bank seemed jeopardized, he needed to cultivate ties with the Malay elite. Lee, it appears, also came to the conclusion that it would be difficult to use the KL-Kepong group's large land base to move into property development without linking up with an influential Malay. As Multi-Purpose Holdings' chairman in 1982, Lee was aware that the company could not develop three huge tracts of plantation land in prime areas on the outskirts of Kuala Lumpur unless it formed joint-ventures with companies owned by UMNO (Gomez 1990: 157–9).[15]

Both the Hong Leong and KL-Kepong groups now seem to be working more with prominent Malays. This change in the manner of operating appears to be due to the realization, by both Quek and Lee, that there was a need to cultivate ties with influential politicians or well-connected businessmen, given the heavily politicized nature of the corporate sector. Quek, in particular, appears to be working with associates of Anwar Ibrahim. Both Lee and Quek have worked with Wan Azmi, who is one of the few well-connected Malay businessmen to have sought to work with Chinese.

These two brief profiles of Quek and Lee suggest that from the late 1980s, even the most established Chinese businessmen who had previously been independent of Malay patronage were beginning to cultivate influential Malay politicians or well-connected businessmen. By the early 1990s, even medium-scale Chinese companies were starting to incorporate influential Bumiputeras as directors of their enterprises. This pattern of development has influenced the nature of inter-ethnic business cooperation, suggesting a more level playing field between the two communities, even though this may not be the case in reality. Although liberalization initiatives can be partly attributed to the government's recognition of the importance of the Chinese contribution to economic development, Chinese businessmen have found it increasingly necessary to develop inter-ethnic corporate ties given the extent of the UMNO leadership's control of the economy. Most of the themes raised here are obvious from the detailed case study of Francis Yeoh's YTL Corporation and Ting Pek Khiing's Ekran Bhd.

## Francis Yeoh and YTL Corporation Bhd — CASE STUDY

Francis Yeoh's father, Yeoh Tiong Lay, a Hokkien, was born in 1930 in Selangor. Francis' grandfather, Yeoh Cheng Liam, was a timber merchant with some involvement in the construction industry, operating through his family company, Yeoh Cheng Liam Construction Sdn Bhd. In 1950, at the age of 20, Yeoh Tiong Lay[16] secured his first contract, to construct two police explosives magazines in Pahang and Selangor. From this modest start, Tiong Lay's company, Syarikat Pembenaan Yeoh Tiong Lay Sdn Bhd, became involved in bigger construction projects, including high rise buildings in the national capital, like the headquarters of two foreign banks, Citibank and the Hongkong & Shanghai Bank, and the headquarters of the Malaysian-controlled multinational, Sime Darby (*The Diplomat* February 1986; *Malaysian Business* 16 February 1994).[17] In 1984, Tiong Lay gained control of Hong Kong Tin plc, a nearly moribund tin-mining company. Through a spate of shares-for-assets swaps and rights issues, Tiong Lay injected a few subsidiaries owned by his family company, Syarikat Pembenaan Yeoh Tiong Lay – including Buildcon Sdn Bhd, Batu Tiga Quarry Sdn Bhd and Yeoh Tiong Lay Brickworks Sdn Bhd – into the publicly-listed company; the company was renamed Hong Kong Tin Corporation (M) Bhd. Through a reverse takeover, Syarikat Pembenaan Yeoh Tiong Lay was injected in 1988 into Hong Kong Tin, which was then renamed YTL Corporation Bhd (Cheong 1992: 279–84; *Malaysian Business* 16 January 1992). Although YTL Corp had established a reputation as a contractor for turnkey projects by the end of the 1980s, the company still remained a relatively small construction, property development and manufacturing concern. In terms of market capitalization, the company's paid-up capital was just about RM73 million in 1991 (see Table 4.3).

Buildcon Bhd, Malaysia's largest ready-mixed concrete manufacturer, is another company in the YTL Corp group, which was publicly-listed in 1993 on the second board of the KLSE. Buildcon, soon to be renamed YTL Cement, is expected to record annual sales of approximately two million tonnes of cement by 1998; by this time, its market is expected to include the Indochina region (see *The Star* 26 February 1997). In mid-1997, YTL Corp will publicly list YTL Power International (YTLPI) Bhd, which will become the largest independent power producer (IPP) on the KLSE (*The Edge* 17 March 1997).

Table 4.3 YTL Corp Bhd: Share Capital, Turnover and Profit Margins, 1991–96 (RM million)

|  | 1991 | 1992 | 1993 | 1994 | 1995 | 1996 |
|---|---|---|---|---|---|---|
| Paid-Up Capital | 73.08 | 90.37 | 90.51 | 109.20 | 178.99 | 179.18 |
| Turnover | 302.70 | 455.58 | 489.59 | 583.99 | 1025.40 | 1600.00* |
| Pre-Tax Profit | 30.95 | 42.81 | 52.72 | 71.81 | 231.26 | 356.00* |

* Figures were obtained from Far Eastern Economic Review (26 December 1996)
Sources: KLSE Annual Companies Handbook 21 (2), 1996: 257–66; Far Eastern Economic Review (26 December 1996)

Yeoh Tiong Lay has seven children, all of whom were educated abroad. His eldest, third and fourth sons, Francis Yeoh Sock Ping, Yeoh Seok Hong and Yeoh Sock Siong respectively, and second daughter, Yeoh Soo Keng, all qualified as engineers in the UK. The second son, Yeoh Seok Kian, is a quantity surveyor, while Tiong Lay's eldest daughter, Yeoh Soo Min, is an accountant, and his youngest son, Yeoh Seok Kah is a lawyer (*The Diplomat* February 1986). All seven third generation Yeohs are directors of YTL Corp. Tiong Lay is the chairman of the company, while Francis Yeoh, who is currently primarily responsible for the management of the YTL Corp group, is managing director; second son Seok Kian is the deputy managing director. The largest shareholder of YTL Corp, with a 48 per cent stake, is Tiong Lay's family holding company, Yeoh Tiong Lay & Sons Holdings Sdn Bhd. Publicly-quoted Buildcon is also led by Yeoh Tiong Lay (as chairman) and Francis Yeoh (as managing director); three of Yeoh's other children also sit on the board of this company. 53.32 per cent of Buildcon's equity is held by YTL Corp (*KLSE Annual Companies Handbook* 21 (2), 1996: 262; 595–9; *Business Times* 26 November 1993).

Yeoh Tiong Lay & Sons Holdings' company records indicate that the shareholders of this private investment and property holding company, which was incorporated on 31 January 1979 and has an issued capital base of RM40.720 million, are all members of the Yeoh family. Yeoh Tiong Lay owns 8.22 million shares in the holding company, his wife, Tan Kai Yong five million shares, while among the children, Francis, Seok Kian, Seok Hong, Sock Siong, Soo Min and Seok Kah each hold five million shares; Seok Keng owns 1.25 million shares. The directors of Yeoh Tiong Lay & Sons Holdings in December 1996 were Yeoh Tiong Lay, his wife, Francis, Soo Min and Seok Kian. This shareholding pattern reflects Tiong Lay's strong emphasis on family control of the YTL Corp group, with the family forming the core of the group's management (see *The Diplomat* February 1986).

Bumiputera participation in the YTL Corp amounts to 16.29 per cent, of which only 0.68 per cent is held by Bumiputera individuals and 1.39 per cent by Bumiputera nominees. The armed forces' provident fund, the Lembaga Tabung Angkatan Tentera (LTAT), is the main Bumiputera shareholder, with a 13.21 per cent stake. Among the prominent Bumiputera directors of the company are Yahya Ismail, who is well linked to UMNO,[18] and former civil servant Raja Mohar Badiozaman (*KLSE Annual Companies Handbook* 21 (2), 1996: 257–65). Total Bumiputera equity participation in Buildcon is 16.22 per cent, of which Bumiputera individuals, including nominees, account for a third, or 5.16 per cent; LTAT is the largest Bumiputera equity holder with 8.86 per cent equity in Buildcon (*KLSE Annual Companies Handbook* 21 (2), 1996: 595–9). There are no prominent Bumiputeras among Buildcon's directors.

Francis Yeoh is believed to have close relations with the current Perak royal family (see Cheong 1992: 283), as well as with the Prime Minister, with many seeing Francis Yeoh as a 'Mahathir man' (see, for example, *Business Times* 22 June 1992). Francis Yeoh has repeatedly denied that any patronage from the government was attributable to his 'political connections,' and has insisted that he has 'no special relationship with the Prime Minister' (quoted in *Malaysian Business* 16 February 1994), while Mahathir has reportedly justified government contracts to Francis Yeoh on the grounds that 'he got things done' (quoted in *Asiamoney* November 1994).

YTL Corp has certainly benefited from some major government projects. In 1990, the company was awarded a RM840 million contract to design and develop 12 hospitals as part of the government's plans to create a nationwide rural healthcare network. The company also secured the contract to build a RM112 million airport in Sibu, Sarawak. YTL Corp has also been awarded two projects in the state of Perak, a low and medium cost privatized housing scheme and a 120ha light industrial park (*Business Times* 26 November 1993).

YTL Corp rose to prominence, if not notoriety, in 1992 when the government announced that the company would be the first to be awarded an independent power producer (IPP) licence worth RM2.5 billion; YTL Corp had submitted plans to the government to construct two power plants. The announcement was both significant and controversial since YTL Corp was Chinese-controlled and had no experience in power generation. Moreover, the government-controlled privatized electricity company, Tenaga Nasional Bhd, then had power plants in the two sites proposed by YTL Corp, and had its own plans to build new plants to raise power generation (*Malaysian Business* 16 June 1992). The licence was for a privatized build-operate-own (BOO) project involving the construction and operation of two gas-fueled electricity generating plants in Paka, Terengganu and Pasir Gudang, Johore (*The Star* 25 October 1993). The project involved the sale of electricity to Tenaga over a 21-year period, sealed through a power purchase agreement; the price was fixed at 15.5 sen per kilowatt hour. Tenaga was then selling electricity at 18 sen per kilowatt hour to end-users. As one magazine commented, 'that left hardly any margin for the state utility after factoring in the cost of distribution' (*Asiamoney* November 1994). This high sale price was justified by YTL Corp on the grounds that it would help keep inflation costs down (see *Asian Business* October 1994)! Though more IPP licences were to be issued to other companies, the contracts ensured guaranteed minimum sales at high fixed prices, i.e. no increase in competition. Guaranteed sales and the fixed price ensured YTL Corp of profitable income for the duration of the 21-year contract.

The licence was awarded in 1993 to YTL Power Generation Sdn Bhd, in which YTL Corp had a 50 per cent stake. The other shareholders of YTL Power Generation, which had an initial paid-up capital of RM300 million, were Tenaga (20 per cent) and the government's Employees Provident Fund (10 per cent), while the remaining 20 per cent equity was split between the British-based construction company John Laing plc, Mayban Ventures Sdn Bhd, and a Bumiputera company Bara Aktif Sdn Bhd[19] (*The Star* 15 September 1994). To handle the operations and maintenance of the two power plants, YTL Power Services Sdn Bhd was incorporated. YTL Corp owned 51 per cent of this company's equity, while the remaining 49 per cent stake was held by the German-based power equipment supplier, Siemens AG; however, YTL Corp has a buy-back option for Siemens' stake in YTL Power Services, exercisable after six years (*Malaysian Business* 16 February 1994).

A year after securing the IPP contract, YTL Corp achieved another coup when it managed to put together a financing package for the project with loans from local financial institutions; it was then the largest single loan provided by local institutions. This reduced YTL Corp's risks arising from foreign exchange fluctuations.[20] The deal was hailed as a milestone for infrastructure project financing as it was the first time that a bond had been successfully issued to raise a large portion of the funds required to finance a major privatized project. Most of the other funds required were raised through loans from Malaysian banks. The government's EPF was, however, used to subscribe to the bond (*Asian Business* October 1994).

Apart from the sale of electricity to Tenaga, YTL Corp was expected to benefit from the IPP in a number of ways. First, YTL Corp's main subsidiary, Syarikat Pembenaan Yeoh Tiong Lay, was expected to make a profit of approximately RM200 million from the turnkey construction of the two power plants. Second, the management fees from operating the plants were another source of income. Third, since YTL Power Generation was expected to be listed, extraordinary gains were anticipated when a portion of the YTL Corp's stake in the company was sold (*The Star* 7 November 1994). The contract would also provide the YTL group with a recurrent earnings flow, with an expected total income of at least RM1 billion for the duration of the IPP contract. Since YTL Corp was expected to provide 20 per cent of Tenaga's generation capacity, with electricity consumption growth estimated at an average 10 to 12 per cent during the 1990s, and given Malaysia's rapid industrialization program, which caused the demand for power to rise, YTL Corp's involvement in electricity supply was expected to provide the company with a significant portion of the group's profits (see *Malaysian Business* 16 February 1994). The IPP project was completed in September 1995, well ahead of the scheduled completion date. As expected, just a year later, in June 1996, YTL Corp recorded a massive increase of 54 per cent with pre-tax profits of RM356 million on sales of RM1.6 billion (*Far Eastern Economic Review* 26 December 1996).

Not unexpectedly, since this activity proved so profitable (see Table 4.4), YTL Corp hoped that this project would be a stepping stone to becoming an international power supplier. According to Francis Yeoh: 'In future, Malaysia could be the regional center of power exchange with links to Singapore, Thailand and further' (quoted in *The Star* 15 September 1994). Subsequently, in 1994, Francis Yeoh secured a contract to supply electricity to Singapore, and in 1996, a US$600 million power deal in Zimbabwe, which involved the acquisition of a power plant and the development of two new power-generating units at the plant (*Far Eastern Economic Review* 26 December 1996; *The Star* 4 April 1997). YTL Corp has similar deals in Thailand and China, and is exploring possible power supply projects in the Philippines, Vietnam and India (*The Star* 4 April 1997). In October 1996, YTL Corp tried unsuccessfully to take over 80 per cent of Consolidated Electric Power Asia (CEPA), the power supply subsidiary of the Hong Kong-based Hopewell Holdings, controlled by Gordon Wu (*Asiaweek* 6 December 1996). The takeover was seen by YTL Corp as an opportunity to create a YTL-controlled pan-Asian power giant, while the Prime Minister's view of the unsuccessful takeover attempt was that it was 'a very good deal that got away' (quoted in *The Edge* 17 March 1997). Amazingly, the government's investment holding company, Khazanah Holdings, had agreed to provide YTL Corp with RM1 billion as financial backing for the takeover (*Asiaweek* 6 December 1996).

In May 1997, YTL Corp announced plans to list YTL Power International on the main board of the KLSE, which was expected to help the company raise around RM2 billion. Apart from the contracts secured in Singapore and Zimbabwe, YTL Power International's subsidiaries and associate companies will include YTL Power Generation, a 30 per cent stake in Teknologi Tenaga Perlis (Overseas) Consortium Sdn Bhd, which is to supply power to Thailand's Electricity Generating Board, and a 51 per cent stake in YTL-CPI Power Ltd, which is to own a 60 per cent stake in a joint-venture company, Nanchang Zhongli Power Co Ltd, formed in China; the other members of the joint-venture are Jiangxi Provincial Power Electric Corp and Jiangxi Provincial Investment Corp (*The Edge* 14 April 1997). YTL Corp is expected to hold 59 per cent of YTL Power International's equity, while the other major shareholders are expected to include three state-linked entities, the government's

*Table 4.4* YTL Corp Bhd: Sectoral Breakdown in Terms of Turnover and Pre-Tax Profits, 1995 (RM million)

| Sector | Turnover | Pre-Tax Profit |
|---|---|---|
| Construction | 469.3 | 72.2 |
| Manufacturing & Trading | 178.9 | 25.4 |
| Property Development & Management Services | 90.7 | 23.6 |
| Power Generation | 286.5 | 110.0 |

*Source: KLSE Annual Companies Handbook* 21 (2), 1996: 266

holding company, Khazanah, the EPF and the government-controlled Tenaga, an indication of the strong government endorsement of YTL Power International's expected forays abroad (*Business Times* 11 March 1997; *The Star* 4 April 1998).

YTL Corp's emphasis on developing an overseas market, both in terms of building power plants and electricity supply, is suggestive of an ability to build upon the experience gained from developing the IPPs locally. It is also unlikely that the company would secure any more IPP contracts in Malaysia as power generation has become increasingly competitive. By 1997, at least five IPP contracts had been issued and a contract awarded for the privatized construction of a major hydroelectric dam in Sarawak, the Bakun Dam, which would also generate electricity for the peninsula.

YTL Corp has gone on to develop even closer ties with the government, working with a number of other state agencies in different sectors. The company is in a joint-venture with the government's Urban Development Authority (UDA) to build apartments and office towers on prime land in KL's golden triangle. In 1994, YTL Corp also reached an agreement with the government's railway company, Keretapi Tanah Melayu (KTM) Bhd, to develop 1.4 million sq ft of prime land in Brickfields, also in the federal capital (*Business Times* 19 December 1994). YTL Corp entered into joint-venture property development projects with a number of state development corporations (SEDCs); this has given the company access to lucrative housing development projects on land owned by state governments (*Malaysian Business* 16 February 1994). With Pasdec Corporation Sdn Bhd, a company owned by the Pahang state government, Buildcon formed a joint-venture, Pahang Cement Sdn Bhd, to construct a 600,000 tonne fully-integrated cement manufacturing plant near the state capital, ostensibly to catalyze the industrialization of the eastern corridor of the peninsula (*Business Times* 26 November 1993).

YTL Corp's management has attributed its diversification to the increasing competitiveness of its mainstay, construction. Moreover, they claim that the gross profit margins of between five and seven per cent from construction projects are neither lucrative nor contribute much to net asset growth (see *Malaysian Business* 16 February 1994). This has contributed to the group's move into the hotel industry, giving it access to land, building its own hotels and developing its asset base. Apart from power generation, the other sectors that the group is concentrating on are manufacturing (primarily through

Buildcon) and property development. Construction and manufacturing continue to be major contributors to the group's revenue, but even the company's directors acknowledge that the 'earnings contribution' from the two power plants 'will underpin the Group's long term growth' (quoted in *KLSE Annual Companies Handbook* 21 (2), 1996: 262). According to one estimate, at least 70 per cent of the group's earnings will come from its power supply arm, allowing earnings from the sector to provide the capital required to finance further group expansion (see *Asiamoney* November 1994). This indicates the importance of the IPP contracts to the future development of the group.

It is obvious that YTL Corp has benefited substantially from government patronage since the early 1990s. The company's rapid growth, in terms of capitalization, profits and turnover, is primarily attributable to the IPP contracts secured from the government in 1993 (see Table 4.3). But it is also clear that YTL Corp has not depended solely on economic concessions from the state to develop. It has made some moves towards acquiring technology. For example, after obtaining the IPP licence, an area in which it had no experience, the company established ties with the German-based company, Siemens, to implement the project. YTL Corp hopes to take over the running of the power plants in future once it has learnt the

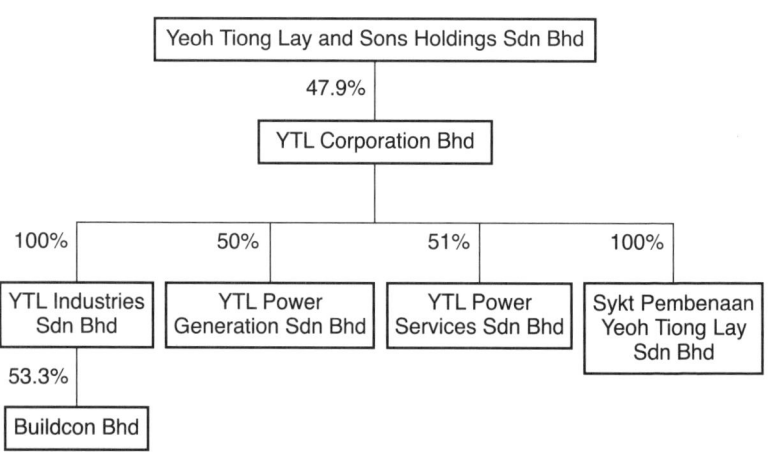

*Figure 4.3* YTL Corporation Bhd: Simplified Corporate Structure, 1995–96
Source: *KLSE Annual Companies Handbook* 21 (2), 1996: 259–62; 596–97

technology from the Germans. Similarly, to implement another major project secured from the government, involving the construction of 12 rural health care nucleus hospitals, YTL Corp has teamed up with the British-based construction company, John Laing plc. With YTL Corp's professionally qualified management, led by Yeoh Tiong Lay's children (referred to as 'the cabinet'), the company's ability to obtain and develop technical expertise and competence augurs well. Diversification rather than specialization in construction alone appears to have been in response to new government-provided opportunities, as its older activities face increasing competition (see Figure 4.3).

| Ting Pek Khiing and Ekran Bhd | CASE STUDY |
|---|---|

Ting Pek Khiing was born in 1941 on the outskirts of Sibu in Sarawak. His father, who had 12 other children, was a farmer and trader in oranges. After completing his secondary education, Ting started out by selling oranges until he had accumulated enough to venture into construction, moving from small projects to bigger housing schemes. To cut down production costs, he acquired a saw mill and subsequently went into logging. By 1980, Ting had created a niche for himself as a turnkey contractor for building timber-based houses and hotels, primarily in Sarawak. Through his main company, Woodhouse Sdn Bhd, he had established a fully integrated timber business, which enabled him to ensure expeditious completion of the projects he undertook. This brought Ting into contact with Sarawak Chief Minister, Abdul Taib Mahmud. In 1989, Ting impressed the Prime Minister when he built two major hotels on Mahathir's favorite island of Langkawi in Kedah in a few months, in time for an international exhibition. The speedy completion of these projects also impressed former Finance Minister and Government Economic Adviser Daim Zainuddin, who chaired the government commission charged with developing Langkawi (*The Star* 22 April 1992 and 22 November 1994; *Malaysian Business* 1 October 1992).

In 1992, Ting injected Woodhouse into a newly established private investment holding company, Ekran Bhd, which was incorporated in September 1991 to become his main publicly-listed company. According to company records, Woodhouse had been incorporated on 24 June 1977, and the original directors were Ting and his wife, Wong Sui Choo.[21] In June 1995, the only two shareholders of the company were Ting (54.288 million shares) and Wong (13.333 million shares). Woodhouse was taken over by Ekran through a share-swap, which increased the latter's paid-up capital from RM2 to RM40 million. In early 1992, Ting re-emerged in the limelight when Ekran was involved in an intense tussle with two well-established publicly-listed companies, Leader Universal Bhd (Malaysia's largest wiring and cable manufacturer) and the politically well-connected telephone terminal equipment manufacturer, Sapura Holdings Bhd (controlled by Shamsuddin Kadir) to take over the profitable, but suspended (since 1987) publicly-listed telephone and electric cable manufacturing company, Federal Cables, Wires & Metal Manufacturing Bhd (FCW). The desire to control FCW arose because cable manufacturers in Malaysia enjoy high tariff protection of 40 per cent (*Malaysian Business* 1 April 1994). To enhance its chances in the takeover bid, Ekran made a restricted share issue to Ting and to two private holding companies, Silara Sdn Bhd and Aneka Aktif Sdn Bhd, increasing Ekran's capitalization by another RM50 million (see Table 4.5). Against the odds, Ekran secured control of FCW through a share-swap, raising its capitalization to RM128.572 million. Ekran also took over FCW's listed status and renamed it FCW Industries Sdn Bhd (*KLSE Annual Companies Handbook* 21 (2), 1996: 453–8; *The Star* 27 April 1992).

Following this reverse takeover, Ekran's main shareholder was Ting, with a 25.25 per cent stake; his wife held another five per cent of the company's equity, while minority shareholders included Shuaib Lazim (0.66 per cent), Rasip Haron (0.99 per cent) and two sons of Taib Mahmud, the Chief Minister of Sarawak, each of whom held one per cent of Ekran's equity (*KLSE Annual Companies Handbook* 19 (2), 1996: 171–4). Shuaib Lazim was an UMNO senator from

*Table 4.5* Ekran Bhd: Share Capital, Turnover and Profit Margins (RM)

|  | 1991 | 1992 | 1993 | 1994 | 1995 |
|---|---|---|---|---|---|
| Paid-Up Capital | 2 | 128.57m | 128.57m | 251.14m | 251.14m |
| Turnover | 34.63m | 163.30m | 219.96m | 257.65m | 313.70m |
| Pre-Tax Profit | 10.57m | 41.34m | 69.14m | 78.05m | 93.43m |

Sources: *Corporate World* April 1994; *KLSE Annual Companies Handbook* 21(2), 1996: 457

Kedah (Mahathir and Daim's home state) and secretary of the UMNO division headed by Daim. Rasip is reputedly also closely associated with Daim (*The Star* 27 April 1992; Gomez and Jomo 1997: 113–14). By December 1995, eight of the top 10 shareholders of Ekran were nominee companies, making it very difficult to identify key shareholders of the company; the other two shareholders were Ting and his wife, who together held a 26.3 per cent stake (*KLSE Annual Companies Handbook* 21 (2), 1996: 453–8).

Ekran's rise was rapid, with almost RM14 billion worth of contracts secured by the company during the period 1991 to 1993 (see also Table 4.6). Some of these were overseas contracts – in Iran, the Philippines, Vietnam and China (*Far Eastern Economic Review* 10 March 1994; *Malaysian Business* 16 March 1994). In early 1997, Ekran secured – from the Kedah state government – a RM8 billion land reclamation contract[22] (*The Star* 21 February 1997). The most important contract Ekran secured, however, was in January 1994, when it was awarded – without tender – a RM15 billion contract to build the Bakun dam in Sarawak, Malaysia's largest ever privatized project. The build-operate-own (BOO) contract was originally to be awarded to the Sarawak government's utility company, Sarawak Electricity Supply Corporation (SESCO). SESCO was then to be involved in a reverse takeover of publicly-listed Dunlop Estates Bhd, controlled by T.K. Lim (who had taken over Multi-Purpose Holdings), giving the Sarawak state government control over a publicly-listed company. However, despite having no experience in the construction of dams, Ekran secured the entire privatized project through Daim's intervention (see *Asian Wall Street Journal* 2 February 1994). Through this contract, Ekran became the only company to receive (from the government) an IPP licence to produce and transmit electricity; the other IPPs issued by the government have only been to produce electricity for sale to Tenaga. Apart from dam construction and revenue from energy supply once the dam is operational, there were expected to be numerous other spin-offs from the project. A 165-kilometre road has to be constructed for RM350 million. The timber revenue from the area to be inundated (bigger than the land area of Singapore) was estimated to be worth about RM2 billion, the cables required for the project have been estimated to cost RM3–5 billion, and the electrical equipment for the project has been estimated to cost at least RM2 billion. There were also plans to build resorts around the man-made lake in the dam area. The project was expected to be completed by August 2003 (*Far Eastern*

*Economic Review* 10 March 1994; *Malaysian Business* 16 March 1994; *The Star* 22 November 1996).

To implement the Bakun dam project, Ekran incorporated two companies – Bakun Hydroelectrical Corporation Sdn Bhd (BHC), which would construct and own the dam, and Bakun Management Sdn Bhd, which would be responsible for overseeing the implementation of the project. Former SESCO chairman, Bujang Nor, was appointed chairman of Bakun Management, while the managing director of the company is a former SESCO engineer, Mohamad Danel Abong (*Asiamoney* March 1995). To raise the funds to finance the construction of the dam, equity in BHC is to be acquired by Ekran (32 per cent), the Sarawak state government (19 per cent), and SESCO (nine per cent), while five per cent of the equity was to be held by each of the following entities linked to the federal government: the Employees' Provident Fund (EPF), the state-owned investment holding company, Khazanah Holdings, and publicly-listed Tenaga.[23] The remaining 25 per cent BHC equity was to be sold with public-listing on the KLSE. BHC would be initially capitalized at RM100 million, with its paid-up equity rising to RM1.5 billion upon stock exchange listing (*The Edge* 21 April 1997). The BHC stock is expected to be priced between RM1.80 and RM2.00 per share.[24]

In June 1996, Ekran announced it would be subcontracting the construction of the dam to a consortium of international companies led by the Swedish-Swiss engineering firm, Asea Brown Boveri (ABB). The other members of the consortium include Cia Brasileira de Projetos e Obras (CBPO), Brazil's largest construction company, South Korea's Hyundai Engineering & Construction, and Mexico's Ingenieros Civiles Associados S.A. de C.V.. This engineering,

Table 4.6 Ekran Bhd: Sectoral Breakdown in Terms of Turnover and Pre-Tax Profits, 1995 (RM million)

| Sector | Turnover | Pre-Tax Profit |
| --- | --- | --- |
| Investment Holding | 2.1 | 0.8 |
| Telecommunications Trading Services | 9.0 | 2.4 |
| Trading & Extraction of Timber | 21.2 | 6.2 |
| Property Development | 281.4 | 82.1 |
| Production of Electricity |  | (0.5) |

Source: *KLSE Annual Companies Handbook* 21 (2), 1996: 458

procurement and construction (EPC) contract involves construction of the dam at an approximate cost of RM2.8 billion, while the cost of building the transmission system from the dam across the South China Sea to the peninsula is estimated at RM10 billion. All four firms were to be involved in the dam construction, while ABB would build the transmission line. However, in July 1996, Ekran issued a statement that 40 per cent of the works to have been awarded to the ABB-led consortium had instead been contracted to four companies controlled by Ting, ostensibly because, according to Ting, 'if you don't take this portion (of the contracts from the EPC contract) now, nobody will get anything. They (ABB) will have all sorts of reasons not to give contracts to local companies' (quoted in *New Straits Times* 13 July 1996). The total value of these contracts amounted to RM9 billion.

In November 1994, Ekran had executed a reverse takeover of an ailing publicly-listed company, Granite Industries Bhd, controlled by Samsudin Abu Hassan, an erstwhile business protégé of Daim. Through a share-swap, 97 million new Granite shares were issued to acquire Ting's company Diamond League Sdn Bhd. In 1996, Ting had 26.28 per cent of Granite's equity, while Samsudin's stake in the company amounted to 11.54 per cent (*KLSE Annual Companies Handbook* 21 (1), 1996: 177–82). The takeover appeared to be an attempt to bail out Samsudin from a business quagmire that he had landed himself in after Granite's attempts to venture into gaming in China failed to materialize. Ekran was believed to have been interested in channeling eco-tourism projects, such as hotels, resorts and recreation parks, in the Bakun vicinity, to the company (see *The Star* 22 November 1994). In July 1996, Ekran awarded Granite two contracts – a RM600 million contract to operate a quarry to produce and supply rocks for construction of the Bakun dam and a RM500 million contract to provide site accommodation for the five thousand workers to be employed during the project (*The Star* 13 July 1996).

In 1995, Ting maneuvered a takeover of a 32.82 per cent stake in another publicly-listed company, Wembley Industries Holdings Bhd, controlled by Ishak Ismail and Mohd Sarit Yusoh, both UMNO members associated with Deputy Prime Minister Anwar Ibrahim (Gomez 1994: 144). Interestingly, Anwar – who had reputedly been at odds with Daim over the award of many privatized contracts to businessmen aligned to Daim – was believed to be privately opposed to the Bakun dam project. Anwar, however, was appointed by Prime Minister Mahathir to head the cabinet committee to implement the project.[25] Since market analysts questioned the wisdom of Ting's decision to buy into Wembley, this acquisition was believed to be an attempt by Ting to ingratiate himself with the Deputy Prime Minister. In 1996, Ekran awarded Wembley a supplies contract for building materials, concrete batching plants and cement containers for the Bakun dam project (*The Star* 13 July 1996).

Wembley is also expected to undertake a RM1 billion contract to supply steel fabrication and structure supports for the construction of the Bakun dam, as well as the supply of cement containers and concrete batching plants. There was some speculation in August 1996 that Wembley would sub-contract this to PPES Concrete Sdn Bhd, a subsidiary of publicly-listed Cement Manufacturers Sarawak Bhd, renamed Cahya Mata Sarawak Bhd (CMS) (see *Malaysian Business* 1 August 1996). CMS is headed by Onn Mahmud, brother of the Chief Minister of Sarawak, Taib Mahmud, who has a 10.3 per cent stake in the company, while two other directors of the company are Taib's sons, Mahmud Abu Bekir Taib and Sulaiman Abdul Rahman Taib, each of whom also has a 12 per cent stake in CMS (*KLSE Annual Companies Handbook* 21 (3), 1996: 88–94).[26]

When Ting acquired FCW in 1992, he was quoted as saying, 'We just wanted FCW. We wanted to diversify our business and the cable business is synergistic to our turnkey timber construction business' (*Malaysian Business* 1 October 1992). Yet, in December 1993, just over a year after its takeover of FCW, and despite securing the Bakun dam project, Ekran had sold FCW Industries to Rasip Haron, Robert Tan Hua Choon and Mohd Noordin Daud, in the process obtaining an extraordinary gain of RM78 million for its brief investment in the company (*Malaysian Business* 16 March 1994). Tan and Rasip were also shareholders of Jasa Kita Bhd, a company listed on the KLSE's second board. Tan, who is also believed to be closely associated with Daim, was also a minority shareholder of Pacific Chemicals Bhd, a publicly-listed company in which he once had majority ownership, before divesting much of his equity in the company to Ting. Tan also has an interest in another listed concern, UCM Industrial Corporation Bhd, a manufacturer of automobile air-conditioning systems.[27] Other shareholders of UCM equity include the Prime Minister's (second) politician-cum-businessman son, Mokhzani Mahathir, and a Daim protégé, Mohd Razali Abdul Rahman, who was involved in the privatized management buy-out of Peremba Bhd (*KLSE Annual Companies Handbook* 21 (4), 1996: 1421; see also Gomez 1995). Through a private company, Spanco Sdn Bhd, Tan was the main beneficiary of a major privatized contract from the government. The contract involved acquisition of government-owned vehicles which would be leased back to the government, with Tan's company responsible for the maintenance of the vehicles. The contract was expected to generate an annual turnover of around RM1.5 billion (*Malaysian Business* 16 August 1993 and 1 April 1994). After securing ownership of FCW Industries from Ting, Tan and Rasip injected the company into publicly-listed Bata (M) Bhd, securing a majority 62 per cent ownership of the company. Bata was renamed FCW Holdings Bhd, giving Tan ownership of another listed company, but the shoe business was re-sold to the original shareholders of Bata (*Malaysian Business* 1 April 1994). FCW was expected to receive part of the contract to supply the cables required for the Bakun dam project (*The Star* 22 November 1996).

Pacific Chemicals was incorporated on 4 December 1968 as a subsidiary of the US-based multinational company, The Dow Chemical Company; it was listed on the KLSE two years later. Pacific Chemicals was originally involved in the manufacture and sale of agricultural chemicals. In 1993, Pacific Chemicals acquired, through a share-swap, Usama Industries Sdn Bhd, whose shareholders included Ting with 55 per cent, and Anuar Abdul Razak with 4.5 per cent, while the remaining 40.5 per cent equity was owned by Majaharta Sdn Bhd (*The Star* 20 June 1995).[28] Majaharta was incorporated on 8 July 1992, and has a paid-up capital of RM14.93 million, which is equally shared by Mahmud Abu Bekir Taib and Sulaiman Abdul Rahman Abdul Taib, sons of the Sarawak Chief Minister, who are also directors of Majaharta, with their sisters, Jailah Hamidah Taib and Hanifah Hajar Taib.[29] Usama Industries is involved in trading logs and production of sawn timber. This gave Ting control of Pacific Chemicals, which ceased its agrochemicals business to concentrate on timber-based activities. As of June 1996, seven of Pacific Chemicals' top 10 shareholders were nominee companies; Ting is the largest shareholder, with 22.14 per cent of the company's equity, while Robert Tan, Pacific Chemicals' deputy chairman, has a 2.46 per cent stake. Majaharta is Pacific Chemicals' second largest shareholder, with a 16.73 per cent stake (*KLSE Annual Companies Handbook* 21 (4), 1996: 235–7). In 1995, Ekran awarded Pacific Chemicals a contract to manage and clear a 17,750ha forest area as part of the Bakun dam project; the total area to be cleared for the project is approximately 69,500ha (*The Star* 20 June 1995). Pacific Chemicals was also awarded a RM1.2 billion contract to supply and install overhead electricity transmission lines, which it is expected to manufacture either on its own or in a joint-venture with foreign investors (*Malaysian Business* 1 August 1996).

PWE Industries was incorporated as PDL (Asia) Sdn Bhd on 8 August 1974 and commenced operations as a subsidiary of PDL Holdings Ltd, a company listed on the New Zealand stock exchange and involved in the manufacturing and marketing of electrical wiring accessories. PWE obtained a manufacturing licence in September 1981 after two companies involved in the manufacture and distribution of electric appliances, the British-based Scholes Group plc and Clipsal (M) Sdn Bhd, acquired interests in PWE. This enabled PWE to expand the range of electrical wiring accessories it manufactures and to widen its market. In March 1996, however, after Ting secured a 56.28 per cent stake in PWE, the manufacturing business of the company was transferred to Clipsal Manufacturing (M) Sdn Bhd, while 60 per cent of the company's equity was divested to Clipsal Industries (Holdings) Ltd. PWE simultaneously acquired timber rights for part of the Bakun dam area from Equitoral Timber Marketing Sdn Bhd, thus moving PWE into the business of extracting and selling timber logs. Ting had a 50 per cent stake in Equitoral Timber Marketing, which in 1992 had three timber licence concessions collectively valued at RM231.25 million (*The Star* 20 June 1995).[30] In July 1996, PWE was awarded sub-contract work for the dam project involving the installation of three submarine cables for approximately RM1.2 billion and a 30-year contract for the operation and maintenance of the dam's hydroelectric facilities estimated to be worth at least RM150 million per annum. As in the case of the other listed companies controlled by Ting, seven of the 10 largest shareholders of PWE are nominee companies, which collectively own almost 32 per cent of the company's equity. The government-controlled Lembaga Urusan and Tabung Haji (LUTH, or Pilgrims' Management and Fund Board) owns 7.49 per cent of PWE stock (*KLSE Annual Companies Handbook* 21 (4), 1996: 1294–8).

Ekran has continued to ensure that it completes the projects it has secured; it has also been growing through a spate of rapid acquisitions, mostly undertaken through reverse takeovers. For example, Ekran's share capital was increased through the injection of Ting's family company, Woodhouse, in return for equity. FCW was taken over through a share-swap, as were Granite and Pacific Chemicals. Companies taken over by Ekran, for instance Pacific Chemicals (Bata can also be included here), were listed, and foreign-

## Chinese Business, Liberalization and Ascendance

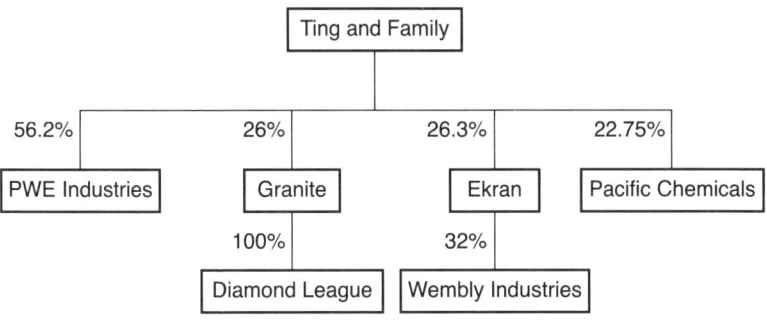

*Figure 4.4* Ekran Bhd: Simplified Corporate Structure, 1995–96

controlled with small capitalization. Ekran's takeover of companies with a small capital base and diffuse shareholdings has been noted from the time of its first major acquisition, i.e. of FCW. When asked why he had acquired FCW and, in the process, secured a backdoor listing for Woodhouse, even though Woodhouse had the track record to secure listing on its own, Ting said, 'Firstly, we wanted to diversify into the cable business. We also found that FCW's shareholding was well spread, so if we succeeded in the takeover, it would mean we would immediately meet the shareholding spread and get listed faster' (quoted in *Malaysian Business* 1 October 1992). Following the takeover of these companies, a number of trends have been noted. Ting channeled lucrative Bakun dam contracts to the each of these companies to increase their profitability. Also, lucrative companies like FCW have been sold off by Ting to business associates for rather hefty capital gains (see Figure 4.4 for structure of Ekran Bhd).

## Conclusion

Both Francis Yeoh and Ting Pek Khiing were sons of businessmen, but while Yeoh's family had established a reputation in construction, Ting's father was a small-scale trader. Thus, while Yeoh had a bourgeois upbringing and received tertiary training in the UK as an engineer, Ting had a more modest background and was only educated up to the secondary level. Although Yeoh took over a well-developed publicly-listed construction company, and Ting built-up a timber-based construction company with a reputation for fulfilling contracts expeditiously, both men have demonstrated an entrepreneurial capability. Yeoh and Ting have built on the economic favors they have secured from the state. With state help, they have also ventured abroad.

Ting originally developed a well-integrated company in his original vocation, timber-based construction. Ting started out with a vertical and horizontal business expansion pattern, developing a manufacturing base for products required for his timber construction business. However, after his involvement in the controversial Bakun dam project, a more diversified style of business expansion has emerged. The YTL Corp group has shown some vertical integration in its construction business, through Buildcon, the country's largest ready-mixed concrete manufacturer. After securing an IPP licence from the government, the YTL Corp group has sought to acquire and develop technological expertise in power supply by entering into joint-ventures with foreign companies. In the case of the Bakun dam project, only jobs which Ting felt he did not have the capacity to undertake himself were sub-contracted.

Ting apparently has much closer business ties with the political elite. Ting's recent business deals appear to be closely associated with companies indirectly linked with UMNO leaders and family members of the Sarawak Chief Minister, particularly in connection with the privatized Bakun dam project. This case study of Ting indicates how 'political business' operates in Malaysia in the 1990s. Ting's apparently impressive capacity for fulfilling contracts put him in good stead with influential politicians. In return, ostensibly as part of the government's desire to channel economic opportunities to businessmen who can fulfill their contractual obligations efficiently, Ting has had access to more government projects. However, Ting has also had to ensure that the gains from these projects are shared with elements of the political elite. For example, after being awarded the potentially lucrative Bakun dam project, the companies that Ekran took over – namely Granite and Wembley – were ailing concerns controlled by businessmen or politicians aligned with UMNO leaders. These companies were awarded sub-contracts to help improve their financial position. Other companies which have secured contracts arising from the Bakun dam project include those in which Chief Minister Taib's family members have interests. This suggests that in return for being awarded the dam contract, Ting has shared some benefits of the projects with some of the politically influential. Clearly, the form of accommodation has changed since the first NEP decade (see Chapters 2 and 3). In the case of YTL Corp, however, although Yeoh has utilized the IPP licence he secured from the state well and although he appears to be close to the Prime Minister and the Perak royal family, there is little evidence that the YTL Corp group is closely associated in business deals involving UMNO politicians or well-connected businessmen. Historically, the YTL Corp group's business deals have involved state agencies; joint-ventures in construction and property development projects have been established with the SEDCs, UDA and KTM.

The varied forms of accommodation are also reflected in the ownership patterns of the groups controlled by Yeoh and Ting respectively. Among the largest Bumiputera shareholders of YTL Corp is a state agency, the armed forces' provident fund, LTAT, which is also the largest Bumiputera shareholder of Buildcon equity. There are no prominent Bumiputeras among the directors of YTL Corp and Buildcon. Ekran's shareholders have included Shuaib Lazim (an UMNO senator closely associated with Mahathir and Daim) and two sons of Taib Mahmud, Chief Minister of Sarawak. When Ekran had achieved prominence as the Bakun Dam contractor in 1995, eight of its top 10 shareholders were nominee companies. The major shareholders of Pacific Chemicals also include Taib's children. Moreover, while the Ekran group now includes companies once associated with UMNO businessmen, this is not the case with companies in the YTL Corp group.

There is no indication that Yeoh and Ting have tried to establish business links with other Chinese businessmen in Malaysia. The only notable ethnic Chinese business partner in Ting's corporate deals is Robert Tan Hua Choon, who has been more closely linked with Daim Zainuddin. Both Ting and Yeoh are more closely associated with prominent Malay leaders. Although Yeoh and Ting have a number of business ventures abroad, including some projects in China, there is little evidence of their attempts to work with other leading Chinese capitalists in the region. Rather, Yeoh was aided by the Malaysian government in his attempted takeover of a power supply company controlled by Gordon Wu. In his business ventures, Yeoh has developed business ties with multinational companies, including German power equipment company, Siemens AG, and the UK-based construction company, John Laing plc. In both cases, YTL Corp seems to have tried to use these joint-ventures to acquire new technology, while the Malaysian company has facilitated the entry of these two multinationals into new markets in Asia.

Although a third generation has emerged in the YTL Corp group, there is no evidence of much dispersion of control, although there has been some division of stock among the family members themselves. There also does not appear to be an appreciable reduction of control of YTL Corp despite the restructuring required to accommodate Bumiputera equity participation. Although it is difficult to gauge the identity of Ekran's shareholders given the large number of nominee companies, Ting evidently remains in control of company policy and management decisions. However, given Ting's close links with the political leadership and the circumstances in which he has taken control of some politically-linked companies, it is unclear if he is holding these companies in trust or if these companies are now under his control. In the YTL Corp group, policy and management decisions still remain in the hands of the family, even though a professional management team has been established. Unlike those who emerged in the 1970s, Yeoh and Ting have not involved the YTL Corp and Ekran groups in an intricate system of crossholdings to consolidate their corporate holdings in Malaysia.

# Conclusion 5

## Chinese Business Networking – Dispelling the Myth

We began this study by questioning how Chinese businessmen have managed to develop their business interests despite operating in an environment apparently hostile to their interests. Since the nominal value of corporate stock owned by Chinese almost doubled during the NEP decades, we also questioned whether intra-ethnic business linkages have been crucial to the development of Chinese capital in Malaysia.

This historical overview reveals that the rise of the most prominent Malaysian Chinese capitalists had little to do with intra-ethnic business networking, locally or abroad. With the exception of Robert Kuok – and Khoo Kay Peng to a much lesser extent – Lim Goh Tong, Loh Boon Siew, William Cheng, Vincent Tan, Francis Yeoh and Ting Pek Khiing have not established, nor are they even attempting to establish, much intra-ethnic business links locally and abroad. Nor is there any evidence of a strong identity among leading Chinese businessmen as an 'interest group' in Malaysia. In fact, there is much evidence that the implementation of the NEP divided Chinese capitalists more than unified them. There is much competition among Chinese businessmen to secure government contracts. It also appears that differences in access to the state among Chinese businessmen has divided the Chinese business community. There is also little evidence of intra-ethnic sharing of these concessions through joint ventures with other Chinese businessmen. Rather, there is much evidence that when big Chinese businessmen have tried to work together, these endeavors have not always been very fruitful or have ended up in acrimony. The well-publicized feuds between Khoo Kay Peng and Tan Chin Nam, Vincent Tan and Khoo

Kay Peng, Vincent Tan and T.K. Lim, as well as Quek Leng Chan and Khoo Kay Peng are some better-known examples.

The significant point that emerges from this study is that in spite of the NEP, the business deals effected by the prominent Chinese capitalists have transcended the ethnic factor. During the corporatization movement, when the MCA tried to overcome the class divisions among the Chinese by propounding arguments along ethnic lines, MCA leaders were, initially at least, successful in getting many Chinese to subscribe to Multi-Purpose Holdings' shares and to participate in the numerous co-operatives that mushroomed under this movement. Yet, even though the corporatization movement attempted to mobilize Chinese capital to counter the growing influence of state capital (perceived by most non-Bumiputeras as Bumiputera capital) during the 1970s, there were business deals between Multi-Purpose Holdings and leading Malays, including Daim Zainuddin, then a prominent businessman, and Ghafar Baba, then a senior vice president of UMNO. In the case of Ghafar, there was even an attempt to jointly secure control of Dunlop Estates Bhd. Thus, it is understandable why Chinese capitalists saw Multi-Purpose Holdings and the new breed of MCA leaders who led the corporatization movement as a threat to their economic interests. Some of the new MCA leaders were of modest class origins and sought to create a business base for themselves through the corporatization movement. The abuses by these politicians contributed to the Pan-El and the deposit-taking co-operatives (DTC) scandals, which led to the demise of the corporatization movement.

Attempts at cultivating long-term business links among the Chinese business elite have not been successful. This is not only attributable to the different business styles of individual businessmen; it has also been a question of trying to retain control or dominance over the business empire created. This desire not to relinquish control has been another reason why leading Chinese businessmen have not been willing to support the corporatization movement. This trait, however, is not attributable only to ethnic Chinese, but is common among owners of most large business enterprises.

Chinese co-operation along dialect or clan lines has diminished significantly. For example, even though most of the businessmen studied here are Hokkien, common sub-ethnic identity has not contributed to significant networking among them, even though Hokkiens have had some history of business cooperation, especially in response to economic crisis. The Singapore-based OCBC Bank, a

## Conclusion

merger of three Hokkien-owned banks, was established to deal with the impact of the Great Depression on Chinese companies during the early 1930s. Although the Southern Bank and Ban Hin Lee Bank are both Hokkien-owned banks, they have been subject to takeover bids by other Hokkiens. Khoo Kay Peng attempted a takeover of Southern Bank, while the Ban Hin Lee Bank was stalked – for a long period – by Quek Leng Chan, until he gained control of MUI Bank from Khoo.

Such predatory attempts on Chinese banks by other ethnic Chinese have transpired during a period when public enterprises and well-connected Bumiputeras have been making significant inroads into the finance sector. In 1970, before implementation of the NEP, Malay ownership in banking and insurance amounted to a mere 3.3 per cent, while Chinese held 24.3 per cent. By the late 1980s, Bumiputeras owned of more than 50 per cent of the equity in 10 of the 22 domestic banks, most of which had been incorporated by Chinese. In 1988, the five largest banks accounted for 53 per cent of total bank resources, 55 per cent of total bank deposits, and 50 per cent of total bank loans (Gomez and Jomo 1997: 60–1). The largest two local banks then were Malayan Banking and Bank Bumiputra, both government controlled, the next three were UMBC, Public Bank and the D&C Bank. Of these five banks, only Bank Bumiputra was not Chinese incorporated. Yet, with the exception of Public Bank, the other three banks had fallen under Bumiputera or state control by the mid-1980s.

Despite this remarkable increase in Bumiputera and state ownership and control of the banking sector during the NEP era, there were minimal attempts by the Chinese to combine their then vast banking, finance and insurance activities. Presently, even though the government has been encouraging banks to merge their activities to create more formidable financial corporations, there have been no attempts by Chinese-owned banks to create ethnic-based alliances. One reason for this could be the impact of the DTC scandal on the Chinese. The scandal appears to have made the Chinese very cautious of venturing into ethnic collaborative efforts in the face of the growth of Bumiputera capital. This scandal, which badly affected many Chinese, is probably one reason why Chinese banks have refrained from undertaking efforts to merge their activities.

Malaysian Chinese businessmen do not appear to be concentrating on developing business ties with other Southeast Asian Chinese businessmen, though there have been a few business deals among some of them. Even during the 1970s, when there was much movement of Chinese capital abroad in response to NEP policies, there was little evidence that Malaysian Chinese were working together overseas, or with other ethnic Chinese in East Asia. During the 1970s, their overseas investments tended to concentrate on real estate and hotels, rather than on more productive enterprises. Although there is much more investment abroad in the case of the big businessmen studied, the reasons for overseas ventures in the 1990s appear to be different. Their ventures offshore are, in many instances, for vertical-type corporate growth and expansion, with some companies investing in manufacturing. For example, Lim has been concentrating on the leisure industry, Yeoh is trying to develop an international empire in power generation, while Cheng, despite his much-diversified operations, has invested heavily in manufacturing, particularly in China. Investments in China have been growing, with all eight involved in ventures there. However, most of these investments in China are in businesses that are independently owned and managed. There is little evidence of much networking by Malaysian Chinese with other ethnic Chinese businessmen in the region in their attempts to seek out business opportunities in China.

## Corporate Growth: Patronage and Entrepreneurship

This brings us back to the question: how has Chinese capital managed to grow in Malaysia? In the case of all the businessmen studied here, with the exception of Loh, a combination of factors has contributed to the growth of their companies: productive, entrepreneurial deployment of economic benefits secured from the state, effective use of the stock market to secure funds to finance the expansion of their groups, and cultivation of patrons from the political leadership. Loh, however, had no direct links with the Malay political elite, did not secure even one concession from the state, nor did he use the stock market much to develop his corporate base.

Although the seven other Chinese businessmen have benefited from some form of state patronage, there have evidently been varying degrees of dependence on the Malay leadership among them to secure benefits from the state. In the case of Lim and Cheng, for instance, one crucial licence from the state was sufficient to build a large business empire. It appears that companies which have established business ties with influential politicians have had greater success in securing licences and contracts from the state. The

## Conclusion

politically well-connected Tan has been privy to numerous privatized contracts and licences from the state, while the Ting case study suggests that companies linked to family members of the Sarawak Chief Minister and business associates of Daim have also benefited from the Bakun dam project. YTL Corp's recent forays into power generation have been attributed to Yeoh's close ties with the Prime Minister. However, unlike the case of Ting, there is little evidence that companies owned by UMNO leaders or their relatives have benefited from the IPP licence or projects awarded to YTL Corp. Clearly, most of these businessmen have been competent enough to build on the benefits they have received from the state.

All eight Chinese businessmen have shown an ability to seize and exploit opportunities that have emerged, indicating their entrepreneurial dynamism, although there have been significant variations in entrepreneurial style. Kuok, Loh and Cheng have acquired a strong reputation in a particular industry and have also developed manufacturing interests. Kuok, recognizing the niches to be cornered in sugar and flour milling, secured licences to virtually monopolize this sector and even held monopolies for short periods. Loh recognized the potential market for Honda motorcycles in the Malaysian economy, and introduced Japanese (Toyota) motor cars in Malaysia. Cheng built on his early experience in the steel industry to develop well-integrated steel manufacturing operation. Ting and Yeoh have done well in construction, while YTL Corp has successfully diversified into power generation. Even in the case of Khoo and Tan, reputedly the two best politically-connected businessmen, the former developed MUI Bank while Tan sought and captured the lucrative McDonald's and Singer franchises for the Malaysian market. Although there is evidence to suggest that Tan has not tapped the maximum potential for the privatized projects he has secured from the state, particularly the Sports Toto gaming operations, Tan ensured that the group has not been too dependent on gaming. Lim recognized the potential that Genting Highlands offered in the leisure industry, though he has benefited most from the group's casino monopoly. However, Lim's involvement in other ventures in plantations, manufacturing and power generation still do not contribute significantly to the Genting group's total turnover.

All eight cases studies showed diversification in growth, usually in the pursuit of potentially profitable ventures. The rise of politically well-connected Bumiputera capitalists who have ventured into all key economic sectors, and the need for Chinese capitalists to accommodate them, has had a bearing on the latter's desire to diversify their interests in various economic sectors. In the 1990s, the state has increased competition in some areas to improve efficiency. The only group among the eight to have a monopoly is Genting through its casino licence, but even here, the group is always under threat of having its licence revoked.

These case studies also reveal the complexities of and diversities in 'political business' interactions. The actual experiences of these businessmen with politicians and political parties defy any easy categorization as there are significant differences in the nature of the political ties cultivated by Chinese businessmen. Loh was rather independent of Malay politicians, and basically relied on his own business acumen to develop. While Kuok and Cheng have shown similar independence, they have better ties with the Malay elite, and have secured important concessions from the state. Such ties are further complicated by the role played by influential Malays in these Chinese companies. The KL-Kepong group has had links with Razaleigh Hamzah, but Lee Loy Seng has not been privy to major concessions from the state, even during the long period that Razaleigh served as Finance Minister. On the other hand, the Hong Leong group's links to Finance Minister Anwar Ibrahim are indirect, but the group managed to gain control of a major bank under rather favorable terms. Finally, there are those businessmen who are so closely associated with UMNO politicians and well-connected businessmen that it is difficult to differentiate between those corporate assets that belong to them and those that appear to be held in trust for others; this, to some extent, appears to be the case for Tan and Ting. How political patronage has been reciprocated is even more difficult to ascertain, although some businessmen have acknowledged that they have contributed to UMNO's coffers. In the case of the Bakun dam project, family members of the Sarawak Chief Minister acquired substantial interests in the potentially lucrative project.

Although there has been a need to ensure Bumiputera equity participation, as required under the NEP, all eight businessmen do not appear to have lost appreciable control of their companies. In some cases, i.e. Perlis Plantations, Genting, Oriental Holdings and YTL Corp, a second or third generation has emerged, and although this has led to some diffusion of corporate stock among family members, policy and management decisions still remain in the hands

## Conclusion

of one individual or family. The use of professional managers has, however, been on the rise since the late 1980s.

Another question needs to be answered: Are the Chinese still as widely resented by the Malays for the extent of their ownership and control of the Malaysian economy? There is adequate evidence that after 27 years of the NEP, enough political and economic power has been channeled to the Bumiputera community, albeit to an elite minority, to reduce the scale of resentment that has prevailed prior to 1970 (see Gomez and Jomo 1997). The new Bumiputera middle class is increasingly confident and capable of managing on its own. Thus, many of them, especially politicians in UMNO who see the party as a means to secure access to concessions, do not like to see Chinese being awarded the concessions they expect to be reserved for Bumiputeras. Government leaders, however, recognize the importance of Chinese capital for economic growth, as underlined during the mid-1980s recession, which was exacerbated by capital flight and limited investment by Chinese businessmen. Moreover, the Barisan Nasional leadership has found it desirable to cultivate non-Bumiputera political support, in part by providing Chinese with more avenues to secure contracts and other business opportunities from the state (see Gomez, 1996c). With growing authoritarianism and greater concentration of power in the hands of the executive since the mid-1980s, and with Mahathir Mohamad consolidating his position in government, the Prime Minister seems to be less concerned with the politics of patronage than those at lower echelons of the party (see Munro-Kua 1996; Gomez and Jomo 1997). Thus, Mahathir can also afford to distribute economic favors to his favorite non-Malays without too much fear for his own political position. Having entrenched his political position, Mahathir seems more concerned with achieving his development agenda, particularly in taking Malaysia to fully developed status by the year 2020. With this objective in mind, he appears to be increasingly rewarding those who show entrepreneurial skills. This can be seen, to some extent, in the case of Yeoh and Ting, which would account for why this new breed of Chinese businessmen are quickly emerging as major corporate players. However, the uncertain future of Malay politics means that Chinese groups can never be totally sure of the consequences of factional rivalry, particularly in the post-Mahathir era. The objections of UMNO members to state economic privileges and benefits accorded to Chinese businessmen continue to persist, and how this issue is addressed by future UMNO leaders struggling to consolidate their positions is obviously a matter of considerable concern to Chinese businessmen. In these circumstances, in order to continue to accumulate and ascend, most big Chinese capitalists in Malaysia may well have to continue to accommodate well-connected Malays.

# Postscript

Just as this study was being completed, Malaysia – along with a number of other countries in East Asia – was engulfed in a financial crisis which resulted in a fall in the value of its currency, the ringgit, and a precipitous drop of the stock prices of publicly-listed companies. Between July 1997 and early 1998, the ringgit fell from RM2.4 to the US dollar to a record low of RM4.9. The Composite Index of the Kuala Lumpur Stock Exchange (KLSE) lost more than half its value when it plunged by nearly 800 points, from a high of 1271 in February 1997 down to around 480 at the turn of the new year. Much of the blame for this crisis in Malaysia was attributed by Prime Minister Mahathir Mohamad to currency speculators and international investors, who had, at astonishing speed, pulled out from the region. To a large extent, the Prime Minister was right. Between August and September 1998, about a month after Thailand was first affected by a massive currency devaluation, it was estimated that between US$25 billion and US$40 billion had flowed from Asia's equity and currency markets (*Newsweek* 15 September 1997).

Malaysia's phenomenal economic progress from 1988 had been largely due to such capital flows. The government's economic liberalization efforts in response to the mid-1980s recession had led to a phenomenal increase in direct foreign investment (DFI), particularly in the manufacturing sector (see Table 4.1). Economic liberalization also enabled foreign ownership of corporate equity to increase from 24.6 per cent to 27.7 per cent between 1988 and 1995.[1] As mentioned in Chapter 1, Malaysia had the highest rate of net capital inflows as a percentage of gross domestic investment in East Asia, which contributed to the remarkable rise of the KLSE's market capitalization during the 1990s (see Tables 1.3 and 1.4). However, until the crisis erupted, there had been little state subservience to foreign – or Chinese – capital, thus catching the government unawares of the potential repercussions of such liberalization, particularly the inadequate regulations to check rapid capital flows. The financial crisis also exposed many of the problems that had existed in the Malaysian economy, in spite of the consistent growth it had registered since 1988. Many of these issues have already been dealt with here, in particular the impact of political patronage – popularly referred to as cronyism – involving the abuse of the state by UMNO leaders for vested interests (see Chapter 4). One issue which needs further elaboration in the light of this crisis is the abuse of financial institutions, controlled by the government or by politically well-aligned businessmen, to lend aggressively, and allegedly imprudently, to select individuals to fund the rapid expansion of their corporate empire.

In December 1997, Malaysia's outstanding debt-to-GDP ratio was 153 per cent, one of the highest in the world; however, the bulk of its debt was in local, not foreign, currency (*Far Eastern Economic Review* 30 April 1998). A massive RM39 billion was loaned by banks for share acquisition, almost 45 per cent of which was given to individuals (*Euromoney* April 1998). When stock prices plunged, the impact of loan defaults on the financial sector was significant. The inherent weaknesses in the Malaysian financial sector which permitted such unsound disbursement of loans was a consequence of the politics of patronage. Figure 1 provides a simplified model of how such patronage has been practiced within the economy, the repercussions of such abuse, and the benefits accruing to ruling politicians from the practice of political patronage.[2]

Politicians abuse their hegemony to distribute to party members state-controlled concessions in the form of licenses, contracts, subsidies and privatized projects. Funds to acquire these concessions are secured through favorable loans from banks and other financial institutions owned or controlled by the government. Distribution of such concessions to party members helps leaders secure or promote their positions. Some recipients of these concessions may use numerous corporate maneuvers, most commonly shares-for-assets swaps and reverse takeovers, to capture control of publicly-listed companies. These companies are, in turn, used for other types of corporate maneuvers, including mergers, acquisitions and takeovers, to develop their business interests. As share prices escalate, the stock is used as security to secure more bank loans for further acquisitions. Such corporate strategies were one primary factor that appreciably

*Postscript*

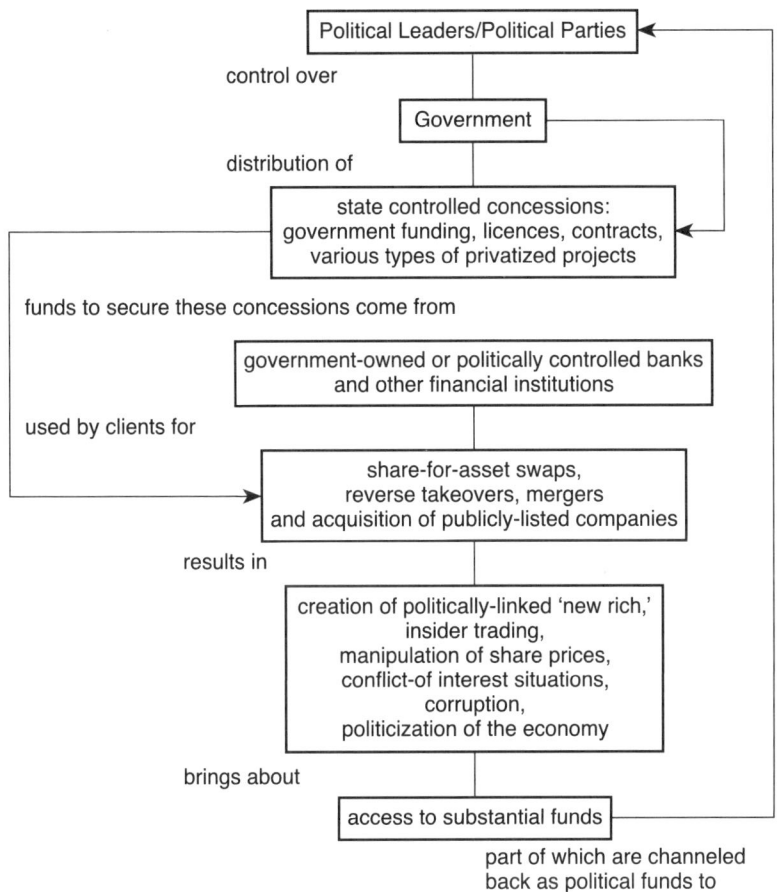

*Figure P.1* Simplified Model of the Practice of Political Patronage

helped to increase the KLSE's market capitalization from the late 1980s.[3]

Political patronage, sophisticated but unproductive corporate maneuvers, and the rise in market value of quoted stock have contributed to the emergence of a politically well-connected 'new rich', most of whom are Malays (see Table 4.2). The emergence of this new rich has led to a concentration of corporate wealth, while selective distribution of state concessions has resulted in corruption, business scandals and conflict-of-interest involving senior government leaders. Companies controlled by well-connected businessmen have been involved in insider trading and manipulation of stock prices. Such political patronage creates avenues for politicians to gain access to large sums of money for political activities, particularly to fund campaigns during party and general elections.

The extent to which financial institutions had been abused became evident when two state-owned banks, Bank Bumiputra Bhd and Sime Bank Bhd, declared huge losses in 1998. Bank Bumiputra announced that it needed a capital injection of RM750 million to stay afloat, while Sime Bank declared a loss of RM1.8 billion and required a recapitalization of at least RM1.2 billion (*The Star* 5 March 1998). This was the third time that the government had to bail out Bank Bumiputra. In 1984, the government had to channel RM2 billion to Bank Bumiputra when it declared enormous losses after its Hong Kong-based subsidiary, Bumiputra Malaysia Finance Bhd (BMF), chalked up huge bad loans, most of which had to be written off; the scandal implicated a number of UMNO leaders (see Hassan 1989). In 1989, Bank Bumiputra declared a loss of RM1.06 billion, necessitating another capital injection of about RM980 million by the government.

Sime Bank (the former United Malayan Banking Corporation Bhd [UMBC]) had been bought over by the government-controlled Malaysian multi-national corporation Sime Darby Bhd in 1996 from publicly-listed Datuk Keramat Holdings Bhd, owned by Mahathir's former political secretary Mohd Noor Yusof. During the period that Sime Bank was under the Datuk Keramat Holdings group, numerous allegations had been made of financial impropriety, including the disbursement of questionable loans (see Gomez and Jomo 1997: 56–9). In December 1997, for the first time in its recent history, the Sime Darby group declared pre-tax losses of RM1.1 billion, most of which were attributed to Sime Bank. If Sime Bank's losses were not consolidated in the group's accounts, Sime Darby would have registered a pre-tax profit of RM625 million, a 13 per cent gain compared to the pre-tax profits registered the previous year (*The Star* 8 March 1998). Eventually, the Sime Bank was divested by Sime Darby at a huge loss, to the politically well-connected Rashid Hussain, who controls the financial conglomerate Rashid Hussain Bhd (RHB) group.[4] Another major shareholder of Sime Bank before its takeover by the RHB group was UMNO's co-operative-now-turned public company, KUB (M) Bhd, which had a 30 per cent stake. The sale of Sime Bank to the RHB Group was widely seen as an attempt to bail-out the UMNO co-operative (see *The Star* 12 March 1998). Although Prime Minister Mahathir announced the suspension of some major projects, including that of the privatized Bakun Dam, his government also permitted preferential treatment for some projects and businessmen affected by the crisis. Among the projects into which state funds were pumped included Malaysia's new international airport and one of Mahathir's pet heavy industrialization projects, the steel producer Perwaja Steel Bhd, which had long been a loss-making concern. The government agreed to take over the Bakun Dam project from Ting Pek Khiing's Ekran Bhd after the latter reportedly objected to the indefinite delay in the construction of the dam (*Asian Wall Street Journal* 22 November 1997). In the process, the government also agreed to paying Ekran a compensation for the work already done on the dam project. The compensation, Deputy Prime Minister Anwar Ibrahim insisted, was 'no bailout. We will be tough on what compensation is due' (ibid.). The compensation is expected to amount to about RM700 million.[5] Ting's business problems, even before the crisis, had steadily been mounting. Ekran's long-standing dispute with its main contractor, ABB, over subcontracts which had been awarded to Malaysian companies, mainly those in the Ekran group, had come to a head, when ABB was dismissed from the project (*Asian Wall Street Journal* 8 September 1997). Even before the KLSE slump, it was becoming increasingly unlikely that Ekran would have been able to raise sufficient funds through the stock market to fund the Bakun Dam project (see *Asian Wall Street Journal* 18 June 1997). In early 1998, Wembley Industries Holdings Bhd, a listed company controlled by Ting, went into receivership. Wembley, a long-ailing company, had been acquired by Ting in 1995 from the business associates of Anwar.

A number of the newly-emerged and politically well-connected Bumiputera businessmen were also adversely affected by the crisis, the value of their corporate stock shrinking rapidly, leaving them with a severe gearing problem. Among the most prominent of these Malays, some of whom found that the value of the corporate stock had shrunk by almost 70 per cent, included Halim Saad and Mahathir's son Mirzan Mahathir. Mirzan's main public-listed company, the shipping concern Konsortium Perkapalan Bhd (KPB),[6] which was barely afloat with huge debts – one estimate was RM1.7 billion (*Far Eastern Economic Review* 19 February 1998) – was bailed out when state-owned and publicly-listed Malaysian

International Shipping Corporation Bhd (MISC) acquired, for cash, subsidiaries owned by KPB; most of these KPB subsidiaries were the companies that had been saddled with loans (*The Star* 7 March 1998). Halim Saad's public-listed construction company, United Engineers (M) Bhd, which wholly-owns the north–south highway toll-operator PLUS Bhd, took on a huge loan to acquire a 32.6 per cent stake in its quoted holding company, Renong Bhd, at a reportedly inflated price of RM2.34 billion (*The Star* 13 March 1998). Renong was reported to have debts amounting to a massive RM1.4 billion (see *Far Eastern Economic Review* 19 February 1998). Following implementation of this deal to help Renong, as UEM now found itself loaded with a huge debt burden, it was announced that the government-controlled Employees' Provident Fund (EPF) would acquire a 20 per cent stake in PLUS from UEM, reportedly for cash RM1.5 billion (see *The Star* 13 March 1998). The economic plight of businessmen like Halim Saad and Mirzan Mahathir reflected another characteristic of businessmen who had developed through significant political patronage. Many of them had concentrated their attention on services and other non-tradeables, such as construction, real property and infrastructure, all sectors that were badly affected by the crisis.

As the financial crisis deepened, the government announced that some Chinese would be allowed to take over companies owned by Malays to prevent the latter from going bankrupt. Most of the Chinese identified as possible candidates for the takeover of Malay-owned companies were those who had benefited from state patronage. Among these were Francis Yeoh, the beneficiary of the highly lucrative power generating licence, and Lim Goh Tong, who depends heavily on the renewal of his lucrative casino licence to sustain his business (*Far Eastern Economic Review* 19 February 1998). This, however, was not the first time that UMNO leaders had called upon Chinese businessmen who had benefited from state patronage to bail-out well-connected Malay businessmen who had found themselves in a business quagmire. Ting Pek Khiing had acquired the publicly-listed and debt-ridden Granite Bhd from Government Economic Advisor Daim Zainuddin's business protégé Samsudin Abu Hassan in 1994 when the latter ran into severe financial problems. Ting, as mentioned, had also acquired the ailing Wembley from businessmen linked to Anwar in 1995. Since the Chinese businessmen called in to aid near-bankrupt Malay businessmen have benefited from state patronage, it is probably doubtful if they will be allowed to hold on to these corporate assets in the long term. This was hinted at by Daim when he said, 'I'd allow them [the Chinese] to rescue ailing companies. After they recover, they can talk about ownership' (ibid.). This use of some Chinese businessmen to help bail out some well-connected Malay businessmen is further indication of the subservience of Chinese capital to Malay hegemony.

The government has taken some measures to address the problems that have arisen following the crisis, including suspending or canceling some major infrastructure projects, intensifying its longstanding endeavor to get Malaysia's numerous financial institutions to merge, curbing bank lending growth appreciably, restricting new public listings of companies and rights issues, deferring investments abroad and checking imports (*Asian Wall Street Journal* 8 December 1998). However, the government has also persisted in bailing out ailing companies controlled by well-connected businessmen, despite the rhetoric to the contrary. The government continues to encourage well-managed companies to take over bad companies rather than let the latter go under, and might still pursue some other uneconomical mega projects (see *Far Eastern Economic Review* 21 May 1998). One of the contributory factors to the crisis was the lack of transparency in corporate deals and accountability in government. This remains one of the key issues that has to be resolved to restore public confidence and attract foreign investment to regenerate growth. The attempts, however, of the Mahathir administration to bail out well-connected businessmen suggests that it is unlikely that there will be much change in market operations in spite of the crisis.

# Notes

## Chapter 1 – Chinese Business: Culture, Entrepreneurship or Patronage?

1 Nominee services are provided by banks, finance and stockbroking companies and other financial institutions. These organizations hold shares on behalf of their owners, enabling the latter to conceal their ownership of corporate stock. An investor who acquires more than five per cent of a company's shares is, however, required, under the Companies Act 1965, to publicly disclose his total shareholding. Some investors also use family members or close allies – sometimes refered to as 'proxies' (Gomez 1990) – to hold corporate stock on their behalf. Such methods of shareholding makes it extremely difficult to quantify the extent of corporate ownership and control of a company by a particular individual.

2 In this study, the determining factor for identifying a company as 'Chinese' is based solely on whether majority share ownership is in the hands of ethnic Chinese.

3 Under the government's ten-year Second Outline Perspective Plan, 1991–2000 (OPP2), manufacturing was projected to grow at 10.5 per cent a year, which would increase its contribution to GDP by the end of the decade to almost 37 per cent; this figure was surpassed by 1996. Manufacturing's contribution to total exports is expected to increase from 60 per cent in 1990 to 81 per cent by the year 2000.

4 Weidenbaum and Hughes' (1996:25) own estimate of the total economic output of such ethnic Chinese by the mid-1990s is close to US$600 billion and associated with the economic boom in East Asia!

5 The case studies in this volume confirm the prominence of the Hokkiens in the Malaysian economy. However, other Chinese sub-ethnic communities also established niches in the economy, particularly during the colonial period. The Teochews then dominated the pepper and gambier plantations and trade, the Cantonese played a prominent role as shopkeepers, the Hainanese dominated the coffee shop catering business and the shipping industry, while the Hakkas had a good presence in agriculture (Yong 1987: 10).

6 Even this, however, has to be qualified. The number of Foochows in Sarawak, for example, is rather high and they control a number of sectors of the state's

*Notes*

economy. Yet, there are also significant divisions among Foochow businessmen. Such divisions are most obvious in attempts by individual Foochows to secure greater access to Sarawak's lucrative timber resources.

7 The ethnic Chinese population figures for the Philippines, Thailand and Indonesia and their corporate ownership figures have been adopted from various sources, and are very rough estimates. For a concise discussion of Chinese capital in Southeast Asia, see Mackie (1992: 161–90) and Lim (1996). Lim (1996), the source of some of these figures, also stresses that these ethnic Chinese ownership figures need to be verified.

8 Among those professing a culturalist perspective, Redding has provided some of the most nuanced arguments. See, in particular, his *The Spirit of Chinese Capitalism*.

9 Lee, however, has qualified his advocacy. According to him: 'And China is not the same as the Chinese diaspora or the overseas Chinese. There is the momentary glow of fraternity. It is as this stage, when China has not established clarity and transparency of law, that the Chinese diaspora can play a critical role. They have proved that if you can develop *guanxi* (connections), you can make up for the lack of rule of law. But I don't think there will be a supranational kinship that will hold the economic loyalties of these overseas groups to China' (quoted in *Business Week* 29 November 1993).

10 This extract is taken from his speech delivered in Kuala Lumpur, carried in full by the *New Straits Times* (5–6 October 1991).

11 In 1989, 97.72 per cent of the 773,511 registered companies in Taiwan were considered SMEs. SMEs also constituted 99 per cent of the companies in the manufacturing sector (Hsiao 1994: 83–4).

This dynamism among Chinese SMEs has been described by Lam and Lee (1992) as a form of 'guerrilla capitalism'. Lam and Lee (1992) also suggest that what constitutes 'Chinese capitalism' is more prevalent in the business practices of the SMEs – they are primarily family-based, have not yet incorporated modern management styles and tend to involve more intra-ethnic co-operation. The Chinese SMEs also share resources and information, have mutually interlocking ownership and have managed to operate and develop outside of state control and without state aid. This is an hypothesis that has not been tested in Malaysia.

12 Some research on medium-sized publicly-listed enterprises (in terms of market capitalization) suggests that there may be some justification for the argument that such Chinese companies are rather entrepreneurial. See, for example, the case study on Kanzen Bhd by Leong (1993) and reports on Pilecon Engineering Bhd (*Malaysian Business* 1 August 1996) and LKT Industrial Bhd (*Malaysian Business* 16 September 1996).

13 Vertical growth occurs when the company acquired is involved in a different stage of production in the same general line of business, for example, when a company involved in the construction of timber-based structures acquires a saw mill company to process the timber required. Horizontal growth occurs when a company acquires another company involved in the same business, for example, when a bank acquires another bank. Conglomerate growth occurs when the company acquired is in a totally different business, for instance, when a construction company acquires a bank.

14 Changing ownership patterns in the construction sector have been particularly interesting. In 1970, the Chinese had control of this sector, owning 52.8 per cent of construction-based companies, while Malays had

only 2.2 per cent. By the 1990s, some of the leading construction-based companies were under Malay control, mainly through state patronage. Most of the country's major privatized projects have been awarded to Bumiputera companies. In the 1990s, some Chinese companies, including those owned by Tan, Ting and Yeoh, have also secured major privatized projects. Thus, the case studies of Berjaya Group, Ekran and YTL Corp will help shed light on why government leaders currently seem more open to sharing with Chinese lucrative contracts which would normally have gone to politically well-connected Malay businessmen.

15 Five of the eight men selected for case studies were identified in 1989 by the Chinese language magazine, *Shang Hai*, as the 'ten biggest Chinese businessmen' in Malaysia (quoted in Hara 1991). The five businessmen were Kuok, Lim, Loh, Cheng and Yeoh's father, Yeoh Tiong Lay. Among the other Chinese businessmen in this list who will be dealt with in this study, though not in such depth, are Lee Loy Seng and Teh Hong Piow. The three other businessmen in Hara's (1991) list were the late Loy Hean Heong (of the MBf group), the late Lim Geok Chan (who once held the Kentucky Fried Chicken franchises in Singapore and Malaysia) and Wong Tok Chai (who had been involved in iron and can manufacturing and had once served as managing director of the *Shin Min Daily News*).

16 Berle and Means (1967) distinguish five types of control: private ownership, majority control, minority control, management control and control through a legal device without majority ownership. The last three types of control are not dependent on ownership of a majority of a company's equity, but rather on relations among those with influence in the company. Under private ownership, control and ownership are identical. Majority control differs from private ownership in that a number of shareholders are devoid of control because control is held by the owner(s) of the majority of the shares. Minority control refers to a situation in which an individual or group of associates owns enough stock to ensure control. Minority control ordinarily rests on a relatively even distribution of the remaining shares among many small stock owners, so that no rival has enough stock to challenge the controlling stock owners successfully.

17 For a more detailed discussion of Mahathir's views on the development of Bumiputera capitalism, see Khoo (1995). See also Gomez and Jomo (1997) for a study of how state patronage facilitated the rapid rise of some of the most prominent Malay businessmen in the country.

18 Ahmad Sebi is well-connected to UMNO leaders. It appears from his business deals that he is now most closely associated with Deputy Prime Minister and Finance Minister Anwar Ibrahim. See Chapter 3 for more information on Ahmad Sebi.

19 In 1994, the market capitalization of quoted equity as a percentage of GDP in Malaysia was significantly higher than other East Asian countries – China (8.6 per cent), Indonesia (30.2 per cent), Korea (50.9 per cent), the Philippines (86.9 per cent), and Thailand (93.1 per cent) (World Bank 1996: 105).

20 Among the state agencies listed on the KLSE included the airlines monopoly Malaysia Airlines Bhd, the power and telecommunications monopolies Tenaga Nasional Bhd and Telekom (M) Bhd respectively, and HICOM Holdings Bhd, Malaysia's largest public enterprise which had been established to lead the country's heavy indiustrialization drive. See *Privatizing Malaysia* for a more detailed account of the privatization policy.

*Notes*

21 See Kahn (1996) for a concise discussion on the emergence Malaysian middle class following rapid economic development.
22 In his study of the top hundred companies in Malaysia during the 1970s, Lim (1981) suggested that the role of Bumiputera directors was generally not business-related, but had more to do with providing protection and securing prompt and favorable responses from the bureaucracy on business matters.

## Chapter 2 – Chinese Business, Colonialism and Accumulation

1 Over the next four decades, the other states in the peninsula fell under British control. By 1914, in addition to Penang, Singapore and Malacca (collectively known as the Straits Settlements, or SS), British Malaya comprised the Federated Malay States (FMS) of Perak, Negri Sembilan, Selangor and Pahang, and the Unfederated Malay States (UMS) of Johore, Kelantan, Perlis, Terengganu and Kedah.
2 The Babas are also known as Peranakan Chinese. Although these Straits-born Hokkien Chinese were originally identified with Malacca, Baba families also emerged in Singapore and Penang. See Tan (1983) for a more detailed discussion on the Baba community.
3 The British had dominance over the rubber plantation sector after introducing the industry to the peninsula. Rubber plantations were primarily established on the west coast of the peninsula. The British were also responsible for the mass immigration of Indians into Malaya to work in the fledgling rubber plantation sector. See Stenson (1980) for an excellent history of the Indians in Malaysia.
4 It is noteworthy that none of the descendants of these men presently own or control major publicly-listed companies in Malaysia. The Lee family, however, owns a major interest in the Singapore-based Oversea-Chinese Banking Corporation (OCBC) group, which still has substantial business interests in Malaysia.
5 Tan Jiak Lim's grandfather, Tan Kim Seng, who was born in Malacca in 1805, had founded the prominent trading and shipping company Kim Seng & Company. The shareholders of Kim Seng & Co had helped found the Straits Steamship Company Ltd, a venture which also involved the Europeans, particularly T.C. Bogaardt (Khoo 1988; Yoshihara 1988: 221).
6 For a more detailed discussion of the rise of the OCBC group and the role Lee played in the incorporation of this bank, see Chapter 3.
7 Although the British had collaborated during the Japanese Occupation with the MCP – when the party gained a following among Chinese Malayans for its role in opposing the Japanese – they were fearful of the growing impact of the party and the influence of other 'left-leaning' parties. As tension mounted between the British and the MCP, the Emergency was declared and the party was banned in 1948, the need for an alternative conservative Chinese party became imperative.
8 Tan Cheng Lock, the first president of the MCA, a Straits-born Chinese with a family heritage stretching back several generations in the country, spoke no Chinese. A number of the other original leaders of the MCA were English-speaking professionals, among them Yong Shook Lin and Leong Yew Koh, both British-trained lawyers, Y.C. Kang, a British-trained accountant, and Ng Sui Cam, an engineer trained in the United States (Heng 1988: 63–5). See Heng (1988) for a early history of the MCA.

9 The mass-based UMNO had been formed in 1946 and was first led by Malay aristocrats. The party secured strong support among Malays after it managed to successfully galvanize the community to oppose the Malayan Union scheme proposed by the British colonial government. The Malayan Union was a unitary constitutional scheme to amalgamate, under one government, the nine federated and unfederated states and the two Straits Settlements of Penang and Malacca. Singapore, the other Straits Settlement, which had emerged as the commercial center of the British empire in Southeast Asia, was to be excluded. The proposal was seen by the Malays as an attempt to dispense with the nine Malay sultans as sovereign heads of their respective states, and to provide citizenship and equal political rights to non-Malays. Following widespread Malay opposition to the Malayan Union, the scheme was replaced in 1948 by the Federation of Malaya agreement. See Firdaus (1985) and Funston (1980) for an account of the early history of UMNO.

10 Malaya's first Prime Minister, Tunku Abdul Rahman, would later acknowledge his 'unwritten accord' with the British – in return for early independence, his government would protect British commercial interests (Funston 1980: 12).

11 H.S. Lee had previous experience as a banker. In 1949, he had helped found the Overseas Union Bank (OUB) in Singapore. Lee had a directorship at OUB until his appointment as Finance Minister (Gomez 1991: 31–2). The D&C Bank was incorporated in October 1965 and commenced business the following year.

12 During the period 1955 to 1970, almost half of total public development expenditure was invested in developing infrastructure, particularly for transport, power and communications.

13 Between 1961 and 1970, British capital in Malaysia increased by 77 per cent, from RM946.9 million to RM1439.8 million (Junid 1980: 25).

14 MARA was a reconstituted version of the Rural Industrial Development Authority (RIDA), established in 1950 to enhance Malay participation in business. RIDA had been the first concerted attempt by Malay leaders to develop Malay entrepreneurs by providing them with access to credit facilities and business training. By 1954, however, although RIDA had been converted to a public corporation and given enlarged responsibilities and funds, its efforts at promoting Malay capitalism were not very successful (Golay 1969: 366).

15 Other public enterprises were established to help rural Malays; apart from the Federal Agricultural Marketing Authority (FAMA), established in 1956, these included the Federal Land Consolidation and Rehabilitation Authority (FELCRA) and the Rubber Industry Smallholders Development Authority (RISDA).

16 In 1997, the Barisan Nasional coalition had 14 constituent members, of which UMNO was the largest party. UMNO has a membership totaling almost 2.7 million. In contrast to this, the MCA, the second largest party, has only around 715,000 members, while the MIC has approximately 350,000 members and the Gerakan about 250,000 members (*New Straits Times* 8 April 1996, 1 August 1996). UMNO also has a very substantial party machinery, due to its access to considerable funds from business interests. See Gomez (1996b) for a detailed discussion on the funding sources of political parties in Malaysia.

17 See Gale (1981) for a detailed studied of some of the major public enterprises established to participate in business.

*Notes*

18 See Chapters 3 and 4 for a more detailed discussion of the corporatization movement and a review of Lee's attitude to the development of Malay and state capital.
19 As there is little published material on Kuok, it is difficult to provide an accurate account of his early history, particularly of when he was sent to England. Lever-Tracy *et al.* (1996: 127–30) suggest that Kuok's stint in London was, in fact, a period of self-exile when the Kuok family came under suspicion of the colonial authorities after Kuok's second brother, William, joined the Malayan Communist Party (MCP). Lever-Tracy *et al.* do not cite the source of their information. William Kuok, reportedly a prominent member of the MCP, was killed in 1952 during the Emergency (1948–60) (see *Far Eastern Economic Review* 7 February 1991).
20 Taib Andak, a British-trained barrister who became Registrar of the Supreme Court, also served as chairman of the Federal Land Development Authority (FELDA), the government's land development and redistribution scheme (Tan 1982: 291).
21 Other government-owned enterprises to which Kuok was appointed director included the Malaysian Industrial Development Finance Bhd (MIDF), Malayawata Steel Bhd and Malaysia Shipyard & Engineering Sdn Bhd (Tan 1982: 173)
22 Peremba was established by Daim in 1979, but was owned by the government's Urban Development Authority (UDA) until it was privatized in 1990. Peremba had been the grooming ground for some of the leading Malay businessmen associated with Daim, including Halim Saad (Renong Bhd), Tajudin Ramli (Technology Resources Industries Bhd and Malaysia Airlines Bhd) and Wan Azmi Wan Hamzah (Land & General Bhd). See Gomez (1990) for a detailed account of the development of Peremba by Daim.
23 Peremba's stake in the Shangri-La Hotel was held though its listed company, Landmarks Bhd, which still owns almost 27 per cent of the company's equity (*KLSE Annual Companies Handbook* 21 (4), 1996: 838). Peremba was involved in a privatization management buy-out in 1990 and was taken over by two of Daim's protégés. See Gomez (1995) for a case study of the controversy surrounding the management buy-out of Peremba.
24 Kuok's almost 13 per cent stake in Citic Pacific was to have been acquired by two companies in the Perlis Plantation group – publicly-listed Federal Flour Mills and Malaysian Sugar Manufacturing Sdn Bhd (see *Far Eastern Economic Review* 8 August 1991). However, Kuok's interest in Citic Pacific now amounts to about 10 per cent and is held through his companies in Hong Kong (*Business Times* 14 September 1993).
25 A longer account of this episode by Kuok (quoted in Perlis Plantations' 1975 Annual Report) is carried by Cheong (1992: 45–6). Cheong also suggests Kuok's experience of the impact of state regulation on potentially profitable business ventures as a possible reason for his move to Hong Kong.
26 Further evidence of Kuok's desire for minimal state interference in market activities is provided in another statement made by him in 1993; he is reported to have stated, 'This (Hong Kong) is really a good place to set up business headquarters. Hong Kong's rule of law by international standards is good, the government exercises effective management. After the principles are established, you are free to do business without interference' (see *Business Times* 14 September 1993).

27 Kuok's daughter, Sue Kuok, is married to Abdul Rashid Hussain, the majority shareholder of the publicly-listed stockbroking company, Rashid Hussain Bhd, a company he first developed with another stockbroker Chua Ma Yu (*Far Eastern Economic Review* 20 April 1995). There is, however, no evidence of any major business deals between Rashid and Kuok, or between the Malaysian companies they own. Rashid Hussain has emerged as a major force in the Malaysian financial sector. He acquired a controlling stake in two banks, DCB Bank (formerly the D&C Bank) and the Kwong Yik Bank, and merged them to form RHB Bank (see *Corporate World* August 1997). Both D&C Bank and the Kwong Yik Bank had been first incorporated by Chinese businessmen. See Gomez and Jomo (1997: 60–6) for a case study of the banking sector in Malaysia, particularly for a discussion of the takeover of a number of Chinese-owned banks by state- and Bumiputera-owned enterprises.
28 Frank Tsao, however, is still a shareholder of MISC equity, and is currently the company's deputy chairman. Presently, the government's Pension Fund is the majority shareholder, with almost 30 per cent of MISC's equity (*KLSE Annual Companies Handbook* 21 (3), 1996: 206–12).
29 According to company records, Genting Highlands Sdn Bhd was incorporated on 27 April 1965 and is currently wholly owned by Resorts World. The directors of the company include Lim and two of his sons, Tee Keong and Kok Thay.
30 Apart from this, Resorts World also appointed another company in the Genting group, Genting International Ltd, as its international marketing and sales agent (*Malaysian Business* 1 March 1990).
31 Genting International was listed in Luxembourg after Lim failed to get the company quoted on the Hong Kong Stock Exchange in 1987.
32 The present owners of the New Straits Times Press, reputedly linked to Deputy Prime Minister Anwar Ibrahim, gained control of the newspaper publishing company in 1993 with the help of the Hong Leong group. It is believed that, in return, Hong Leong was allowed to take over the MUI Bank. See Chapter 3 for further details on Hong Leong's takeover of MUI Bank. For a detailed discussion of the links between the Hong Leong group and members of the UMNO elite, see Gomez (1994) and Gomez and Jomo (1997: 66–71).
33 The cruise vessels ply short routes from Singapore to Langkawi in Kedah, Phuket in Thailand and Medan in Indonesia (*The Straits Times* (Singapore) 22 October 1993).
34 Tunku Abdul Rahman, the Prime Minister responsible for giving Lim the casino licence, justified it on the grounds that Lim had shown a capacity to perform (see *Malaysian Business* 1 December 1987).
35 Oriental Assemblers was originally known as General Motors (M) Sdn Bhd. The company was incorporated on 1 May 1967 to assemble vehicles. Among the other current shareholders of Oriental Assemblers are Honda Motor Co. Ltd and Syarikat S.M. Aidid Sdn Bhd. This information was obtained from company records.
36 Information obtained from records filed at the Registrar of Companies.
37 The information was primarily obtained from Oriental Holdings' annual report for the year 1992.
38 The information was obtained from the report by Arab-Malaysian Securities on Oriental Holdings in 1995.
39 The information was obtained from company records.

*Notes*

40  Before the 1970s, when the MCA had more influence in government, cases can be cited of MCA leaders benefiting from government patronage. One example was the banking licence given to H.S. Lee when he left government to establish the D&C Bank in 1965. Lee, an MCA leader and prominent businessmen, was the country's first Finance Minister. More information is provided on Lee and the D&C Bank later.

Individual MCA leaders who do not have significant business interests appear to have benefited from the government though. When the current MCA President, Ling Liong Sik, was sacked from the party during a factional dispute in 1984, he obtained a brokerage licence from then Finance Minister Razaleigh Hamzah (Gomez 1991: 101). More often, state patronage has been in the form of company directorships. When Richard Ho, a former deputy leader of the party, was forced out of the MCA, he became a director of the government-owned Malayan Banking. It is not uncommon for MCA leaders to secure directorships in Chinese companies after leaving office, as was the case of Lee Kim Sai, another deputy leader of the MCA maneuvered out of office in 1995. More recently, in late 1996, Ling Hee Leong, the 27-year-old son of Ling Liong Sik, has emerged as a major corporate player with interests in 11 publicly-listed local and foreign companies (see *The Star* 31 December 1996). Ling's meteoric rise involved a rapid succession of takeovers, probably facilitated by access to bank loans.

41  The Malaysian Chinese companies in this list by *Asiaweek* (21 November 1997) include Vincent Tan Chee Yioun's Berjaya Group Bhd and William Cheng's Amsteel Corporation Bhd (see Chapter 3). The Malaysian companies that secured the highest ranking are all government-controlled: Petroliam Nasional Bhd, the national oil corporation, and its listed trading concern, Petronas Dagangan Bhd, the multinational Sime Darby Bhd, the privatized utilities giants, Tenaga Nasional Bhd and Telekom (M) Bhd, Malaysia Airlines Bhd, the car assembler UMW Holdings Bhd, Malaysia LNG Bhd, and two companies controlled by the privatized heavy industries corporation, HICOM Holdings Bhd, the national car manufacturer and distributor, Proton Bhd and EON Bhd respectively (see *Asiaweek* 21 November 1997).

## Chapter 3 – Chinese Business, The NEP and Accommodation

1  In the case of some of these Chinese and Indian banks, their management had come under investigation by the authorities for alleged malpractices or violation of banking regulations. This contributed to the eventual takeover of these banks by the government before it was divested to state agencies or to select Bumiputeras.

2  See below for a detailed discussion on the incorporation and development of OCBC.

3  In this election, the MCA had won only 13 of the 33 parliamentary seats it contested. In the previous general election in 1964, the party won 27 of the 33 seats it contested. Two of the party's incumbent Cabinet ministers were defeated; it had lost the state government and chief ministership of Penang, and was all but obliterated in Perak and Selangor where it won only one seat each.

4  Following the 1969 general election, the MCA leaders felt that divisions within the Chinese community were to blame for the party's poor electoral

performance. This prompted the formation of the Chinese Unity Movement in 1971, and later the Perak Task Force, to help revive waning support for the MCA. In the next two years, growing support for the Chinese Unity Movement and the Perak Task Force led to a factional struggle between the leaders of the MCA and the two movements. Siew Sin, in particular, felt that his position was under threat. This eventually led to the suppression and demise of the two movements in 1973. Many of the leaders of these two movements left the MCA to join the Gerakan. See Loh (1982) and Means (1991) for a detailed account of the formation and demise of the Chinese Unity Movement and the Perak Task Force.

5 Lee's KL-Kepong group had sold MPHB a highly lucrative 1445-acre site on the outskirts of Kuala Lumpur for development of a housing and commercial project. It was MPHB's first acquisition, following its original 30 million issue of RM1 shares, and a major boost for its expansion drive (*Far Eastern Economic Review* 13 January 1978).

6 The first Malay bank, the Malay National Banking Corporation, was incorporated in Kuala Lumpur in 1947, almost 50 years after the first Chinese bank was established, but ceased operations in 1952 (Lim 1969: 233).

7 Yeap Chor Ee was born in 1867 in Fujian province and migrated to Penang at the age of 17. He started out as a barber, but went on to establish a major commodities trading company, Chop Ban Hin Lee, which later diversified into shipping, property development and banking. Yeap died in 1952, but the Ban Hin Lee Bank remains under the control of his family (Yoshihara 1988 211–12; Lee and Chow 1997: 190–1).

8 A qualification is required here. Although the Babas trace their roots back to Hokkien traders, the Babas had emerged as a community distinct from more recent Chinese migrants.

9 See the case study on the MUI group in this chapter for more details on the takeover and development of MUI Bank by Khoo, his fall-out with UMNO leaders in the late 1980s and his apparent attempts to win back their favor in the early 1990s. See Chapter 4 for a profile on Quek Leng Chan, his takeover of MUI Bank in 1993, and how this was facilitated after he appeared to have cultivated close ties with UMNO leaders.

10 See the case study on Khoo Kay Peng for details on the takeover of MUI Bank and how this was linked to the Pan-Electric scandal.

11 Other Chinese-owned banks in Malaysia fell under state or Bumiputera control following allegations of impropriety, including the United Malayan Banking Corporation Bhd (UMBC) and the D&C Bank. UMBC was established by Chang Ming Thien, went on to become one the leading banks in Malaysia, but was taken over by the government following a run on the bank in 1976. UMBC is currently owned by the plantations giant, Sime Darby Bhd, which, in turn, is majority owned by the government trust agency PNB, which also has direct majority ownership of Maybank.

The D&C Bank Bhd was established by Henry H.S. Lee and controlled by his family; they lost control of the bank following allegations of impropriety by his son Alex Lee. See Gomez (1991: 31–43) for a study of the controversy involving Alex Lee and the D&C Bank. The D&C Bank was later taken over by the well-connected Rashid Hussein, who also got control of the Kwong Yik Bank.

12 It has been noted, for example, that during Ronald Reagan's term of office as President of the United States, the number of merger and acquisition

## Notes

activities was two-and-a-half times the level recorded in the last five years of the 1970s (see Fallon and Srodes 1988: 5).

13 For a study of the rise of Malaysia's 'new rich,' and how the emergence of their companies as leading corporations was largely achieved through a series of acquisitions, see Gomez and Jomo (1997). See also Gomez (1990 and 1994) for a detailed studies on the rise and near demise of Fleet Group Sdn Bhd, UMNO's investment holding company which was managed by Daim.

14 In Malaysian Chinese politics, the number of Chinese parties that profess to protect ethnic Chinese interests is an indication of Chinese difficulty in transcending various divisions, even in the face of growing Malay political hegemony. See Lee (1987) for an analysis of the three parties in Malaysia that have much Chinese support – the MCA, Gerakan and the opposition Democratic Action Party (DAP).

15 Among the other original shareholders of UMBC was Kang Kock Seng, who had served as managing director of UMBC; he was a former MCA member of parliament ((Tan 1982: 159; Lee 1997: 56).

16 Daim's acquisition of UMBC raised much controversy as his takeover of the bank was announced just before his appointment as Finance Minister. Daim tried to get his predecessor, Razaleigh Hamzah, to approve the deal retroactively, but failed (*Asian Wall Street Journal* 30 April 1986).

Daim subsequently sold his stake in UMBC to Pernas, reportedly at a huge profit. Pernas held on to the UMBC equity for a few years, then sold it to a company owned by Mohd Noor Yusof, the former political secretary of Prime Minister Mahathir. Mohd Noor later sold his interests in UMBC to Sime Darby, controlled by the government trust agency PNB. This equity in the bank seemed to be going about in circles among influential private businessmen and state agencies. UMBC has since been renamed Sime Bank. See Gomez and Jomo (1997: 56–9) for a detailed study of UMBC.

It was well known that Daim did not harbor political aspirations, and his main interests have always appeared to be his involvement in the corporate sector. All Daim's senior positions in UMNO and in government, as party treasurer and Finance Minister, were appointments determined by UMNO president, Mahathir; Daim is reputedly Mahathir's closest confidante. Daim could, thus, afford to undertake potentially profitable business ventures with MPHB – or with other Chinese businessmen – even though it may not have gone down well with some UMNO members. In 1987, during the height of a factional dispute in UMNO, party members had alleged that Daim had abused his position as UMNO Treasurer to channel party assets to his family companies. See Gomez (1990) for a detailed account of Daim's control of UMNO's corporate assets.

17 In 1983, MPHB acquired an interest in two publicly-listed companies in Hong Kong – a 75 per cent stake in New Star Development Co Ltd (later renamed Mulpha Enterprise (Hong Kong) Ltd) and a 75 per cent interest in Promptship Holdings. MPHB's acquisition of Promptship, an ailing company with an antiquated fleet of ships, surprised most market analysts (Gomez 1994: 206–8).

18 The impact of the Pan-El crisis on other Chinese businesses, particularly those associated with friends of Koon Swan, are dealt with in the case study on Khoo Kay Peng.

19 For a detailed account of the DTC scandal, see Gomez (1991: 47–104).

20 Lee Loy Seng served as chairman of MPHB from 1975 to 1983. He is

believed to have relinquished the chairmanship after a fall-out with Koon Swan (Gomez 1994: 209–10).
21 Information obtained from company records.
22 The remaining 20 per cent stake in SFI was retained by the Sabah state government. Lion Corp managed to secure this privatized contract after a protracted struggle with other influential companies, including the Sabah-based Suniwang Sdn Bhd, owned by Joseph Ambrose Lee (see Gomez and Jomo 1997: 132).
23 Until July 1995, Lion Corp held a 30 per cent stake in Natvest, before divesting this equity to Chocolate Products.
24 Bright Steel was incorporated on 11 October 1973 as Standard Steel Sdn Bhd. It is currently wholly-owned by Amalgamated Containers. The directors of the company include two former senior officials in the armed forces, General Tahir Ismail and Admiral M.W. Alvisse. The information was obtained from company records.
25 Lion Corp has an 80 per cent stake in this joint-venture while the remaining 20 per cent equity is divided between two Japanese companies (*KLSE Annual Companies Handbook* 21 (2), 1996: 156).
26 Khoo apparently ventured into construction and property development in Kuala Lumpur during the mid-1970s. The profits Khoo made from this facilitated his takeover of MUI. In this regard, there are similarities in his early career with that of another prominent Chinese banker, Teh Hong Piow.
27 Alex Lee is the son of Henry H.S. Lee, the country's first Finance Minister, a former MCA leader and founder of the D&C Bank. Alex Lee was an MCA leader, but left the party in 1973 after a bitter factional dispute to join the Gerakan, another party in the ruling Barisan Nasional. Lee eventually became a vice-president of the Gerakan, was elected to parliament for two terms (1986–1995) and served as a Deputy Minister in Mahathir's cabinet.

In 1982, Alex Lee had joint control of the D&C Bank with Syed Kechik, but two years later, after he was embroiled in a major scandal involving abuse of the bank's funds, Lee had to relinquish his control over the bank's management. For details of this controversy, see Gomez (1991: 31–43).
28 Syed Kechik was an UMNO lawyer from the state of Kedah. He was later sent to Sabah, where he became the powerful adviser to Mustapha Harun, the state's autocratic Chief Minister from 1965 to 1976. Syed Kechik ran the Sabah Foundation, a powerful patronage institution in the state. On his return to the peninsula, Syed Kechik emerged as a major corporate figure controlling a number of companies including the D&C Bank Bhd and Sri Hartamas Bhd, and established close business ties with the H.S. Lee family. He was, however, badly affected by the economic recession of the mid-1980s, and eventually had to relinquish ownership of much of his business interests.
29 Killinghall was then controlled by the Ramuda group, reportedly owned by Selangor royalty (see *The Star* 8 December 1982). Southern Bank, however, still remained under the control of the Saw family (*New Straits Times* 8 December 1982).
30 Similar rhetoric was voiced when companies linked to the MCA established ties with UMNO companies during the 1980s, most of which favored the latter (see Gomez 1990: 157–60).
31 The reasons behind this deal were revealed by Syed Kechik: 'D&C Bank does not have a diversified vehicle which MUI is, and they (MUI) want what we have – a banking group' (*Business Times* 10 May 1982).

*Notes*

32 As the economy recovered from the recession of the mid-1980s, the companies in the MUI group involved in property development, hotels, banking, finance and manufacturing (especially cement manufacturing due to increasing demand with the construction boom) had begun to perform better.
33 Azman Hashim, an accountant by training, was an UMNO member. In 1980, he was appointed chairman of the Kwong Yik Bank, then under the control of Malayan Banking. Azman was also one of the original shareholders of UMNO's investment holding company, Fleet Holdings Sdn Bhd. The other shareholders of Nautilus included Danny Tan Chee Sing and Azlan Hashim, the brothers of Tan and Azman.
34 Apart from these two franchises, Tan also secured the franchise for another American fast-food chain, the Kenny Rogers Roasters Restaurants.
35 Daim was then believed to be trying to divest his stake in Cold Storage to close allies following his ministerial appointment. By the end of 1986, Daim's stake in Cold Storage had come under the control of publicly-listed Aokam Tin Bhd (now Aokam Perdana) which, in turn, was acquired by an UMNO investment holding company, Halimtan Sdn Bhd (subsequently renamed Waspavest). In the early 1990s, Daim protégé Samsudin Abu Hassan secured a controlling interest in Cold Storage. See Gomez (1990: 116–27) for a detailed account of the development of Waspavest and how Daim's stake in Cold Storage was passed around among his close business allies.
36 Ahmad Sebi, once reputedly a close associate of Daim, but now more associated with Deputy Prime Minister Anwar, also served as a director of the New Straits Times Press Bhd, the newspaper publishing company controlled by UMNO's Fleet Holdings. Ahmad also acquired an interest in other UMNO-linked companies like Kinta Kellas plc (controlled by United Engineers (M) Bhd (UEM)) and Kampung Lanjut Tin Dredging Bhd (controlled through Waspavest). In 1991, Ahmad Sebi acquired a controlling stake in another listed company, Batu Lintang Rubber Company Bhd – he renamed it Advance Synergy – which has emerged as one of his main listed holding companies (Gomez 1994: 101–2).
37 Since the late 1980s, the Berjaya Group has also been involved in the acquisition and sale of a number of other publicly-listed companies including Prudential Assurance Bhd, South Pacific Textiles Industries Bhd (later renamed Berjaya Textiles), Far East Assets Bhd (renamed Berjaya Sports Toto), Singer Holdings (M) Bhd (subsequently renamed Berjaya Singer), IGB Corporation Bhd, Magnum Corporation Bhd, Dunlop Estates Bhd (renamed Sarawak Enterprises), Malayan United Industries (MUI), SIG Holdings Bhd (renamed Berjaya South Island Bhd) and Tropical Veneer Company Bhd (renamed Intiplus Bhd). For another detailed case study of the growth of the Berjaya Group, see Gomez and Jomo (1997: 152–9).
38 According to another report, Kuok and Tan Chin Nam 'are old friends . . . . As a token of mutual support, each holds a small stake in the other's publicly-listed companies' (*Asiaweek* 9 June 1989).
39 Kuok, as a director of Multi-Purpose Holdings, had indirect control over Magnum. However, he relinquished this position as director in January 1988.
40 For a detailed case study of T. Ananda Krishnan, see Gomez and Jomo (1997: 159–65). Ananda Krishnan developed the Tanjong group into a well-diversified enterprise within less than half a decade after receiving a licence to operate the Pan Malaysian Pools lottery.

41 In the event, Sports Toto's gaming operations were sold by Berjaya Leisure (formerly known as Sports Toto Bhd) to Far East Asset Bhd, an ailing, listed property company, for RM600 million. The amount was settled through a cash payment of RM209.03 million and the issue of 390.97 million Far East Asset convertible unsecured loan stock valued at RM1 each. Berjaya Leisure was to eventually sell the entire 390.97 million convertible unsecured loan stock to Berjaya Leisure shareholders, Far East Asset's minority shareholders, and through private placement in the market. However, in November 1992, Berjaya Leisure announced its acquisition of a 12.95 per cent stake in Far East Asset, thus allowing it to have indirect control over the Sports Toto gaming operation (*Business Times* 14 July 1992; *New Straits Times* 18 November 1992). In May 1993, Far East Asset was renamed Berjaya Sports Toto. See Gomez and Jomo (1997: 155–7) for a more detailed account of this market transaction.

42 During the height of the feud between Khoo and Vincent Tan, one report stated that MUI executives felt that Berjaya Group's gearing ratio in 1991 was so high that the Sports Toto operations would be divested to reduce debt if MUI secured control of Berjaya Group. According to MUI's calculations, the total borrowings of the companies in the Berjaya Group exceeded RM1 billion (see *The Star* 16 September 1991).

43 According to another report in *The Sun* (10 December 1993), '[I]n the last eight years, Khoo has been keeping a relatively low profile . . . . Its growth, compared to a lot of main board companies, has been very much stilted, much to the chagrin of minority shareholders who believed in the magic of Khoo . . . . Ever since Khoo's mentor, Tengku Razaleigh left UMNO to start Semangat 46, Khoo's counters have languished.'

44 When Ishak Ismail's Sanorex acquired its 3.5 per cent stake in MUI, it made an application to the central bank to increase its interest in MUI to 30 per cent (*Asian Wall Street Journal* 22 July 1991). Although Sanorex did not eventually get to increase its equity in MUI, this suggests that there was a concerted alliance to oust Khoo from MUI.

45 See Gomez 1994 (219–20) for more details on this disagreement between Lim and Tan.

46 JMI was then used to buy a 5.72 per cent interest in Insas Bhd, another publicly-listed company associated with Vincent Tan and Thong Kok Kee. Insas was, in turn, used to acquire a 20 per cent interest in the Ayer Molek Rubber Company Bhd, a quoted company once involved in rubber plantations, but now primarily an investment holding concern controlled by the family of Lee Kong Chian of the Lee Rubber group (Cheong 1995: 79–82, 19–53, 179).

47 Danny Tan Chee Sing is also the managing director of another publicly-listed company, Diperdana Corporation Bhd (formerly known as Shapadu Kontena Bhd) (*KLSE Annual Companies Handbook* 21 (4), 1996: 372).

## Chapter 4 – Chinese Business, Liberalization and Ascendance

1 The president of the MCA, Ling Liong Sik, is the Minister of Transport, while other senior party leaders hold the Labor, Health and Housing portfolios in cabinet.

2 Vision 2020's nine objectives are to establish:

*Notes*

    (i) a united, peaceful, integrated and harmonious Malaysian nation;
    (ii) a secure, confident, respected and robust society committed to excellence;
    (iii) a mature, consensual and exemplary democracy;
    (iv) a 'fully moral' society with citizens strongly imbued with spiritual values and the highest ethical standards;
    (v) a culturally, ethically and religiously diverse, liberal, tolerant and unified society;
    (vi) a scientific, progressive, innovative and forward-looking society;
    (vii) a caring society with a family-based welfare system;
    (viii) an 'economically just' society with inter-ethnic economic parity; and
    (ix) a 'fully competitive, dynamic, robust, resilient and prosperous' economy.

3 There are, of course, other factors which also contributed to this significant increase in support for the Barisan Nasional. The redelineation of constituencies undertaken just before the 1995 general election had an impact on voting patterns. The Barisan Nasional's dominance over the electronic and print media, which was effectively used to portray the opposition negatively and to expound the government's 'achievements,' was another factor. The Barisan Nasional also had far greater access to funds, which allowed it to mount a much more effective campaign. See Gomez (1996a) for an in-depth study of this general election.

4 One HICOM joint-venture, however, included one of Cheng's companies. In 1987, Amsteel Corp, HICOM and Suzuki Motors Co. Ltd of Japan formed a joint-venture, HICOM-Suzuki Manufacturing (M) Sdn Bhd, to manufacture Suzuki motorcycle engines locally. Cheng had secured the franchise to assemble and sell Suzuki motorcycles in Malaysia in 1985.

5 After Chia lost control of UMW, in 1988 Mahathir appointed him managing director of Perwaja Steel Bhd, then a HICOM subsidiary responsible for developing Malaysia's steel production industry. Perwaja Steel had been declaring phenomenal losses, and although Chia's management style initially appeared to have a positive impact on the company, it was disclosed in 1996 that the company was in severe financial crisis. Perwaja Steel had accumulated losses of almost RM2.5 billion and huge debts; its debt to government-owned Bank Bumiputra alone was a massive RM860 million (see *Asian Wall Street Journal* 16 February 1996; *Far Eastern Economic Review* 7 March 1996). Allegations were made, even in parliament, that Chia had mishandled Perwaja Steel's funds. Chia relinquished his position at Perwaja Steel in August 1995, when rumors began spreading of the dire financial situation of the company.

6 Prior to the privatization of HICOM Holdings, the group had an interest in ten publicly-listed companies. Before his takeover of the HICOM Holdings group, Yahya Ahmad had control of four other publicly-quoted companies. At that time, the total market capitalization of all these 14 quoted companies was almost RM21 billion! Through his takeover of HICOM Holdings, Yahya also gained control of a bank, EON Bank, a finance company, EON Finance, an insurance company and a stockbroking firm. Yahya Ahmad had thus emerged as one of Malaysia's leading capitalists within less than a decade (see *Malaysian Business* 1 December 1995).

7 See Gomez (1990, 1991 and 1994) for in-depth studies on the theme of 'political business' and the impact of money on Malaysian politics.

8 For an excellent account of the highly divisive 1987 UMNO elections which eventually resulted in the deregistration of the party, see Kershaw (1989). For another account of this party election, see Shamsul (1988).
9 See Gomez and Jomo (1997) for a detailed study of the politics of patronage in Malaysia.
10 For a detailed discussion of the divisions among Malays, reflected in the 1995 general election, see Gomez (1996a).
11 OYL Industries, founded in 1974 by Ong Yoke Lin, who is still the chairman of the company, has been developing its markets overseas. To move into the market in China, the company established a joint-venture, Shenzhen OYL Electrical Co. Ltd in 1992, to manufacture air-conditioners, and is planning to further expand its operations to the north of the country. In Southeast Asia, OYL Industries is moving into Thailand and the Philippines (*Malaysian Business* 16 November 1992; *Business Times* 12 November 1993).
12 Another major shareholder of Perdana Merchant Bank is Vincent Tan's Berjaya Group. Tan is also a close business associate of Ahmad Sebi (see Chapter 3).
13 The KL-Kepong group also had a 24 per cent stake in Heveafil Sdn Bhd, the largest manufacturer of latex threads in the world (*Investors' Digest* January 1992).
14 Joseph Ambrose Lee controls Suniwang Sdn Bhd, the largest private landowner in the Federal Territory of Labuan island, once part of the state of Sabah. Lee's partner in Suniwang is the UMNO Member of Parliament for Labuan, Abdul Mulok Awang Damit, who claims 'access' to the influential Daim Zainuddin (see Gomez and Jomo 1997: 132). In 1993, Lee and Mulok used Suniwang to gain control of CASH (and another listed company, Pengkalan Industrial Holdings Bhd). Lee Loy Seng had sold CASH to Syed Ibrahim Mohamed, who had injected some property development projects into the company (Cheong 1995: 30–1). CASH, however, was badly effected by the mid-1980s recession and had been faring badly for some time before it was bought by Joseph Lee.
15 Two joint-ventures in property development involving companies owned by Multi-Purpose Holdings and Permodalan Bersatu Bhd (PBB), the holding company of UMNO cooperative, Koperasi Usaha Bersatu Bhd (KUB), were Multi-Purpose Bersatu Development Sdn Bhd and Bersatu Raya Development Sdn Bhd. Another joint-venture was established between these two holding companies to develop the West Country Estate. See Gomez (1990: 157–60) for a detailed discussion of how Multi-Purpose Holdings could not secure permission from the state to redesignate these tracts of plantation land for housing and commercial purposes until these joint-ventures were established. Multi-Purpose Bersatu Development was subsequently renamed Sri Damansara and is currently under the control of Wan Azmi Wan Hamzah.
16 Very much like other Chinese businessmen of his generation, Yeoh Tiong Lay went into business without much technical training. He later secured professional qualifications from the UK and Australia which conferred upon him the title of 'Chartered Builder' (*The Diplomat* February 1986).
17 Other major government construction projects that Yeoh Tiong Lay has been involved in include the Bukit Aman Police Headquarters in Kuala Lumpur and the Sri Iskandar sub-campus for Universiti Sains Malaysia (USM) (*Malaysian Business* 16 January 1992).
18 Yahya Ismail was a director of United Engineers (M) Bhd (UEM), owned by

*Notes*

an UMNO investment holding company before being taken over by Halim Saad, a self-acknowledged UMNO business proxy. Yahya is a director of Cement Industries of Malaysia Bhd (CIMA), in which UEM has a majority controlling stake (Gomez 1994: 100).

19 Company records reveal that the shareholders and directors of Bara Aktif, an investment holding company incorporated on 26 April 1993, are Raja Wahid Raja Kamaralzaman and Mohd Zainal Abidin Haji Abdul Kadir. Both men are also directors of Batu Tiga Quarry, a company incorporated on 26 October 1967 and owned by the Yeoh family through YTL Industries Bhd.

20 The implications of securing local financing for the IPP contract was well captured by the following report: 'By raising the total project cost in local currency from Malaysian banks and institutions, not only cut out the foreign exchange risk of converting ringgit-denominated revenues into US dollars to repay the debt, but also reduced financing costs and eliminated a demanding foreign partner' (*Asian Business* October 1994).

21 On 27 July 1992, Ahmad Hisham bin Zainal Abidin was appointed a director of Woodhouse, and by June 1994, he owned around seven per cent of the company's stock. He resigned as director on 30 August 1994, relinquishing his equity in Woodhouse at the same time.

22 The project, involving almost three thousand hectares of land, situated in Kuala Kedah, facing the island of Langkawi, entails development of a modern township in the area (see *The Star* 21 February 1997).

23 The original plan for BHC's shareholding structure involved Ekran and the Sarawak state government (jointly owning 51 per cent), EPF (10 per cent), SESCO (nine per cent), Tenaga (25 per cent) and another publicly-listed company controlled by the government, Malaysia Mining Corporation Bhd (MMC) (five per cent). MMC eventually backed out, claiming that 'it was busy with other projects' (see *The Edge* 21 April 1997). It is widely believed that most government-linked agencies, like EPF, Tenaga and MMC, have been reluctant to invest in the Bakun dam project (see Gomez and Jomo 1997: 111–12).

24 It was reported that Ekran had hoped to issue four billion BHC shares for sale, which, if all the shares are subscribed to, would help raise RM8 billion for immediate use in the dam project (see *Business Times* [Singapore] 14 June 1996). The scaling down of BHC's share capital, and the number of shares eventually acquired by government-owned agencies and the Sarawak state government reflected the controversy surrounding the means used to raise funds to finance the project. See Gomez and Jomo (1997: 110–16) for an indepth discussion of the controversies surrounding the privatization of the Bakun dam.

25 As recently as July 1996, Anwar had to deny allegations that he was opposed to the Bakun dam project and claimed that these were rumors spread by those intent on causing friction between him and Mahathir. Undoubtedly, there is much political infighting within UMNO, caused partly by a desire by some members within the party to speed up the succession process, partly to facilitate their own greater access to business opportunities.

26 Another major shareholder of CMS is the Sarawak state government's development corporation with 11 per cent equity. The other major shareholders of CMS are disguised by six nominee companies, which collectively own almost 37 per cent of the company's equity (*KLSE Annual Companies Handbook* 21 (3), 1996: 90–1).

27 UCM has diversified into stockbroking, futures trading and asset management (*KLSE Annual Companies Handbook* 21 (4), 1996: 1420–1).
28 When Pacific Chemicals was taken over in 1993, it had a paid-up capital of just RM2.08 million. By 1995, this figure was increased to RM10.367 million, raised through two bonus issues, with the new shares created for the share-swap used to acquire Usama Industries.
29 This information was obtained from company records filed at the Registrar of Companies.
30 Before Ekran undertook the reverse takeover of Granite through Diamond League, a number of companies and assets owned by Ting were injected into Diamond League. Among these assets was part of the timber rights owned by Equitorial Timber Marketing (Cheong 1995: 66–7).

## Postscript

1 Under the New Economic Policy (NEP), between 1971 and 1990, foreign ownership of corporate equity had decreased from 63.4 per cent to 25.4 per cent (see Table 1.1).
2 For a more detailed account of the ways in which political patronage influenced the concentration and accumulation of wealth, see Gomez and Jomo (1997).
3 As mentioned in Chapter 1, the KLSE's market capitalization increased from about 80 per cent of GDP in 1980 to 265 per cent of GDP in 1995.
4 Rashid Hussain is believed to be close to both Mahathir and his deputy, Anwar. Another shareholder of RHB is public-listed Malaysian Resources Corporation Bhd (MRCB), controlled by Anwar's business associates. The RHB group's banking concern, RHB Bank Bhd, is to be merged with Sime Bank. RHB Bank was itself the product of merger of two other Chinese-founded banks, the D&C Bank Bhd and Kwong Yik Bank Bhd. Rashid Hussain had, in effect, gained control of a huge segment of Malaysia's financial sector within a span of less than a decade.
5 The trading of Ekran shares on the KLSE was suspended in November 1997 when the government announced that it was taking over the Bakun Dam project. When trading of Ekran shares resumed in mid-January 1998, its value plummeted by 51 per cent. Other publicly-listed companies in the Ekran group, i.e. Wembley Industries Holdings Bhd and Granite Industries Bhd, which had also been suspended, experienced an almost similar percentage plunge in share price (*Asian Wall Street Journal* 21 January 1998).
6 In March 1997, before the financial crisis, KPB's share price was RM17.30; by February the following year, its price had fallen to RM3.78.

# References

Basch, L., Glick Schiller, N. and Szanton Blanc, C. (1995) *Nations Unbound: Transnational Projects, Postcolonial Predicaments and Deterritorialized Nation-States*, Basel: Gordon and Breach.
Berle, A. A., and Means, G.C. (1967) *The Modern Corporation and Private Property*, New York: Harcourt, Brace and World, Inc.
Bonacich, E. and Modell, J. (1980) *The Economic Basis of Ethnic Solidarity: Small Business in the Japanese-American Community*, Berkeley: University of California Press.
Bonbright, J.C. and Means, G.C. (1969) *The Holding Company: Its Public Significance and Its Regulation*, New York: Augustus M. Kelly.
Bowie, A. (1991) *Crossing the Industrial Divide: State, Society and the Politics of Economic Transformation in Malaysia*, New York: Columbia University Press.
Brown, R.A. (1994) *Capital and Entrepreneurship in South-East Asia*, New York: St. Martin's Press.
Brown, R.A. (ed.) (1996) *Chinese Business Enterprise: Critical Perspectives on Business and Management*, London: Routledge.
Brown, R. (1994) *The State and Ethnic Politics in Southeast Asia*, London: Routledge.
Callen, T. and Reynolds, P. (1997) 'Capital Market Development and the Monetary Transmission Mechanism in Malaysia and Thailand', in Hicklin, J., Robinson, D. and Singh, A. (eds), *Macroeconomic Issues Facing ASEAN Countries*, Washington DC: International Monetary Fund.
Chan, A.B. (1996) *Li Ka-shing: Hong Kong's Elusive Billionaire*, Hong Kong: Oxford University Press.
Chan K.K., W. (1992) 'Chinese Business Networking and the Pacific Rim: The Family Firm's Roles Past and Present', *Journal of American-East Asian Relations* 1 (2).
Chan, K.B. and Chiang, C. (1994) *Stepping Out: The Making of Chinese Entrepreneurs*, Singapore: Prentice Hall.
Chandler, A.D., Jr. (1977) *The Visible Hand: The Managerial Revolution in American Business*, Cambridge: Harvard University Press.
Chee, S. (1991) 'Consociational Political Leadership and Conflict Regulation in Malaysia', in Chee, S. (ed.), *Leadership and Security in Southeast Asia: Institutional Aspects*, Singapore: Institute of Southeast Asian Studies.
Cheong, S. (1992) *Chinese Controlled Companies in the KLSE: Industrial Counter*, Kuala Lumpur: Corporate Research Services Sdn Bhd.

Cheong, S. (1995) *Changes in Ownership of KLSE Companies*, Kuala Lumpur: Corporate Research Services Sdn Bhd.
Chia, O.P. (1990) 'The Chinese in Kuala Krai: A Study of Commerce and Social Life in a Malaysian Town', Ph.D. diss., University of Malaya, Kuala Lumpur.
Chirot, D. and Reid, A. (eds) (1997) *Essential Outsiders: Chinese and Jews in the Modern Transformation of Southeast Asia and Central Europe*, Seattle: University of Washington Press.
Clad, J. (1989) *Behind the Myth: Business, Money and Power in Southeast Asia*, London: Unwin Hyman.
Clark, C. and Chan, S. (eds) (1992) *The Evolving Pacific Basin in the Global Political Economy*, Boulder: Lynne Rienner.
Clegg, S.R. and Redding, S.G. (1990) 'Introduction: Capitalism in Contrasting Cultures', in Clegg, S.R., Redding, S.G. and Cartner, M. (eds), *Capitalism in Contrasting Cultures*, Berlin: Walter de Gruyter.
Clement, W. (1977) *Continental Corporate Power: Economic Elite Linkages between Canada and the United States*, Toronto: McClelland and Stewart.
Crouzet, F. (1985) *The First Industrialists: The Problem of Origins*, Cambridge: Cambridge University Press.
Cushman, J.W. and Gungwu, W. (eds) (1988) *Changing Ethnic Identities of the Southeast Asian Chinese Since World War II*, Hong Kong: Hong Kong University Press.
Dirlik, A. (1996) 'Critical Reflections on 'Chinese Capitalism' as a Paradigm', in Brown, R.A. (ed.), *Chinese Business Enterprise: Critical Perspectives on Business and Management*, London: Routledge.
East Asia Analytical Unit (1995) *Overseas Chinese Business Networks in Asia*, Parkes: Department of Foreign Affairs and Trade, Commonwealth of Australia.
Edwards, C. and Jomo, K.S. (1993) 'Policy Options for Malaysian Industrialisation', in Jomo, K.S. (ed.), *Industrialising Malaysia: Policy, Performance and Prospects*.
Esman, M. (1985) 'The Chinese Diaspora in Southeast Asia', in Sheffer G. (ed.), *Modern Diasporas in International Politics*, London: Croom Helm.
Fallon, I. and Srodes, J. (1988) *Takeovers*, London: Pan Books.
Faridah, A. (1997) *Effective Stock Market Investment in Malaysia*, Kuala Lumpur: Berita Publishing.
Firdaus Haji Abdullah (1985) *Radical Malay Politics: Its Origins and Early Development*, Petaling Jaya: Pelanduk.
Fisk, E.K. and Osman-Rani, H. (eds) (1982) *The Political Economy of Malaysia*, Kuala Lumpur: Oxford University Press.
Freeman, M. (1996) 'Human Rights, Democracy and 'Asian Values'', *The Pacific Review* 9 (3): 352–66.
Fukuda, S. (1995) *With Sweat and Abacus: Economic Roles of Southeast Asian Chinese on the Eve of World War II*, Singapore: Select Books.
Fukuyama, F. (1995) *Trust: The Social Virtues and the Creation of Prosperity*, London: Hamish Hamilton.
Funston, N.J. (1980) *Malay Politics in Malaysia: A Study of the United Malays National Organisation and Party Islam*, Kuala Lumpur: Heinemann Educational Books.
Gale, B. (1981) *Politics and Public Enterprise in Malaysia*, Singapore: Eastern Universities Press.
Gale, B. (1985) *Politics and Business: A Study of Multi-Purpose Holdings Berhad*, Singapore: Eastern Universities Press.

# References

Gates, Hill (1996) *China's Motor: A Thousand Years of Petty Capitalism*, Ithaca: Cornell University Press.
Ghazali, A. (1994) 'Foreign Investment', in Jomo K.S. (ed.), *Malaysia's Economy in the Nineties*, Kuala Lumpur: Pelanduk Publications.
Gill, R. (1985) *The Making of Malaysia Inc.: A Twenty-five Year Review of the Securities Industry of Malaysia and Singapore*, Singapore: Pelanduk Publications.
Godley, M.R. (1981) *The Mandarin-Capitalists From Nanyang: Overseas Chinese Enterprise in the Modernization of China, 1893–1911*, Cambridge: Cambridge University Press.
Golay, F.H., Anspach, R., Pfanner, M.R. and Ayal, E.B. (1969) *Underdevelopment and Economic Nationalism in Southeast Asia*, Ithaca: Cornell University Press.
Gomez, E.T. (1990) *Politics in Business: UMNO's Corporate Investments*, Kuala Lumpur: Forum.
Gomez, E.T. (1991) *Money Politics in the Barisan Nasional*, Kuala Lumpur: Forum.
Gomez, E.T. (1994) *Political Business: Corporate Involvement of Malaysian Political Parties*, Townsville: Centre for Southeast Asian Studies, James Cook University of North Queensland.
Gomez, E.T. (1995) 'Management Buy-outs', in Jomo (ed.), *Privatizing Malaysia: Rents, Rhetoric, Realities*, Boulder and London: Westview Press.
Gomez, E.T. (1996a) *The 1995 Malaysian General Elections: A Report and Commentary*, Singapore: Institute of Southeast Asian Studies.
Gomez, Edmund Terence (1996b) 'Electoral Funding of General, State and Party Elections in Malaysia', *Journal of Contemporary Asia* 26 (1).
Gomez, E.T. (1996c) 'Changing Ownership Patterns, Patronage and the NEP', in Muhd. Ikmal Said and Zahid Emby, (eds) *Malaysia: Critical Perspectives*, Petaling Jaya: Malaysian Social Science Association.
Gomez, E.T. (1996d) 'Philanthropy in a Multiethnic Society: The Case of Malaysia', in Tadashi, Y. (ed.), *Emerging Civil Society in the Asia Pacific Community*, Singapore and Tokyo: Institute of Southeast Asian Studies and Japan Center for International Exchange.
Gomez, E.T. (1997a) 'Political Business in Malaysia', Occasional Paper No. 8, Department of Intercultural Communication and Management, Copenhagen Business School, Frederiksberg.
Gomez, E.T. (1997b) 'Privatized Patronage: The Economics and Politics of Privatization in Malaysia', *Journal of the Asia Pacific Economy*, 2 (2).
Gomez, E.T. and Chee, P.L. (1994) 'Malaysian Sogoshoshas: Superficial Cloning, Failed Emulation', in Jomo, K.S. (ed.) *Japan and Malaysian Development: In the Shadow of the Rising Sun*, London: Routledge.
Gomez, E.T. and Jomo, K.S. (1997) *Malaysia's Political Economy: Politics, Patronage and Profits*, Cambridge: Cambridge University Press.
Goody, J. (1996) *The East in the West*, Cambridge: Cambridge University Press.
Hamilton, G.G. (1996) 'Competition and Organization: A Reexamination of Chinese Business Practices', *Journal of Asian Business* 12 (1).
Hamilton, G.G. (1997) 'Organization and Market Processes in Taiwan's Capitalist Economy', in Orru, M., Woolsey Biggart, N. and Hamilton, G.G. (eds), *The Economic Organization of East Asian Capitalism*, London: Sage Publications.
Hara, F. (1991) 'Malaysia's New Economic Policy and the Chinese Business Community', *The Developing Economies* 29 (4).
Hara, F. (ed.) (1993) *Formation and Restructuring of Business Groups in Malaysia*, Tokyo: Institute of Developing Economies.

Hara, F. (ed.) (1994) *The Development of Bumiputera Enterprises and Sino-Malay Economic Cooperation in Malaysia*, Tokyo: Institute of Developing Economies.
Hassan, A.K. (1989) 'BMF – The People's Black Paper', in Jomo, K.S. (ed.), *Mahathir's Economic Policies*, Kuala Lumpur: Insan.
Heng, P.K. (1988) *Chinese Politics in Malaysia: A History of the Malaysian Chinese Association*, Singapore: Oxford University Press.
Heng, P.K. (1992) 'The Chinese Business Elite of Malaysia', in McVey, R. (ed.), *Southeast Asian Capitalists*, Ithaca, N.Y.: Cornell South East Asian Studies Program.
Herman, E.S. (1981) *Corporate Control, Corporate Power*, Cambridge: Cambridge University Press.
Hicks, G.L. (ed.) (1993) *Overseas Chinese Remittances from Southeast Asia 1910–1940*, Singapore: Select Books.
Hiscock, G. (1997) *Asia's Wealth Club*, London: Nicholas Breasley Publishing.
Ho, K.L. (1995) 'Recent Developments in the Political Economy of China-Malaysia Relations', in Suryadinata, L. (ed.) *Southeast Asian Chinese and China: The Politico-Economic Dimension* Singapore: Times Academic Press.
Hodder, R. (1996) *Merchant Princes of the East: Cultural Delusions, Economic Success and the Overseas Chinese in Southeast Asia*, Chichester: John Wiley & Sons.
Hsaio, H.H., M. (1994) 'The State and Business Relations in Taiwan', in Fitzgerald, R. (ed.), *The State and Economic Development: Lessons from the Far East*, Singapore: Toppan.
Hua, W.Y. (1983) *Class and Communalism in Malaysia: Politics in a Dependent Capitalist State*, London: Zed Books.
Huff, W.G. (1994) *The Economic Growth of Singapore: Trade and Development in the Twentieth Century*, Cambridge: Cambridge University Press.
Hutchcroft, P. (1994) 'Booty Capitalism: Business-Government Relations in the Philippines', in MacIntyre, A. (ed.), *Businesss and Government in Industrialising Asia*, Sydney: Allen & Unwin.
Jesudason, J.V. (1989) *Ethnicity and the Economy: The State, Chinese Business, and the Multinationals in Malaysia*, Singapore: Oxford University Press.
Jesudason, J.V. (1997) 'Chinese Business and Ethnic Equilibrium in Malaysia', *Development and Change*, 28 (1).
Jomo, K.S. (ed.) (1989) *Mahathir's Economic Policies*, Kuala Lumpur: Insan.
Jomo, K.S. (1990) *Economic Growth and Structural Change in the Malaysian Economy*, London: Macmillan.
Jomo, K.S. (ed.) (1993) *Industrialising Malaysia: Policy, Performance and Prospects*, London: Routledge.
Jomo K.S. (1994) *U-turn? Malaysian Economic Development Policies After 1990*, Townsville: Centre for Southeast Asian Studies, James Cook University of North Queensland.
Jomo, K.S. (ed.) (1995) *Privatizing Malaysia: Rents, Rhetoric, Realities*, Boulder and London: Westview Press.
Jomo, K.S. (1997) 'A Specific Idiom of Chinese Capitalism in Southeast Asia: Sino-Malaysian Capital Accumulation in the Face of State Hostility', in Chirot, D. and Reid, A. (eds), *Essential Outsiders: Chinese and Jews in the Modern Transformation of Southeast Asia and Central Europe*, Seattle: University of Washington Press.
Jomo, K.S. and Gomez, E.T. (1997) 'Rents in Multi-ethnic Malaysia', in Aoki, M., Kim H.K., and Okuno-Fujiwara, M. (eds), *The Role of Government in East*

# References

*Asian Economic Development: Comparative Institutional Analysis*, Oxford and Washington D.C.: Clarendon Press and the World Bank.

Jomo, K.S. and Todd, P. (1994) *Trade Unions and the State in Peninsular Malaysia*, Kuala Lumpur: Oxford University Press.

Junid, S. (1980) *British Industrial Development in Malaysia, 1963–1971*, Kuala Lumpur: Oxford University Press.

Kahn, J.S. (1996) 'Growth, Economic Transformation, Culture and the Middle Classes in Malaysia', in Robison, R. and Goodman, D.S.G. (eds), *The New Rich in Asia: Mobile Phones, McDonalds and Middle-Class Revolution*, London: Routledge.

Kao, J. (1993) 'The Worldwide Web of Chinese Business', *Harvard Business Review*, March–April.

Keenan, M. and White, L.J. (eds) (1982) *Mergers and Acquisitions: Current Problems in Perspective*, Lexington, MA: D.C. Heath & Co.

Kershaw, R. (1989) 'Within the Family. The Limits of Doctrinal Differentiation in the Malaysian Ruling Party Election in 1987', *Review of Indonesian and Malaysian Affairs*, 23: 125–93.

Khoo, B.T. (1995) *Paradoxes of Mahathirism: An Intellectual Biography of Mahathir Mohamad*, Kuala Lumpur: Oxford University Press.

Khoo K.J. (1992) 'The Grand Vision: Mahathir and Modernisation', in Kahn, J.S. and Loh, K.W., F. (eds), *Fragmented Visions: Culture and Politics in Contemporary Malaysia*, Sydney: Allen & Unwin for Asian Studies Association of Australia.

Khoo, K.K. (1988) 'Chinese Economic Activities in Malaya: A Historical Perspective', in Nash, M. (ed.), *Economic Performance in Malaysia: The Insider's View*, New York: Professors World Peace Academy.

Khor, K.P. (1983) *The Malaysian Economy: Structures and Dependence*, Kuala Lumpur: Maricans.

King, Y.C., A. (1994) 'Kuan-shi and Network Building: A Sociological Interpretation', in Tu W.M. (ed.), *The Living Tree: The Changing Meaning of Being Chinese Today*, Stanford: Stanford University Press.

Kotkin, J. (1993) *Tribes: How Race, Religion, and Identity Determine Success in the New Global Economy*, New York: Random House.

Kuala Lumpur Stock Exchange (1996) *Annual Companies Handbook*, 21 (1–4), Kuala Lumpur: Kuala Lumpur Stock Exchange.

Lam, K.K., D. and Lee, I. (1992) 'Guerrilla Capitalism and the Limits of Statist Theory: Comparing the Chinese NICs', in Clark, C. and Chan, S. (eds), *The Evolving Pacific Basin in the Global Political Economy*.

Lazonick, W. (1991) *Business Organization and the Myth of the Market Economy*, Cambridge: Cambridge University Press.

Lee, E. (1976) *The Towkays of Sabah*, Singapore: SingaporeUniversity Press.

Lee, K.H. (1987) 'Three Approaches in Peninsular Malaysian Chinese Politics: The MCA, the DAP and the Gerakan', in Zakaria H.A. (ed.), *Government and Politics in Malaysia*, Singapore: Oxford University Press.

Lee, K.H. and Chow, M.S. (1997) *Biographical Dictionary of the Chinese in Malaysia*, Kuala Lumpur: Institute of Advanced Studies, University of Malaya and Pelanduk Publications.

Lee, P.P. (1978) *Chinese Society in Nineteenth-Century Singapore*, Kuala Lumpur: Oxford University Press.

Leong, S. (1993) 'From Dreamland to Kanzen: A Perfect Switch', in Hara, F. (ed.), *Formation and Restructuring of Business Groups in Malaysia* Tokyo: Institute of Developing Economies.

Lever-Tracy, C., Ip, D. and Tracy, N. (1996) *The Chinese Diaspora and Mainland China: An Emerging Economic Synergy*, London: Macmillan.

Light, I.H. (1980) 'Asian Enterprise in America: Chinese, Japanese and Koreans in Small Business', in Cummings, S. (ed.) *Self-Help in Urban America: Patterns of Minority Economic Development*, Port Washington, NY: Kennikat Press.

Lim, L.L. (1988) 'The Erosion of the Chinese Economic Position', in L.S. Ling *et al.* (eds), *The Future of the Malaysian Chinese*, Kuala Lumpur: Malaysian Chinese Association.

Lim, Y.C., L. (1996) 'The Evolution of Southeast Asian Business Systems', *Journal of Asian Business* 12 (1).

Lim, Y.C., L. and Gosling, L.A.P. (eds) (1983) *The Chinese in Southeast Asia* (2 volumes), Singapore: Maruzen Asia.

Lim, Y.C., L. and Gosling, L.A.P. (1997) 'Strengths and Weaknesses of Minority Status for Southeast Asian Chinese at a Time of Economic Growth and Liberalization', in Chirot, D. and Reid, A. (eds), *Essential Outsiders: Chinese and Jews in the Modern Transformation of Southeast Asia and Central Europe*, Seattle: University of Washington Press.

Lim, M.H. (1981) *Ownership and Control of the One Hundred Largest Corporations in Malaysia*, Kuala Lumpur: Oxford University Press.

Lim, M.H. (1983) 'The Ownership and Control of Large Corporations in Malaysia: The Role of Chinese Businessmen', in Lim, Y.C., L. and Gosling, L.A.P. (eds), *The Chinese in Southeast Asia*, Singapore: Maruzen Asia.

Limlingan, V.S. (1986) 'The Overseas Chinese in Asean: Business Strategies and Management Practices', Ph.D. diss., Harvard University, Cambridge, MA.

Loh, K.W. (1982) *The Politics of Chinese Unity in Malaysia: Reform and Conflict in the Malaysian Chinese Association 1971–1973*, Singapore: Institute of Southeast Asian Studies.

Low, K.Y. (1985) 'The Political Economy of Restructuring in Malaysia: A Study of State Policies with Reference to Multinational Corporations', M.Ec. diss., University of Malaya, Kuala Lumpur.

Machado, K.G. (1992) 'ASEAN State Industrial Policies and Japanese Regional Production Strategies: The Case of Malaysia's Motor Vehicle Industry', in Clark, C. and Chan, S. (eds), *The Evolving Pacific Basin in the Global Political Economy*, Boulder: Lynne Rienner.

Malaysia (1971) *Second Malaysia Plan, 1971–1975*, Kuala Lumpur: Government Printers.

Malaysia (1976) *Third Malaysia Plan, 1976–1980*, Kuala Lumpur: Government Printers.

Malaysia (1991) *Second Outline Perspective Plan, 1990–2000*, Kuala Lumpur: Government Printers.

Malaysia (1996) *Seventh Malaysia Plan, 1996–2000*, Kuala Lumpur: Government Printers.

Mackie, Jamie (1992) 'Changing Patterns of Chinese Big Business in Southeast Asia', in McVey, R. (ed.), *Southeast Asian Capitalists* Ithaca, N.Y.: Cornell South East Asian Studies Program.

Maxfield, S. and Schneider, B.R. (eds) (1997) *Business and the State in Developing Countries*, Ithaca: Cornell University Press.

McVey, R. (ed.) (1992) *Southeast Asian Capitalists*, Ithaca, NY: Cornell South East Asian Studies Program.

McVey, R. (1992) 'The Materialization of the Southeast Asian Entrepreneur', in

# References

McVey, R. (ed.), *Southeast Asian Capitalists*, Ithaca, NY: Cornell South East Asian Studies Program.
Means, G.P. (1991) *Malaysian Politics: The Second Generation*, Singapore: Oxford University Press.
Min, C. (1995) *Asian Management Systems: Chinese, Japanese and Korean Styles of Business*, London: Routledge.
Ministry of Finance, Malaysia (1989) *Economic Report, 1989/1990*, Kuala Lumpur: Government Printers.
Moore, M. (1997) 'Societies, Polities and Capitalists in Developing Countries: A Literature Survey', *The Journal of Development Studies* 33 (3): 287–363.
Munro-Kua, A. (1996) *Authoritarian Populism in Malaysia*, London: Macmillan.
Nado, M. (1996) 'Research Institutions in Malaysia', in Tadashi, Y. (ed.), *Emerging Civil Society in the Asia Pacific Community*, Singapore and Tokyo: Institute of Southeast Asian Studies and Japan Center for International Exchange.
Nasbitt, J. (1995) *Megatrends Asia: The Eight Megatrends That Are Changing The World*, London: Nicholas Breasley.
Nonini, D. (1997) 'Shifting Identities, Positioned Imaginaries: Transnational Traversals and Reversals by Malaysian Chinese', in Ong, A. and Nonini, D. (eds), *Ungrounded Empires: The Cultural Politics of Modern Chinese Transnationalism*, New York: Routledge.
Pan, L. (1990) *Sons of the Yellow Emperor: The Story of the Overseas Chinese*, London: Mandarin.
Park, K. (1997) *The Korean Dream: Immigrants and Small Business in New York City*, Ithaca: Cornell University Press.
Parmer, J. Norman (1969) 'Malaysia', in Kahin, G.M. (ed.), *Government and Politics in Southeast Asia*, Ithaca: Cornell Univeristy Press.
Pennings, J.M. (1980) *Interlocking Directorates: Origins and Consequences of Connections Among Organizations' Board of Directors*, San Francisco: Jossey-Bass Publishers.
Phang, C.N. (1981) 'The Malaysian Chinese Press and the Malaysian Chinese Community', in Loh, K.W., Nyap, P.C. and Saravanamuttu, J. *The Chinese Community and Malaysia-China Ties*, Tokyo: Institute of Developing Economies.
Portes, A. and Manning, R.D. (1986) 'The Immigrant Enclave: Theory and Empirical Examples', in Olzak, S. and Nagel, J. (eds), *Competitive Ethnic Relations*, Orlando, FL: Academic Press.
Purcell, V. (1951) *The Chinese in Southeast Asia*, London: Oxford University Press.
Puthucheary, J.J. (1960) *Ownership and Control in the Malayan Economy*, Singapore: Eastern Universities Press.
Ratnam, K.J. (1965) *Communalism and the Political Process in Malaya*, Kuala Lumpur: University of Malaya Press.
Redding, S.G. (1990) *The Spirit of Chinese Capitalism*, Berlin: Walter de Gruyter.
Reid, A. (1996) *Sojourners and Settlers: Histories of Southeast Asia and the Chinese*, Sydney: Allen & Unwin.
Robison, R. (1986) *Indonesia: The Rise of Capital*, Sydney: Allen & Unwin.
Rowher, J. (1995) *Asia Rising*, Singapore: Butterworth-Heinemann Asia.
Rugayah, M. (1994) 'Sino-Bumiputera Business Cooperation', in Hara, F. (ed.), *The Development of Bumiputera Enterprises and Sino-Malay Economic Cooperation in Malaysia*, Tokyo: Institute of Developing Economies.
Rugayah, M. (1995) 'Public Enterprises', in Jomo, K.S. (ed.), *Privatizing Malaysia: Rents, Rhetoric, Realities*, Boulder and London: Westview Press.

Rutten, M. (1994) *Asian Capitalists in the European Mirror*, Amsterdam: VU University Press.
Sato, Y. (1993) 'The Salim Group in Indonesia: The Development and Behaviour of the Largest Conglomerate in Southeast Asia', *The Developing Economies*, December.
Scott, J. (1985) *Corporations, Classes and Capitalism*, London: Hutchinson.
Shamsul, A.B. (1988) 'The Battle Royal: The UMNO Elections of 1987', *Southeast Asian Affairs*, Singapore: Institute of Southeast Asian Studies.
Sia, I. (1993) 'Robert Kuok: Taipan Incorporated', in Hara, F. (ed.), *Formation and Restructuring of Business Groups in Malaysia*, Tokyo: Institute of Developing Economies.
Sieh, L.M.L. (1982) *Ownership and Control of Malaysian Manufacturing Corporations*, Kuala Lumpur: UMBC Publications.
Sieh, L.M.L. (1992) 'The Transformation of Malaysian Business Groups', in McVey, R. (ed.), *Southeast Asian Capitalists*, Ithaca, NY: Cornell South East Asian Studies Program.
Snodgrass, D.R. (1980) *Inequality and Economic Development in Malaysia*, Kuala Lumpur: Oxford University Press.
Stenson, M. (1980) *Class, Race and Colonialism in West Malaysia: The Indian Case*, Queensland: University of Queensland Press.
Suehiro, A. (1989) *Capital Accumulation in Thailand, 1855–1985*, Tokyo: Centre for East Asian Cultural Studies.
Suryadinata, L. (ed.) (1989) *The Ethnic Chinese in the ASEAN States*, Singapore: Institute of Southeast Asian Studies.
Suryadinata, L. (ed.) (1995) *Southeast Asian Chinese and China: The Politico-Economic Dimension*, Singapore: Times Academic Press.
Suryadinata, L. (ed.) (1995) *Southeast Asian Chinese and China: The Socio-Cultural Dimension*, Singapore: Times Academic Press.
Suryadinata, L. (ed.) (1997) *Ethnic Chinese as Southeast Asians*, Singapore: Institute of Southeast Asian Studies.
Tadashi, Y. (ed.) (1996) *Emerging Civil Society in the Asia Pacific Community*, Singapore and Tokyo, Institute of Southeast Asian Studies and Japan Center for International Exchange.
Tan, C.B. (1983) 'Acculturation and the Chinese in Melaka: The Expression of Baba Identity Today', in Lim, Y.C., L. and Gosling, L.A.P. (eds), *The Chinese in Southeast Asia*, Singapore: Maruzen Asia.
Tan, T.W. (1982) *Income Distribution and Determination in West Malaysia*, Kuala Lumpur: Oxford University Press.
Tong, C.K. (1996) 'Centripetal Authority, Differentiated Networks: The Social Organization of Chinese Firms in Singapore', in Hamilton, G.G. (ed.), *Asian Business Networks*, Berlin: Walter de Gruyter.
Torii, T. (1991) 'Changing the Manufacturing Sector, Reorganizing Automobile Assemblers and Developing the Auto Component Industry under the New Economic Policy', *The Developing Economies*, 29 (4).
Useem, M. (1984) *The Inner Circle: Large Corporations and the Rise of Business Political Activity in the U.S. and the U.K.*, New York: Oxford University Press.
Wang, G. (1988), 'Trade and Cultural Values: Australia and the Four Dragons', *ASAA Review*, 11 (3).
Wang, G. (1991) *China and the Chinese Overseas*, Singapore: Times Academic Press.
Wang, G. (1992) *Community and Nation: China, Southeast Asia and Australia*, Sydney: Allen & Unwin.

## References

Wang T.P. (1994) *The Origins of Chinese Kongsi*, Petaling Jaya: Pelanduk Publications.
Ward, R. and Jenkins, R. (eds) (1984) *Ethnic Communities in Business: Strategies for Economic Survival*, Cambridge: Cambridge University Press.
Weber, M. (1971) *The Protestant Ethnic and the Spirit of Capitalism*, London: Unwin University Books.
Weidenbaum, M. and Hughes, S. (1996) *The Bamboo Network*, New York: The Free Press.
Whitley, R. (1992) *Business Systems in East Asia: Firms, Markets and Societies*, London: Sage Publications.
Wickberg, E. (1994) 'Overseas Chinese Adaptive Organizations, Past and Present', in Skeldon, R. (ed.) *Reluctant Exiles? Migration from Hong Kong and the New Overseas Chinese*, Armonk, NJ: M.E. Sharpe.
Wong, S. (1985) 'The Chinese Family Firm: A Model', *British Journal of Sociology*, 36.
World Bank (1996) *Managing Capital Flows in East Asia*, Washington DC: World Bank.
Wu, Y.L. and Wu, C.H. (1980) *Economic Development in Southeast Asia*, Stanford: Hoover Institute.
Yasuda, N. (1991) 'Malaysia's New Economic Policy and the Industrial Coordination Act', *The Developing Economies*, 29 (4).
Yen, C.H. (1986) *A Social History of the Chinese in Singapore and Malaya*, Singapore: Oxford University Press.
Yen, C.H. (1995) *Community and Politics: The Chinese in Colonial Singapore and Malaysia*, Singapore: Times Academic Press.
Yong, C.F. (1987) *Tan Kah-Kee: The Making of an Overseas Chinese Legend*, Singapore: Oxford University Press.
Yong, P.A. (1995) 'Singapore's Investments in China', in Suryadinata, L. (ed.) *Southeast Asian Chinese and China: The Politico-Economic Dimension*, Singapore: Times Academic Press.
Yoshihara, K. (1988) *The Rise of Ersatz Capitalism in South-East Asia*, Singapore: Oxford University Press.
Zeitlin, M. and Ratcliff, R.E. (1988) *Landlords and Capitalists: The Dominant Class of Chile*, Princeton, NJ: Princeton University Press.
Zysman, J. (1983) *Governments, Markets and Growth*, Ithaca: Cornell University Press.

# Index

Abdul Hamid Omar, 146, 147–148
Abdul Hamid Pawanteh, 146
Abdul Kadir Jasin, 143
Abdul Kadir Yusof, 112
Abdul Mulok Awang Damit, 144
Abdul Rashid Mohd Hussain, 25
Abdul Razak Hussein, 24, 34, 50, 56, 82, 106
Abdul Taib Mahmud, 171, 172, 176, 177, 180, 181, 187, 188
Abdul Wahab Zainuddin, 90
Abdullah Ahmad, 56
Abdullah (Tunku), Tuanku Abdul Rahman, 24, 114, 117, 129, 143
Abu Talib Othman, 24, 106, 118, 146, 147
Acidchem Bhd, 5, 25
Adnan Tengku Mansor, Tengku, 117, 143
Advance Synergy Bhd (*formerly* Batu Lintang Rubber Co Bhd), 18, 116, 142, 156, 160
Ahmad Johari Tun Razak, 24
Ahmad Nazri Abdullah, 143
Ahmad Razali Ali, 145
Ahmad Rithaudden, 146
Ahmad Sebi Abu Bakar, 18, 108, 114, 115–116, 117, 129, 142, 148, 149, 151, 156, 160
Ahmad Zahid Hamidi, 144
Aidid, S.M., 60
Aishah Ghani, 146, 147
Alliance, 32–33, 36
Alwi Jantan, 24
Amalgamated Containers Bhd, 93, 98–99, 100, 101

Amanah Saham Nasional (ASN), 45
Amin Shah Omar Shah, 143, 144
Amsteel Corporation Bhd (*formerly* Amalgamated Steel Mills Bhd), 4, 15, 25, 93–101, 130, 131
Amsteel Mills Sdn Bhd, 96
Ananda Krishnan, T., 122, 131, 151
Aneka Aktif Sdn Bhd, 172
Angkasa Marketing Bhd, 93, 95–96, 100, 101
Antah Holdings group, 117
Anuar Abdul Razak, 177
Anuar Othman, 144, 160
Anwar Ibrahim, 24, 108, 123, 124, 136, 141, 142, 143, 144, 145, 148, 150–151, 155, 156, 160, 162, 175–176, 188
Aokam Perdana Bhd (*formerly* Aokam Tin Bhd), 142, 143, 148
Arab-Malaysian Corporation Bhd, 113, 144, 145, 147
Arab-Malaysian Merchant Bank Bhd, 114, 146
Asea Brown Boveri (ABB), 174–175
Ashman Shah Azlan Shah, Raja, 25
Asia Commercial Finance Bhd, 94, 100
Asia Pacific Land Bhd, 147
Asian 'democracy', 139–140
Asiatic Development Bhd, 4, 24, 52–53, 56, 57
Asola Sdn Bhd, 56
Associated Pan Malaysia Cement Sdn Bhd (APMC), 103, 104, 111
Austral Amalgamated Bhd, 142
Avenel Sdn Bhd, 97
Azman Hashim, 113, 114, 129, 144

## Index

Babas, 28, 32, 76
Baharuddin Musa, 56
Bakun Dam, 169, 173–179, 180, 187, 188
Bakun Hydoelectrical Corporation Sdn Bhd (BHC), 174
Bakun Management Sdn Bhd, 174
Ban Hin Lee Bank Bhd, 18, 19, 75, 142, 151, 155, 156, 185
Bandar Raya Developments Bhd, 86
Bangkok Bank, 49
Bank Bumiputra (M) Bhd, 35, 40, 64, 72, 78, 79, 102, 128, 185
Bank Negara, 39, 123
Bank of Commerce Bhd (BCB), 67
Bara Aktif Sdn Bhd, 166
Barisan Nasional, 1, 3, 36, 43, 57, 71, 72, 74, 90, 92, 133, 136–137, 140, 151, 152, 189
Basir Ismail, 144
Batu Kawan Bhd, 20, 145, 158, 161
Batu Tiga Quarry Sdn Bhd, 163
Bayview Hotel Sdn Bhd, 61
B&B Eenterprise Sdn Bhd, 114, 115
Berjaya Capital Bhd (*formerly* Intiplus Bhd), 117
Berjaya Group Bhd, 15–16, 20, 108, 112–127, 129, 130, 131, 143, 148, 162
Berjaya Industrial Bhd (*formerly* Berjaya Corporation Bhd), 113, 114, 115, 120, 122, 127, 129, 143
Berjaya Kawat Bhd (*renamed* Berjaya Corporation Bhd *and then* Berjaya Industrial Bhd)
Berjaya Leisure Bhd, 114, 115, 122, 127
Berjaya Singer Bhd, 117, 127, 143
Berjaya Sports Toto Bhd, 4, 24, 127
Berjaya Textiles Bhd (*renamed* Jaya Tiasa Holdings), 4, 124–125
Berjaya Universal Casino, 124
Berle, A.A. and G.C. Means, 17
Best World Land Bhd, 143, 148
Bonbright J.C. and G.C. Means, 19
Boon Siew Sdn Bhd, 58, 59, 61, 62
Bowie, A., 12–13
Bright Steel Sdn Bhd, 99, 101
Buildcon Bhd (*renamed* YTL Cement Bhd), 163, 164, 165, 169, 170, 180, 181
Bujang Nor, 174

Cahya Mata Sarawak Bhd (CMS) (*formerly* Cement Manufacturers Sarawak Bhd), 176
Cantonese, 7, 28, 29
Capital Issues Committee (CIC), 70, 71
Chai Siew Phin, Pauline, 112
Chan, Dick, 5
Chan Kang Swi, 29, 76
Chandler, A.D., 17, 66
Chang, Brian, 145
Chang Ming Thein, 87
Charoen Pokphand, 8
Cheah Fook Ling, 5
Chemical Company of Malaysia Bhd (CCM), 5, 25
Chen Yeng Khan, 5
Cheng Chwee Huat, 93
Cheng Heng Jem, William, 2, 4, 15–16, 20, 93–101, 128–132, 138, 183–190
Cheng Theng Kee, 93
Cheng Yang Liang, 97
Cheng Yu Tung, 10
Chia, Eric, 138
China International Trust and Investment Corporation (Citic), 41
Chinese immigration to Malaya, 27–29
Chinese Commercial Bank, 30, 31, 75
Chocolate Products Bhd, 93, 96–97, 100, 101
Chong Chek Ah, Joseph, 2, 144, 148
Chong Hon Nyan, 147
Choo Ching Hwa, 83
Chun Yuan Steel Industry Co Ltd, 98
Chung Khiaw Bank, 30
Citic Pacific, 41
Clarity Crest Sdn Bhd, 159, 161
Clipsal Industries (Holdings) Ltd, 178
Clipsal (M) Sdn Bhd, 178
Cold Storage Bhd, 113, 144
Consolidated Electric Power Asia (CEPA), 168
Construction and Supplies House Bhd (CASH) (*formerly* Ulu Benut Consolidated Rubber Co (M) Bhd), 144, 160
corporatization movement, 2, 13, 67–75, 83–93, 161
Cycle & Carriage Bintang Bhd, 5, 25, 142, 144, 145, 146
Cycle & Carriage Ltd, 5, 138, 144

225

# Index

Daim Zainuddin, 41, 84, 87, 88, 90, 91, 113, 114, 115, 118, 120, 129, 141, 142, 143, 144, 149, 150, 154, 160, 171, 173, 175, 181, 184, 187
Dao Heng Bank, 154
Dara Naqiah, Tunku, 24
Democratic Action Party (DAP), 137, 147
deposit-taking cooperatives (DTC) scandal, 89, 92, 184, 185
Development & Corporation Bank Bhd (D&C Bank) (*renamed* DCB Bank), 33, 67, 79, 103, 106, 143, 185
Diamond League Sdn Bhd, 175, 179
Dirlik, A., 9
Diversified Resources Bhd, 139, 142
DMIB Bhd, 147
Dunham-Bush (M) Bhd (*formerly* Topgroup Holdings Bhd), 117, 127, 130, 143
Dunlop Estates Bhd (*renamed* Sarawak Enterprise Corporation Bhd), 86, 88, 91, 125, 173, 184

E Kong Guan, 29
Edaran Otomobil Nasional Bhd (EON), 138, 142
Eka Tjipta Widjaja, 8
Ekran Bhd, 4, 16, 24, 144, 151, 162, 171–179
Employees' Provident Fund (EPF), 166, 167, 169, 174
Eng Technology Bhd, 135
Equitorial Timber Marketing Sdn Bhd, 178
Eswaran, Kenneth, 148
Eu Kong, 29
Eu Tong Sen, 29–30
Everpeace Corporation Bhd (*formerly* Supreme Plantations Industries Bhd), 85, 86
export-oriented industrialization (EOI), 68–70

FACB Bhd, 146, 148
FCW Holdings Bhd, 142, 177, 178
FCW Industries Sdn Bhd (*formerly* Federal Cables, Wires & Metal Manufacturing Bhd), 172, 176, 177, 179

Federal Flour Mills Bhd, 40, 43, 44, 45, 46, 65, 130
Fima Corporation Bhd, 138, 144
Fleet Group Sdn Bhd, 85, 88, 114, 149–150, 154
Fleet Holdings Sdn Bhd, 144
Foochows, 8, 40
Four Seas Communications Bank, 75
free trade zone (FTZ), 68, 69
Free Trade Zone Act, 68
Fukuyama, F., 6

Gadek Bhd, 142
Ganz Technologies Bhd, 146, 147
Geh Ik Cheong, 43
General Corporation Bhd, 146, 147
Genting Bhd, 4, 15, 24, 26, 49–58, 73, 74, 84, 122, 130, 131, 146, 147, 187, 188
Genting Australia Investment Holdings, 54
Genting Highlands Hotel Sdn Bhd, 50, 51
Genting Hotel & Resorts Management Sdn Bhd, 51
Genting International Ltd, 53, 55, 57
Genting Sanyen Newsprint Sdn Bhd, 54, 58
Genting Sanyen Power Sdn Bhd (GSP), 54–55
Gerakan Rakyat Malaysia (Gerakan), 3, 36, 144, 147
Ghafar Baba, 85, 87, 88, 91, 145, 147, 150, 151, 184
Ghazali Mohd Seth, 24, 25
Ghazali Shafie, 154, 161
Glenealy Plantations (M) Bhd, 20, 158, 160
Goh Ban Huat Bhd, 143, 148
Goh family, 148
Goh Tjoei Kok, 77
Gokongwei, John, 8
Golden Arches Restaurant Sdn Bhd, 112–113
Golden Hope, 53
Golden Plus Holdings Bhd, 143, 145
Grand United Holdings Bhd (*formerly* Textile Corporation of Malaysia Bhd), 85, 86
Granite Industries Bhd, 142, 175, 178, 179, 180

226

# Index

Great Eastern Life Assurance Company, 76
Guoco Group Ltd, 153

Hainanese, 7, 28, 83
Hakkas, 7, 28, 30, 83
Halim Saad, 142, 148–149, 150, 154, 160
Hamzah Abu Bakar, 146
Hamzah Sendut, 25, 60, 62
Hang Lung Bank, 154
Hanifah Hajar Taib, 177
Haniff Omar, 24, 56, 146, 147
Hap Seng Consolidated Bhd, 5, 25, 62
Hara F., 13
Hashim Mohd Ali, 24, 145
Hassan Abas, 25, 144
Hatibudi Sdn Bhd, 149–150
Heavy Industries Corporation of Malaysia (HICOM), 95, 137, 138, 139, 142, 146
Heng P. K., 13
Henghwa, 28
Highlands & Lowlands Bhd, 39
HLG Capital Bhd (*formerly* Zalik Bhd), 145, 153, 154, 155, 156, 157
H'ng family, 4
Ho Hong Bank, 75, 76
Ho, Richard, 147
Ho, Stanley, 121, 125
Hokchia, 28
Hokchiu, 28
Hokkiens, 7, 28, 30, 49, 58, 63, 74, 75–83, 101, 163, 184–185
Hong Leong Bank Bhd (*formerly* MUI Bank Bhd), 4, 24, 26, 108–109, 153, 156, 157
Hong Leong Co (M) Bhd, 18, 54, 59, 63, 89, 90, 92, 102, 108–109, 142, 143, 148, 150–151, 152, 153–157, 161, 188
Hong Leong Credit Bhd, 4, 24, 145, 153, 154, 155, 157
Hong Leong Finance Bhd, 153, 154, 157
Hong Leong Industries Bhd, 4, 24, 25, 153, 157
Hong Leong Properties Bhd, 4, 24, 153, 157
Hopewell Holdings, 168

Huaren Holdings Bhd, 103, 128
Hume Industries (M) Bhd, 4, 24, 89–90, 153, 154
Hussein Onn, 40, 50, 82, 106

Ibrahim Abdul Rahman, 145
Ibrahim Mohamed, 145
ICI (M) Holdings Sdn Bhd, 5
Idris Hydraulic Bhd, 143, 146
IGB Corporation Bhd, 49, 107, 108, 117–124, 129, 146, 147, 159
IJM Corporation Bhd, 18, 49, 118
import-substituting industrialization (ISI), 33–34, 46, 68–70, 137
Indah Water Konsortium Sdn Bhd, 115
independent power producer (IPP), 55, 163, 165, 166, 167, 169, 170, 173, 180, 181, 187
Industrial Coordination Act (ICA), 70–71
Industrial Oxygen Incorporated Bhd (IOI), 145
Institute of Strategic and International Studies (ISIS), 139
interlocking directorates, 22–26
interlocking stock ownerships, 19–22
Intiplus Bhd, 116
Investment Incentives Act, 1968, 68
IOI Properties Bhd, 4, 24
Ishak Ismail, 123, 143, 148, 160, 175
Ismail Abdul Rahman, 40

Jaffar Mohd Ali, 25, 145
Jaguh Mutiara Sdn Bhd, 154
Jailah Hamidah Taib, 177
Jasa Kita Bhd, 176
Jasa Megah Industries Bhd (JMI), 126
Jaya Tiasa Holdings, 4, 24, 124–125
JCG Finance Co Ltd, 80, 81
Jesudason, J., 7, 12–13
John Laing plc, 166, 171, 181

Kah Motor Co Sdn Bhd, 59–60, 61, 62
Kamaruddin Jaffar, 144, 148
Kamaruddin Mohamad Nor, 144
Kamunting Corporation Bhd, 4, 20, 24, 90, 91, 92, 125
Kazzon Ltd, 53, 57
Kerry Financial Services Ltd, 110

# Index

Kerry Trading, 41
KFC Holdings Bhd, 143, 146, 148
Khalid Haji Ahmad, 143
Khazanah Holdings Bhd, 168, 169, 174
Khee San Bhd, 143, 148
Khir Johari, 24, 146, 147
Khoo Kay Peng, 2, 4, 15–16, 20, 35, 43, 49, 78, 79, 82, 83, 101–112, 117–124, 126, 127, 128–132, 155, 183–190
Khoo Teck Puat, 33, 39, 77–78, 79, 82, 83, 102, 104
Khoo Yang Tin, 77
Kian Joo Can Factory Bhd, 5, 25
Kien Huat Construction Sdn Bhd, 50
Kien Huat Realty Sdn Bhd, 52, 56, 57
Kilang Gula Felda Perlis Sdn Bhd, 45
Killinghall Tin (M) Bhd, 103
Kinabalu Motor Assembly Sdn Bhd, 97
KKP Enterprise Sdn Bhd, 111–112
KKP Holdings Sdn Bhd, 111–112
KL-Kepong Bhd, 4, 24, 39, 83, 142, 145, 148, 152, 153, 158–162, 188
KLOFFE Capital Sdn Bhd, 156
Koperasi Usaha Bersatu Bhd (KUB), 106, 128
Koperatif Serbaguna (M) Bhd, 72, 73, 74, 83, 84, 89, 102
Kotkin, J., 9, 10
Kuala Lumpur Stock Exchange (KLSE), 3, 20–22, 23, 39, 43, 49, 50, 51, 108, 114, 117, 156, 163, 168, 174, 176, 177
Kuok Brothers Sdn Bhd, 40, 46, 64
Kuok Hock Nien, Robert, 4, 8, 10–11, 15, 33, 34, 35, 39, 40–49, 64, 65, 66, 71, 78, 89, 102, 108, 110, 111, 119, 120, 125, 129, 130, 131, 132, 183–190
Kuok Keng Kang, 40
Kwong Lee Bank Bhd (*renamed* MUI Bank), 103, 106
Kwong Yik Banking Corporation Ltd, 30, 75
Kwong Yik Bank Bhd, 67, 143
Kwongsai, 28

Land & General Bhd, 113, 117, 125, 142, 154, 159–160

Lau family, 148
Lau Gek Poh, 5
Lau Pak Khuan, 29, 30, 32
Leader Universal Bhd, 4, 24, 172
Lee, Alex, 103, 106, 147
Lee, Henry H.S., 32, 33, 79, 106
Lee, Joseph Ambrose, 144, 160
Lee Keng Hee, 29
Lee Kim Sai, 147
Lee Kong Chian, 29, 30–31, 39, 75–76
Lee Kuan Yew, 10
Lee Lam Thye, 147
Lee Loy Seng, 4, 20, 39, 63, 71, 74, 83, 89, 152, 153, 157–162
Lee Oi Hian, 160
Lee Rubber group, 31, 75
Lee San Choon, 72–73, 74, 89, 90
Lee Shau Kee, 8, 10
Lee Wah Bank, 29, 75
Lee Yan Lian, 83
Leisure Management Bhd, 91, 146, 147
Lembaga Tabung Angkatan Tentera (LTAT), 45, 52, 94, 95, 99, 165, 181
Lembaga Urusan Tabung Haji (LUTH), 45, 46, 178
Li Ka Shing, 8, 10, 41, 47, 49, 104, 132
Liem Sioe Liong, 8, 49
Lien Hoe Corporation Bhd, 146, 148
Liew Sip Hon, 147
Light, I.H., 9
Lim Chee Wah, 55, 56
Lim Chong Eu, 147
Lim Goh Tong, 4, 15, 33, 39, 49–58, 63, 64, 65, 66, 73, 103, 122, 129, 130, 183–190
Lim Keng Kay, 5
Lim Kim Hua, 55
Lim Kok Thay, 55, 56
Lim Say Chong, 5
Lim Siew Lay, 55, 56
Lim Su Tong, 61, 62
Lim T.K., 2, 4, 20, 90, 91, 125, 130, 131, 142, 173, 184
Lim Tee Keong, 55, 56
Lim Tow Seng, 98
Lim Tow Yong, 98
Ling Liong Sik, 2, 3

## Index

Lingui Developments Bhd, 4, 24
Lion Asia Investment Pte Ltd, 96
Lion Asia Ltd, 98, 100
Lion Coropration Bhd, 20, 59, 93–101, 129, 145
Lion Land Bhd (*formerly* Supreme Corporation Bhd), 86, 93, 95–96, 100, 145, 147
Lion Metal Manufacturing Sdn Bhd, 93
Lion Sankyu Tekko Sdn Bhd, 99
Lippo group, 8, 110, 132
Loh Cheng Yean, 60, 61, 62
Loh Boon Siew, 5, 15, 39, 58–63, 64, 65, 66, 103, 129, 130, 138, 183–190
Loh Boon Siew Holdings Sdn Bhd, 58, 61, 62
Loh Gim Ean, 62
Loh Kar Bee, 62
Loh Kim Teow (LKT) Bhd, 135
Loh Say Bee, 61
Loke Wan Tho, 77
Loke Yew, 29–30, 77
Long Huat group, 147
Loy Hean Heong, 4, 143

Magnum Corporation Bhd, 4, 24, 25, 86, 91, 102, 120, 125, 129, 130, 131, 146, 147
Mahathir Mohamad, 11, 18, 24, 25, 43, 87, 114, 115, 134, 135, 137, 138, 139, 140, 141, 142, 143, 144, 145, 151, 152, 155, 156, 165, 173, 175, 181, 187, 189
Mahmud Abu Bekir Taib, 176, 177
Majaharta Sdn Bhd, 177–178
Majlis Amanah Rakyat (MARA), 35, 72
Malayan Banking Bhd (Maybank), 33, 49, 76, 77–78, 79, 80, 82, 83, 92, 102, 104, 109, 128, 147, 185
Malayan Communist Party (MCP), 31
Malayan Sugar Manufacturing Company Bhd, 43, 45
Malayan United Industries Bhd (MUI), 4, 20, 24, 26, 49, 101–112, 117–124, 128, 129, 130, 146, 147, 161
Malayan United Manufacturing Bhd (MUM), (*formerly* Central Sugars, *now renamed* MUI Properties Bhd)
Malaysia Airlines Bhd (MAS), 142
Malaysia Mining Corporation Bhd (MMC), 38, 90
Malaysian Chinese Association (MCA), 1, 2, 13, 15, 16, 31–33, 36, 37, 39, 43, 63, 66, 71, 72, 73, 74, 76, 83, 84, 86, 87, 88, 89, 90, 102, 105, 128, 129, 133, 147, 149, 159, 161, 184
Malaysian French Bank Bhd (*renamed* Multi-Purpose Bank)
Malaysian Indian Congress (MIC), 1, 32, 33
Malaysian Institute of Economic Research (MIER), 139
Malaysian International Shipping Corporation Bhd (MISC), 40, 46, 64
Malaysian Newsprint Industries Sdn Bhd, 54
Malaysian Pacific Industries Bhd, 4, 24, 54, 153, 157
Malaysian Plantations Bhd, 20, 91
Malaysian Resources Corporation Bhd (MRCB), 143, 153, 155
management buy-out (MBO), 5, 155
MBf Capital Bhd, 4, 24, 143
McDonald's Corporation, 112–113
McDonald's franchise, 15–16, 112–113, 128, 187
Megat Fairouz Junaidi, 145
Megat Junid, 145
Mekar Idaman Sdn Bhd, 5
Melewar Corporation Bhd, 114, 115, 143
Metal Containers Ltd, 99, 100
Metro Kajang Holdings Bhd, 147
Metrojaya Bhd, 109, 111, 146, 147
Metroplex Bhd, 5, 25
Ming Court Hotel group, 104, 105, 109, 111
Mirzan Mahathir, 94, 101, 145, 148
Mohamad Amin Osman, 24, 56
Mohamad Danel Abong, 174
Mohamad Farid Ariffin, 146
Mohamad Noah Omar, 50, 82, 106
Mohamad Noor Mutalib, 143
Mohamad Noordin Daud, 176
Mohamad Razali Abdul Rahman, 176

## Index

Mohamad Sarit Haji Yusoh, 143, 148, 175
Mohamad Shah Abdul Kadir, 112–113, 114, 128–129
Mohamad Sofi Ghafar, 145
Mohamed Noor Yusof (Mohamed Noor Azam), 144
Mohamed Sheriff Mohd Kassim, 25
Mohamed Yassin Jaffar, 24
Mokhzani Mahathir, 145, 176
'money politics', 149–151
MUI Bank Bhd (*renamed* Hong Leong Bank Bhd), 4, 15–16, 35, 76, 78, 79, 82, 104, 105, 106, 108–109, 110, 128, 151, 155, 156, 185, 187
MUI Continental Insurance Bhd, 108
MUI Finance Bhd (*renamed* United Merchant Finance Bhd), 15–16, 104–105, 108–109, 110, 123, 124, 128, 151, 155
MUI Hikari Construction Sdn Bhd, 109
MUI Properties Bhd (*formerly* Central Sugars Bhd *and then* Malayan United Manufacturing (MUM) Bhd), 102–103, 109, 111, 122, 128, 146
Mukhriz Mahathir, 145
Mulpha International Bhd, 5
Multi-Purpose Bank Bhd (*formerly* Malaysian French Bank), 41, 86, 146, 147, 155
Multi-Purpose Holdings Bhd, 2, 4, 13, 20, 24, 39, 43, 73, 74, 83–93, 103, 105, 107, 120, 125, 128, 142, 146, 147, 154–155, 159, 161, 162, 184
Murdoch, Rupert, 110–111
Musa Hitam, 96, 101, 145, 147, 150
Mutiara Telecommunications Sdn Bhd, 116
Mycom Bhd, 153

Nanyang Press Bhd, 153, 154, 157
Nadzaruddin Tuanku Jaafar, Tunku, 25
Nasruddin Mohamed, 24, 25
National Development Policy (NDP), 136, 137
Natvest Sdn Bhd, 96, 97, 98, 101

Nautilus Corporation Sdn Bhd, 113, 114
Nazri Abdullah, 143
New Economic Policy (NEP), 5, 14, 16, 25, 39, 47, 51, 63, 64, 101, 134, 136, 140, 158, 161, 180–181, 183, 184, 185, 186, 188, 189
 and Chinese business, 67–75, 91
 emergence of 'new rich', 1, 18, 149–150
 implementation, 1, 2, 3, 7, 36–37
New Straits Times Press Bhd (NSTP), 54, 58, 85, 88, 143, 150–151, 155, 156
News Corp Ltd, 110–111
Nik Ahmad Kamil, 78, 82
Nik Hashim Nik Yusoff, 24, 25, 26
Nizam Tun Razak, 24
Northwest Water Ltd, 115

Oh Kim Sum, 5
Olympia Industries Bhd, 146, 147
Omali Corporation Sdn Bhd, 99
Ong Beng Seng, 8, 54, 66
Ong Lay Wah, 62
Onn Mahmud, 176
Oriental Assemblers Sdn Bhd, 59, 60, 61
Oriental Holdings Bhd, 5, 15, 25, 58–63, 65, 130, 138, 188
Oriental Smelting Company, 30
Osman Tuanku Temenggong Ahmad, Tunku, 106
Oversea Chinese Bank, 75
Oversea-Chinese Banking Corporation Ltd (OCBC), 31, 39, 72, 75–79, 82, 87, 101, 102, 103, 104, 128, 184–185
'Overseas Chinese', 6, 11
Overseas Trust Bank, 154
Overseas Union Bank, 30
OYL Industries Bhd, 4, 24, 153, 157
Ozly Shoe Sdn Bhd, 98

Pacific Bank Bhd, 76
Pacific Carriers Ltd, 46, 177–178
Pacific Chemicals Bhd, 4, 24, 176, 178, 179, 181
Palm-Oleo Sdn Bhd, 159
Palmco Holdings Bhd, 113

## Index

Pan-Electric Industries Ltd, 83, 85, 86, 88–89, 92, 106–107, 109, 184
Pan Malaysia Cement Works Bhd (PMCW), 4, 24, 103, 104, 107, 109, 111, 122
Pan Malaysian Industries (PMI, *formerly* Pan Malaysia Rubber Industries Bhd (PMRI), 103, 104, 109, 110, 111, 119, 122
Pan Malaysia Rubber Industries Bhd (PMRI, *renamed* PMI)
Parit Perak Bhd, 20, 158, 160
Parti Islam Se-Malaysia (PAS), 36, 152
Pathmanaban, K., 147
Pegi (M) Bhd, 87–88
Pembinaan YCS Bhd, 147
Penang Yellow Bus Company Sdn Bhd, 58, 61
Pengkalan Industrial Holdings Bhd, 144
Pennings, J.M., 22–23
Perbadan Nasional Bhd (Pernas), 35, 38, 40, 64, 72, 87
Perdana Merchant Bankers Bhd, 116, 117, 127, 156
Peremba Bhd, 41, 142, 144, 149
Perlis Plantations Bhd, 4, 15, 24, 41, 42, 43, 44, 45, 47, 65, 119, 130, 188
Permodalan Nasional Bhd (PNB), 38, 92, 138
Perusahaan Otomobil Nasional Bhd (Proton), 142
Petroliam Nasional Bhd (Petronas), 50, 87
'political business', 149–151, 180–181, 188
Posim Bhd, 93, 97–98
Post Publishing Co Ltd, 48, 110
PPES Concrete Sdn Bhd, 176
Prime Utilities Bhd (*formerly* Berjaya South Island Bhd), 115–116, 117, 142
Promet Bhd, 143, 145
Promotion of Investments Act, 1986 (PIA), 134
Public Bank Bhd, 4, 33, 39, 76, 78–83, 109, 185
Public Finance Bhd, 80, 81
Public Insurance Company, 30
PWE Industries Bhd, 178, 179

Quek Leng Chan, 4, 8, 63, 78, 89, 102, 152, 153–157, 160–162, 184, 185

Raja Mohar Raja Badiozaman, 24, 165
Raleigh Bhd (*renamed* Berjaya Group Bhd)
Rashid Hussain, 143
Rashid Hussain Bhd, 143, 156
Rasip Haron, 172, 173, 176, 177
Razaleigh Hamzah, 24, 43, 78, 82, 102, 123, 128, 145, 150, 154, 155, 160, 188
Redding, S.G., 9
Regnis (M) Sdn Bhd, 113, 121
Renong Bhd, 90, 142, 154, 155, 156, 160
Resorts World Bhd, 4, 15, 24, 49–58, 146, 147
Rimbunan Hijau Sdn Bhd, 124–125
Robert Hamzah, 24, 145, 160
Rohas Sdn Bhd, 148
Run Run Shaw, 10, 49

Sabah Gas Industries Sdn Bhd, 96
Sabah Forest Industries Sdn Bhd (SFI), 96, 97, 98
Saleha Mohd Ali, 145
Salim Group, 8, 42
Sallehuddin Mohamed, 25, 146
Samling Strategic Corporation Bhd, 4, 160
Samsudin Abu Hassan, 142, 148, 149, 150, 175
Sanorex Sdn Bhd, 123
Sapura Holdings Bhd, 144, 146, 172
Saranan Maju Sdn Bhd, 95
Sarawak Electricity Supply Corporation (SESCO), 173, 174
Sarawak Enterprise Corporation Bhd (*formerly* Dunlop Estates Bhd), 91
Saw Choo Theng, 103
Scholes Group plc, 178
Scott, J., 19, 23
See family, 5
Seimens AG, 166, 181
Semi-Tech Microelectronics Ltd, 120–121, 125
Seri Angkasa Sdn Bhd, 90, 91
Shamsuddin Abdul Kadir, 144, 172

## Index

Shangri-La Hotels (M) Bhd (SHMB), 43, 44, 45
Shin Min Daily News (M) Sdn Bhd, 85, 88
Shuaib Lazim, 144, 172–173, 181
Sigma Metal Bhd, 85, 86
Silara Sdn Bhd, 172
Sime Darby Bhd, 38, 105, 144, 163
Sime-UEP Properties Bhd, 87, 91, 146, 147
Singapore Star Cruise Pte Ltd, 55
Singer Furniture (M) Sdn Bhd, 117, 121
Singer Holdings (M) Bhd (*see* Berjaya Singer)
Singer Sewing Machine Co (SSMC), 113, 121, 125, 129
Sistem Televisyen (M) Bhd (STMB) (*see* TV3)
small- and medium-scale enterprises (SMEs), 11–12, 13, 20, 90–91, 135, 136
Soo Lay Holdings Sdn Bhd, 111–112
Soon Ann Company, 30
Sophonpanich, Chatri, 8, 49
South China Morning Post (Holdings) Ltd (SCMP), 47, 48, 49, 110, 111, 123
South Pacific Textile Industries Bhd (*renamed* Berjaya Textiles Bhd), 113
Southern Bank Bhd, 63, 66, 103, 128, 185
Spanco Sdn Bhd, 176–177
Sports Toto lottery, 15–16, 114, 116, 122, 129, 131, 143
Sports Toto (M) Bhd, (*renamed* Berjaya Leisure Bhd)
Sri Alu Sdn Bhd, 90
Sri Damansara Sdn Bhd (*formerly* Multi-Purpose Bersatu Development Sdn Bhd), 125
Sri Hartamas Bhd, 4, 24
Star Publications (M) Bhd, 116, 117, 129, 143
Steelcorp Sdn Bhd, 96
Straits Echo Press Sdn Bhd, 85, 87, 88
Sucden Kerry International (SKI), 47
Suiwah Corporation Bhd, 147
Sulaiman Abdul Rahman Taib, 176, 177
Suleiman Manan, 117
Sungei Way Holdings Bhd, 5, 25
Supreme Corporation Bhd (*renamed* Lion Land Bhd), 74, 84–85, 92, 95–96, 159
Suzuki Assemblers (M) Sdn Bhd (SAM), 94–95
Sy, Henry, 8
Syarikat Pembenaan Yeoh Tiong Lay Sdn Bhd, 163, 167, 170
Syed Kechik Syed Mohamed, 103, 106
Syed Nahar Shahabuddin, 146
Syed Zaid Syed Jaffar Albar, 24

TA Enterprise Bhd, 4
Taib Andak, 40, 45
Tajudin Ramli, 142, 148, 149, 150
Tan & Tan Development Bhd, 49, 118, 147
Tan Chee Khoon, 56
Tan Chee Sing, Danny, 114, 126
Tan Chee Yioun, Vincent, 2, 4, 15–16, 20, 108, 112–127, 128–132, 142, 143, 148, 151, 183–190
Tan Cheng Lock, 32, 76
Tan Chin Nam, 18, 49, 107, 117–124, 126, 131, 159, 183
Tan Chin Tuan, 39, 76
Tan Chong Motors Bhd, 4, 24, 138
Tan Hua Choon, Robert, 176, 177–178, 181
Tan Jiak Hoe, 29
Tan Jiak Kim, 29
Tan Kah Kee, 29, 30–31
Tan Kah Kee & Company, 30–31
Tan Kai Yong, 164
Tan Kee Peck, 30
Tan Koon Swan, 43, 71–72, 73–74, 83–86, 88, 89, 90, 92, 95, 96, 102, 103, 107, 159
Tan Siew Sin, 32, 72, 73, 76
Tan Teong Hean, 56
Tanjong plc, 122, 131
Tasek Cement Bhd, 63
Tat Lee Bank, 77
Technology Resources Industries Bhd (TRI), 142, 145
Teck Chiang Foundry Co, 93
Teck Chiang Manufactory Ltd, 93
Teck See Plastics Sdn Bhd, 60, 61
Teh Hong Piow, 4, 33, 39, 78, 79–83

## Index

Teh Soon Seng, 2, 142, 148
Teknologi Tenaga Perlis (Overseas) Consortium Sdn Bhd, 168
Television Broadcasts (TVB), 48, 49
Tenaga Nasional Bhd (TNB), 49, 166, 167, 169, 173, 174
Teo Joo Kim, 119
Teochews, 7, 8, 28, 93
Tham, Peter, 106–107
Thong Kok Cheong, 126
Thong Kok Kee, 126
Tiah Thee Kian, 4
Tiong Hiew King, 4, 54, 124–125
Ting, James, 121, 125
Ting Pek Khiing, 2, 4, 16, 142, 144, 148, 151, 162, 171–182, 183–190
Tong Bee Finance (M) Bhd (*renamed* MUI Finance Bhd), 102
Tong Kooi Ong, 2
Tong Seng & Company, 40
Tsao Wen-king, Frank, 46
Tsui T.T., 47, 49
Tuck Heng Manufactory Ltd, 93
TV3 (*see also* STMB), 114, 116, 129, 143, 144, 151

UBN Holdings Sdn Bhd, 41, 43, 44
UCM Industrial Corporation Bhd, 145, 176
Unico Holdings Bhd, 91
Union Paper Bhd, 145, 147
United Asian Bank Bhd (UAB), 67
United Engineers (M) Bhd (UEM), 89–90, 142, 154, 160
United Malacca Rubber Estates Bhd, 76
United Malayan Banking Corporation Bhd (*renamed* Sime Bank), 67, 87, 91, 92, 112, 144, 185
United Malays' National Organization (UMNO), 1, 15, 16, 24, 32, 33, 35, 36, 37, 41, 43, 57, 58, 72, 78, 79, 84, 85, 86, 87, 88, 89, 91, 100, 114, 115, 117, 118, 123, 128, 129, 136, 140, 141, 142, 143, 144, 145, 146, 149, 150, 151, 152, 153, 154, 155, 160, 162, 165, 172, 173, 175, 180, 181, 184, 187, 188, 189
United Merchant Finance Bhd (*formerly* MUI Finance Bhd), 156

United Merchant Group Bhd (UMG), 142, 156
United Motor Works Bhd (UMW), 138
United Oveseas Bank, 75
Unza Holdings Bhd, 127, 143
Urban Development Authority (UDA), 67, 169, 181
Usama Industries Sdn Bhd, 177
Utusan Melayu Press Bhd, 85

Vision 2020, 136, 137

Wan Azmi Wan Hamzah, 117, 125, 142, 148, 149, 154, 159, 162
Waspavest Sdn Bhd, 149–150
Weber, M., 9
Wee Boon Peng, 160
Weidenbaum, M. and S. Hughes, 6
Wembley Industries Holdings Bhd, 175–176, 179, 180
Westmont group, 144, 148
William Cheng Sdn Bhd, 101
Wing Teik Holdings Bhd, 144, 147
Wong Lum Kong, 60, 61, 62
Wong Sui Choo, 172
Woodhouse Sdn Bhd, 171–172, 178, 179
World Bank, 6
World Chinese Entrepreneurs' Conventions, 6
World Chinese Traders' Conferences, 6
Wu, Gordon, 168, 181

Yahya Ahmad, 25, 139, 142, 148
Yahya Ismail, 24, 25, 165
Yahya Talib, 97
Yan family, 148
Yeap Chor Ee, 75
Yeap family, 18, 155
Yeoh Cheng Liam, 163
Yeoh Cheng Liam Construction Sdn Bhd, 163
Yeoh Seok Hong, 164
Yeoh Seok Kah, 164
Yeoh Seok Kian, 164, 165
Yeoh Sock Ping, Francis, 16, 151, 162, 163–171, 179–182, 183–190
Yeoh Sock Siong, 164
Yeoh Soo Keng, 164

*Index*

Yeoh Soo Min, 164
Yeoh Tiong Lay, 4, 151, 163, 164
Yeoh Tiong Lay & Sons Holdings Sdn Bhd, 164–165
Yeoh Tiong Lay Brickworks Sdn Bhd, 163
Yong, C.F., 7
Yoshihara Kunio, 3, 12–13
YTL Corporation Bhd, 4, 16, 24, 151, 162, 163–171, 180–182, 187, 188
YTL-CPI Power Ltd, 168
YTL Industries Bhd, 170
YTL Power Generation Sdn Bhd, 166, 167, 168, 170
YTL Power International Bhd (YTLPI), 163, 168, 169
YTL Power Services Sdn Bhd, 166, 170
Yule Catto & Co plc, 159, 161

Zailah Tun Dr Ismail, 24
Zain Hashim, 25, 97, 101